TERRITORY OF LIES

TERRITORY OF LIES

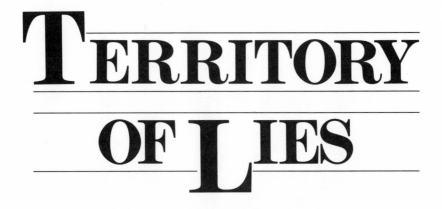

**The Exclusive Story
of Jonathan Jay Pollard:
The American Who Spied on
His Country for Israel
and How He Was Betrayed**

Wolf Blitzer

1817

HARPER & ROW PUBLISHERS, New York
*Grand Rapids, Philadelphia, St. Louis, San Francisco
London, Singapore, Sydney, Tokyo*

FIRST EDITION

Designed by Karen Savary

Library of Congress Cataloging-in-Publication Data

Blitzer, Wolf.
  Territory of Lies.

  1. Pollard, Jonathan J.   2. Espionage, Israeli—
United States—History—20th century.   I. Title.
UB271.I82P653 1989   327.1′2′095694   88-45885
ISBN 0-06-015972-3

89 90 91 92 93 CC/HC 10 9 8 7 6 5 4 3 2 1

To my grandparents, Chaja and Wolf Zylberfuden, and Chaja and Yitzhak Blitzer, whom I never knew because they were killed during the Holocaust. May their memory be blessed.

With my eyes shut and not fully aware of the consequences, I entered the territory of lies without a passport for return.

JONATHAN JAY POLLARD

CONTENTS

INTRODUCTION

Looking into the Abyss

I first met Jonathan Jay Pollard on November 20, 1986, in the Petersburg, Virginia, federal penitentiary, where he was awaiting his sentencing on espionage charges. It was a sensational case that had rocked U.S.-Israeli relations. Charged Secretary of Defense Caspar Weinberger, "It is difficult for me, even in the so-called 'year of the spy,' to conceive of a greater harm to national security than that caused by the defendant in view of the breadth, the critical importance to the United States, and the high sensitivity of the information he sold to Israel." For the American Jewish community, it was a nightmare come true—an American Jew spying for Israel.

The implications were enormous. I had covered the story from the first day it broke on Thursday, November 21, 1985. I remember the details well.

Late that afternoon in Washington, I had received a phone call from Charles Wolfson, a top producer for the "CBS Evening News" and a friend. Earlier in his career, Wolfson had served as the CBS Bureau Chief in Tel Aviv. He said that Rita Braver, CBS's Justice Department correspondent, was about to go on the air with a bizarre story about a U.S. Naval Intelligence analyst's unsuccessful effort earlier that day to receive political asylum at the Israeli Embassy in

Washington. The FBI arrested him after he was thrown out of the embassy. Wolfson wanted to know whether I had any additional details.

I told him that I had not heard of the incident. My first reaction was that the story sounded ridiculous. I think I may have even chuckled. From my years in Washington, I knew that all sorts of crackpots often showed up at the embassy. Some had well-intentioned but weird proposals for peace; others were gung-ho Vietnam War veterans who were anxious to volunteer for service in the Israeli Army. Israeli security officers at the embassy had standing instructions to politely but firmly turn these people away.

Wolfson assured me that the story was serious. He said CBS was running with it in the next ninety minutes. But by the tone of his voice, I sensed that he, too, was still somewhat skeptical. I told him I would look into the story and get right back to him.

My own newspaper, *The Jerusalem Post,* was itself very close to deadline, so I didn't have much time. I called an Israeli Embassy official who immediately confirmed the bare facts—someone by the name of Jonathan Jay Pollard had indeed come to the embassy that morning seeking political asylum. He drove a green Mustang. He claimed he was an Israeli spy. As a Jew, he cited Israel's "Law of Return," which automatically grants citizenship to Jews upon their arrival in Israel. He was accompanied by his wife Anne Henderson Pollard and their cat Dusty. The diplomat said that he knew nothing else about the matter, insisting that the entire thing sounded "crazy." He speculated that the guy may have been "a nut," but he assured me that the embassy was taking the matter very seriously. In fact, he confided, Israel's diplomatic mission in the U.S. capital was in an uproar.

Although still uncertain about the incident, I quickly telephoned the night editor at the *Post.* It was already very late, past midnight in Israel. We didn't have much time to get the story into the paper. He, too, laughed when he heard what I had to say. I explained that CBS News was carrying the story and that Israeli officials in Washington were taking the matter very seriously indeed. With that, he reluctantly agreed to squeeze it into the paper. "But keep it tight," he snapped.

Off the top of my head, I dictated a few paragraphs, quoting CBS News as my source. Based on my years of experience, I suspected that the Israeli military censor might spike this kind of a story unless it were attributed to a foreign news organization. The censor cannot kill stories that have already appeared abroad. Several days later, when I finally received my air-mailed edition of the newspaper, I was pleased to see the story on the front page, although embarrassed that the name of the spy was given as "Jonathan J. Tollard," my "P" somehow becoming a "T" during trans-Atlantic dictation. That, in short, was my inauspicious introduction to the Pollard affair.

In the first year after the arrest, both Pollard and his wife remained publicly silent in the face of numerous accusations against them in the news media; their lawyers had advised them not to talk to the press. The Pollards, they said, should cooperate with the authorities and show great remorse for their crimes. They should simply beg for mercy, admitting their crimes. That was to be their legal strategy. Thus, even though scores of news organizations had sought interviews, those requests were all routinely rejected. My own many phone calls to the Pollards' lawyers were never returned.

The Israelis, deeply embarrassed and anxious to limit the damage to their image and their relationship with the United States, were also comfortable with this strategy since they, too, wanted the entire affair to disappear from the headlines. They were understandably happy to learn that Pollard was going to plead guilty. A long, highly publicized jury trial could be avoided. They assumed—incorrectly—that if Pollard pleaded guilty, all the nasty details of the operation would remain secret. They did not know that the U.S. government would have to submit lengthy papers to the judge in advance of sentencing.

The story appeared to be dying down while the Pollards quietly awaited sentencing. But suddenly, I found myself stirring things up again.

Nearly one year after Pollard was arrested, in early November 1986, Bernard Henderson, Anne Henderson Pollard's father, called me at my Washington office. He asked if he could stop by; he had some information he wanted to give me.

What he came to tell me was that Pollard felt betrayed by Israel. After all, he had been a loyal agent, yet for some inexplicable reason, he had been abandoned. Why had he been denied asylum at the Israeli Embassy in Washington after being instructed to go there? Why had Israel cooperated with the Justice Department's investigation? Why had Israel turned against him? Many of the details Henderson told were incredible and would have to be confirmed. He spent three hours with me in my compact office in the upper Georgetown section of Washington. He sat across from my desk, chain-smoking cigarettes. I was literally nauseous from the smoke, but I did not complain.

Henderson subsequently told me that he had come to my office only after lengthy discussions with his daughter and Pollard. They were concerned that the prosecutors were not living up to the plea-bargaining agreements that had been signed in June. "They started punishing Jay," Henderson said. "They started bringing up other people. They started feeding stories to the papers—stuff like that; fake stories. They just intensified what they were doing before."

" 'I don't care what the lawyers say,' " he recalled his daughter saying, " 'there is something going wrong here. If I get back in jail, I'll be cut off and nobody will know.' "

"You're right," Henderson said he told her. "You're absolutely right."

Over the next few days, they decided to turn to a reporter. They did not consult their lawyers. "We drew up a list," he told me. "Your name was on it. We thought of several people."

Anne drove from Washington to Petersburg to discuss the idea with Pollard. She showed him the list. "Jay wanted this done quietly, discreetly, from day one," Henderson said. "He was the most reluctant of all to open it. Anne had to scream at him a lot of times to do things."

A few days after our first meeting, Henderson called back.

I had apparently impressed him as someone who was sympathetic. At that time, he still did not know what I was writing, but he asked whether I wanted to interview Pollard. I immediately said yes. I knew that the first interview with him would be a worldwide scoop. In Israel and the American Jewish community, it would almost certainly be a sensation.

"Why don't you call the warden at Petersburg?" Henderson said. "I think you should try."

I thanked him for the advice, called the federal prison at Petersburg, Virginia, and then put my request in writing.

I was still very doubtful about the chances for success. But to my amazement, the warden called back within a few days to inform me that my request had been approved. I wasn't sure why but I didn't ask questions.

At the meeting, I was struck by how prison life had transformed the former civilian intelligence analyst for the U.S. Navy since his initial court appearances exactly a year earlier. He wore metal-framed glasses; his brown hair was very thin, with the bald spot on top of his head getting larger; his mustache was growing over his mouth. But what was most dramatic was that in the year since his arrest, he had lost fifty pounds on what he described as the "soul food" diet of chitlins and refried beans that the black cooks prepared for the prisoners, most of whom are also black. Pollard simply couldn't keep the food down. I wasn't surprised to learn that he hadn't been sleeping, but I was chilled by the reason: Every night the sound of prisoners sharpening their spoons against the concrete floor reached him in his cell in solitary where Pollard was put for his own safety. He told me he was under death threat. "We're going to get you, Jew boy, traitor, kike." The shouts were from both the White Aryan Brotherhood and Black Muslim prisoners, two groups who normally couldn't agree on anything. He constantly feared for his life. At Petersburg, he told me, he never even trusted the guards.

The guards permitted me to bring my camera and tape recorder with me. Pollard, wearing a prison-issued khaki shirt, was escorted from his cell. We sat alone on plastic-covered chairs in a large, stark room where visitors (lawyers,

family members, friends) meet with prisoners. A guard
stood nearby watching us and a television set elevated on
the cement wall. For the three hours I spent with Pollard
that day, I kept hearing the sound of game-show applause
in the background. I didn't think the guard could hear our
conversation although I assumed that the table—or Pollard,
for that matter—might have been wired. I didn't know what
was going on but I was growing more suspicious. For a reporter, access of this kind was too good to be true. Was I
being set up or used?

Pollard opened the conversation with some small talk. He
was clearly embittered after a year of physical isolation. But
he still tried to keep the initial part of our meeting relatively
light and relaxed. I complimented him on the loss of weight;
he was of only medium height and had been rather overweight when I first saw him in court immediately after his
arrest.

"I also quit smoking," he said. "I used to smoke about two
packs of Marlboros a day. I decided that I was contributing
to my own demise at an unacceptable rate."

"Are you feeling better now?" I asked.

"Yes," he replied. "Though I had pleurisy, a lung infec-
tion."

I asked Pollard how he wound up in this mess. He quoted
from a Graham Greene novel, *The Quiet American.* He said
he loved spy novels: "I don't know if you ever read any of
his books, but he happens to be one of my favorite authors.
There's a character, an international correspondent, who
characterizes an acquaintance of his—an American diplomat—by saying, 'I've never met a man who had better motives for all the trouble he's caused.' And I suspect that that
aptly characterizes both my motives and my subsequent
involvement in this affair."

Prison life, he told me, was terrible. He said the isolation
was "comparable to the type of experience long-distance
solo yacht racers face—although I would gladly exchange
my environment for the one that they enjoy. At least a shark
represents a known threat to a sailor, whereas in my case the
threats are as frequent as a breath of air."

Pollard clearly was very scared. "The right way to describe where I am is in a pit," he said. "It's totally frustrating and scary." And what he feared even more than the isolation was the thought of being released into the general prison population. "What will happen there?" he asked. "I don't know what will happen if they throw me to the wolves."

He compared his fate to that of an Israeli Air Force navigator who had just been shot down over Lebanon and was being held prisoner by Lebanese Shi'ites. "I think I can appreciate what that navigator is going through right now. I feel very close to him." Prison life, he added, becomes "a daily battle just to rationalize one's existence."

Through me, he was most anxious to address the American Jewish community. "I don't think the American Jewish community fully appreciates what it's like being a Jew in a prison, regardless of whether he was well motivated or whether he was just a crook," he said. The handful of other Jewish prisoners in Petersburg were expressing some sympathy for him. Pollard described them as *mensches,* a Yiddish word for nice, honorable people. At that point, Pollard had received no sympathy whatsoever from an American Jewish community that had clearly been embarrassed and outraged by the entire affair. "It's ironic that I have to get the kind of moral support that I would have expected from reputable members of the American Jewish community from fellow prisoners," he said. The Jewish prisoners may have broken the law, he went on, but many of them had "retained a sense of compassion and race consciousness which is commendable."

I asked Pollard what he was thinking about in jail so that his mind would not go off the deep end. He said that he spent a great deal of time thinking about Israel's economic future. He still loved the country even though he felt abandoned by it. His great hope was to one day live in Israel and to make a personal contribution to Israel's drive for economic self-sufficiency. "One good thing about being in isolation is that it does tend to focus the mind," he said. "I've been consumed with life after prison and what I can do when I get out. I want to become a productive member of that society." He and his wife "unhesitatingly" wanted to live in Israel, he added.

But in the meantime, Pollard was struggling every day. He read and slept a lot—"It's an escape mechanism." His situation was painful. "There are limits and I am fast approaching those limits. I can't do it alone. I'm tired. I'm frustrated. I'm scared as hell for myself and for my wife, and I just want an end to this nightmare."

Nietzsche had written, "When you look into the abyss, the abyss also looks into you." In Pollard, I saw a tormented man, a potentially brilliant young intelligence analyst and rising star in his field—now sitting in jail. The overnight contrast in his lifestyle was total, a complete change for this cosmopolitan, middle-class Jew. This was certainly not Stanford University nor the Notre Dame Law School nor Indiana University nor the Fletcher School of Law and Diplomacy at Tufts University, where Pollard had studied only a few years earlier.

I had come to the interview with many deeply troubling questions about this case that had so shocked the American Jewish community. I had heard the angry accusations of the U.S. government that Pollard was an evil and greedy mercenary, a dangerous traitor, prepared to sell out his country for money. I had also heard the clearly embarrassed and lame explanations put out by the Israeli government about Pollard's being part of a "rogue" or "unauthorized" intelligence-gathering unit. Yet now I heard Pollard's completely different version of the events which led him to become a "walk-in," a volunteer in Israel's supersecret spy network, considered by many to be the best in the world. He bitterly denied that he spied for the money—the money was not his idea. He wanted to get that message out. That was why he was anxious to see me.

Before meeting him, I had assumed that Pollard was weird or crazy. There had been newspaper stories about his bragging in college that he worked for the Mossad, the Israeli intelligence service. Other reports suggested that he used drugs. But, as we talked, I began to suspect that he was no nut. He appeared very intelligent and cogent, telling his story in thoughtful, measured tones. He was articulate and quite impressive. And when he spoke of literature and music—in high school, I later discovered, he was a prize-winning cellist—he demonstrated real sensitivity.

To some extent, Pollard impressed me as a son of the American Jewish community run amok. I felt that American Jewry was partially responsible for having created him. He grew up believing in the centrality of Israel to the Jewish people. And he wanted to help personally.

Pollard, that day at Petersburg, reminded me very much of other bright young Jews for whom religion wasn't necessarily Judaism, but Israel—an ideological passion for the country as a birthright for all Jews. Their image of Israel is often highly exaggerated, not very realistic. But for the grace of God, I said to myself, any one of them could have wound up like Pollard under similar circumstances. And that bothered me.

Before leaving, I asked Pollard why he had agreed to see me. "My decision was based primarily on my belief that you would maintain a high degree of professionalism with regard to checking out my story," Pollard answered. "This is critical for me because the one thing that I have been damaged by most has been the irresponsibility of the press." He felt that he had not been portrayed accurately in the news media. He said he wanted to personally explain his motives in spying for Israel.

"I have been reading your byline for years," he said. "That's really the bottom line."

But Pollard also explained that he selected me because of the audience for which I write. He was especially interested in reaching the people of Israel, as well as the American Jewish community. "I'll be the first to admit that I broke the law," he said. "But give the kid a little empathy. I thought I was helping Israel and the United States."

I had come with a set of expectations that clearly did not fit. I left very confused; so many questions remained unanswered. Why did the Israelis do it? Weren't they getting enough information from the United States officially? Why risk the overall U.S.-Israeli relationship? Was he justified in spying for Israel? Was the United States holding back vital information, necessary for Israel's very survival? Was Pollard part of a rogue operation or did he have high-level authorization? And how high did that authorization go? Was there an official Israeli cover-up? Did he act alone inside the U.S. intelligence community, or was there a mysterious "Mr. X," a second Israeli spy who has still remained at large? What did the Pollard case say about American Jewry's dual loyalty?

I drove away from the prison, leaving behind a huge watchtower and seemingly endless rolls of barbed wire. It was miserably cold and raining—appropriate weather, I thought, to reflect on what I had just seen and heard. I was determined to learn whether Pollard had indeed been a destructive, dangerous spy or whether he was simply an over-bright young man who led a rich fantasy life that centered on his becoming a superhero for the country he idolized.

I stopped at the first pay telephone I could find—it happened to be outside a 7-Eleven convenience store. I had not told my editors about the interview in advance because I was never 100 percent certain that it would in fact materialize. Until I actually saw Pollard, I was afraid that the guards would come up with some last-minute excuse; why get my editors all excited over nothing?

It was Thursday evening in Jerusalem when I reached David Landau, the *Post*'s associate managing editor. Normally he is not very emotional, but he was clearly excited to hear of my scoop. I asked him how he wanted to play the story. I frankly thought it might be a good idea to wait a few days so that I could work thoughtfully and slowly on a lengthy article. Pollard had assured me that he did not plan to meet with any other reporters. I would have his exclusive story—at least for the time being. Landau, to his credit, insisted that I write up the interview right away. The next day, November 21, happened to be the first anniversary of

Pollard's arrest. It was also Friday, when Israeli newspapers publish their biggest editions.

For the next two hours I sat in my car rereading my notes, listening to the tape recording, and writing the story on my Radio Shack lap-top portable computer.

Pollard had told me that he was speaking "on the record" and that it was up to me to decide what to do with the material. "I trust you completely," he said. "I have made a decision to deal with only one journalist, and that's you. You do with the material whatever you want."

The headline in Friday's paper was "BEFUDDLED" POL-LARD: WHY DID ISRAEL ABANDON ME?

Pollard was quoted in my story as saying: "I am heart-broken . . . I feel the same way that one of Israel's pilots would feel if, after he was shot down, nobody made an effort to get him out—not even lifted a finger; in fact, questioned his abilities and his motivations."

The story caused a sensation in Israel. For the first time, Pollard's side of the story had been aired. He had acted out of his love for Israel—not for the money. It was picked up by all the wire services and reported around the world. *The Washington Post* asked me to write a special article about the interview for the paper's Sunday "Outlook" section. It was reprinted in numerous other newspapers. I was invited to discuss the subject on American television and radio in-terview programs. The BBC world service began to call me frequently for telephone interviews. Overnight, I had become the expert on the Pollard affair.

Meanwhile, I continued to pursue various aspects of the case. I rather quickly decided to seek a second interview with Pollard. Permission was granted more slowly this time. I wrote again to the warden. One of his aides wrote back to inform me that there were formal restrictions on prison interviews. "This is necessary to minimize disruption to in-stitutional operations, conserve staff resources necessary to supervise such interviews and to afford all members of the media equal access to the inmate," he said.

In early January 1987, I flew to Israel, where I had a

chance to interview some top Israeli officials with intimate knowledge of the Pollard case. I learned and confirmed some incredible details. An Israeli intelligence official told me that some of the information Pollard had provided was "so breathtaking" that it justified the risk Israel was taking in running an agent in Washington. Another Israeli official confirmed almost everything that Pollard had told me.

Back in Washington, I followed up my letter to the prison authorities with a phone call. I wanted to underline my continued interest in the interview. I was polite but persistent, and this combination paid off. Within a few days, I received approval to come to Petersburg on January 29, which turned out to be another cold and miserable day.

During this second session, Pollard was much more depressed than at our first meeting. He was more nervous and edgy. He told me that he was now convinced he was going to get a life sentence even though the prosecution had promised, as part of the plea-bargaining agreement, not to ask for life. He felt that he had been set up. And he pinned most of the blame directly on Defense Secretary Caspar Weinberger. By then, he had already seen Weinberger's classified pre-sentencing memorandum to the judge outlining the damage to U.S. national security caused by his actions.

On Sunday, February 15, I published an article that appeared simultaneously in *The Jerusalem Post* and *The Washington Post*. The article, for the first time, documented the exact nature of some of the material Pollard had provided to Israel. I reported, for example, that he had given the Israelis U.S. reconnaissance photographs of PLO headquarters in Tunisia, including a description of the buildings there. This and other related data obtained by Pollard enabled the Israeli Air Force to evade detection and to bomb those headquarters on October 1, 1985. I noted that despite Israel's claim that Pollard was part of a rogue operation, "Israeli officials speak of him in terms that suggest he may prove to be one of the most important spies in Israel's history."

Why, I wondered, didn't the United States simply give Israel this kind of important information?

From Israel's point of view, the information Pollard obtained was critical—"superimportant" was a description I repeatedly heard from the highest Israeli leaders.

The interviews clearly had a significant but completely unexpected impact on both of our lives. Because of the stories I wrote, some suggested that I was too sympathetic to a confessed spy. But others would consider me one of Pollard's hangmen because of my disclosures. Those charges against me, and the sense of resentment they built in me, were factors in drawing me to learn as much about the case as possible.

In the government's pre-sentencing memorandum, prosecutors cited Pollard's first interview with me as one reason to justify his receiving a harsh sentence. Pollard, the government said, had "violated an express provision of his written plea agreement." Although the information Pollard gave me was not classified, he had violated procedures simply by talking to me:

> There is every reason to believe that defendant
> would make further disclosures of classified
> information to Israel if given the opportunity. By his
> own account as related to *The Jerusalem Post*
> reporter, defendant considers Israel his "home" and
> intends to live there once released; defendant claims
> he is "as much a loyal son of that country as anybody
> has been;" and the only apology defendant offers is
> that his espionage activity "wasn't the most effective
> from a long-range standpoint."

Defense Secretary Weinberger, in a separate unclassified memorandum to the judge, also referred to Pollard's interviews with me, claiming that Pollard's "loyalty to Israel transcends his loyalty to the United States."

Weinberger referred to my February 15 article in *The*

Jerusalem Post and *The Washington Post.* "That article," he wrote,

> contained information purporting to reflect U.S. intelligence efforts. While I do not intend publicly to confirm or deny the accuracy of those statements, it was beyond cavil that, if true, such information should never be made publicly available. The defendant initially denied having been the source of the information, but when confronted with a polygraph examination on February 25, he acknowledged that he had either provided or confirmed certain of the information contained in that article by talking to a journalist. I have no way of knowing whether he provided additional information not published in that article, but I believe that there can be no doubt that he can, and will, continue to disclose U.S. secrets without regard to the impact it may have on U.S. national defense or foreign policy.

I was shocked. Unwittingly and unhappily, I found myself part of the story. Yet I did not sneak into the prison. I signed U.S. Department of Justice forms on both occasions clearly stating my purpose in meeting with Pollard—and, of course, identified myself as a reporter for *The Jerusalem Post.* If those interviews were not approved, why was I allowed into prison?

I asked that question to the U.S. Attorney for the District of Columbia, Joseph E. diGenova, chief prosecutor in the case, on March 4, only two hours after Pollard was sentenced. We had appeared jointly on the MacNeil/Lehrer Newshour to discuss the case. As we walked outside the studio, I told diGenova that the government's pre-sentencing memorandums, in my opinion, should have pointed out that I had received permission from the Justice Department to interview Pollard.

DiGenova said the government was not blaming me for anything. "You were doing your job," he said. "We understand that." But he insisted that according to Pollard's plea-bargaining agreement, it was up to Pollard to first clear any newspaper interviews with the director of Naval Intelligence. "It wasn't up to the warden to make that kind of decision," diGenova stressed. "It was Pollard's responsibility."

As I considered diGenova's words over the course of subsequent weeks, I began to suspect that the prosecutors had deliberately allowed me to interview Pollard to see exactly what he might say. They probably assumed that he would undermine his own defense by talking too much. I suspected that they also wanted Pollard to commit some technical violation of his plea-bargaining agreement. That would enable the judge to impose a stiffer sentence. And in fact the judge, in announcing his life sentence, cited, among other things, Pollard's interviews with me as having shown that he had no remorse for his crime and that he was still incapable of protecting classified information. A copy of my interview of Pollard was attached to the government's pre-sentencing memorandum as Exhibit A. There were no other exhibits. Was this part of a conspiracy? Or was it part of the fear in the United States that Pollard was only one of a band of Israeli spies at work?

That was March 1987. Since that time, I have been dogged with questions about whether I was used to nail Pollard. His lawyer, Richard Hibey, told me flatly that the interviews very seriously damaged his client. During a visit to Israel in July 1987, several senior Israeli military and intelligence officials said they knew for a fact that I had been used by the prosecution. The more I learned, the more I was motivated to straighten out a story I had perhaps unintentionally muddled by my involvement.

I never felt guilty because I knew that I had behaved as any professional journalist would have behaved under similar circumstances. Would any reporter have refused to interview Pollard? He clearly wanted to see me; he wanted to explain his side of the story. He spoke on the record. The U.S. government authorized my entry into the prison.

With espionage, you hardly ever know what's really going on. In dealing with intelligence services, I subsequently came to learn, you sometimes find that a light at the end of the tunnel leads only to a tunnel at the end of the light. Yet I wanted to find the truth. That's why I wrote this book.

Many people encouraged me to do so. Harriet Rubin, then an editor at Harper & Row, was present at the creation. She made sure this book would get off the ground. A delight to work with, she offered some excellent points that I have incorporated. Arthur H. Samuelson, my editor at Harper & Row, was fortunately very tough in forcing me to rewrite and rethink many sections. A very talented professional, he was enthusiastic and energetic in helping me. I will forever be grateful for his considerable input. Cynthia Barrett, his assistant, was also very helpful to me, as were Jim Fox, Maggie Mulvihill, and Laura Starrett.

My editors at *The Jerusalem Post,* Ari Rath and Erwin Frenkel, were very generous in granting me a leave of absence. Like many other Israelis, they pressed me to write this book even though the Pollard spy scandal does not represent one of Israel's better moments. They felt that I would be careful in putting the story in its proper perspective. Indeed, not one Israeli leader—from the President and Prime Minister on down—tried to discourage me. Very often the exact opposite was the case. To their credit, they said that I had a responsibility to explain to a confused and embarrassed Israeli public exactly where mistakes were made. How else could Israel avoid repeating those mistakes?

Yes, I have personal feelings about the case, but I have tried to put them aside in my researching and writing. I sought to be as professional, honest, responsible, and fair as possible.

I was blessed with access to all sides; top officials in both the U.S. and Israeli governments made very sensitive information available to me. Israeli and American investigators were generous with their time. They, too, felt the public had a right to know what happened. I entered into no deals to obtain this cooperation. But because of the nature of the subject—intelligence—they almost unanimously asked that

I not mention their names. Many could lose their jobs if I did. I could not have written this book without their assistance.

I, of course, interviewed Jonathan Pollard and Anne Henderson Pollard, as well as their families, friends, and lawyers. I am grateful to them for their cooperation, which was also given with absolutely no strings attached. I have not entered into any financial agreements with them. Dr. and Mrs. Morris Pollard, their daughter, Carol, and Bernard Henderson were especially kind in receiving me. They are warm and decent people who have suffered an enormous personal tragedy.

I reviewed thousands of pages of court documents as well as many other declassified documents made available to me for the first time under the Freedom of Information Act. I would especially like to thank Dr. Jeffrey Richelson of the National Security Archive in Washington for helping me weave through this process.

I am also deeply indebted to my agent, Alex Sheftell, and to my lawyer, Victor A. Kovner, for their continuing assistance. They are both fine gentlemen.

Finally, my family and friends have been a constant source of encouragement. I owe much to all of them.

PART ONE

The Spy

CHAPTER ONE

The Bond Salesman

Very early in 1984, Jonathan Jay Pollard, a feisty twenty-nine-year-old civilian analyst for U.S. Naval Intelligence, was told by Steven E. Stern, a wealthy stockbroker and a long-time family friend in New York, of a fascinating lecture he had recently heard. The speaker had been Israeli Air Force Col. Aviem Sella, who was then on leave pursuing a doctorate in computer sciences at New York University. An architect of Israel's very successful air assault against Syrian warplanes during the 1982 war in Lebanon—in air-to-air combat, Israel downed ninety Syrians MiGs while losing none of its own planes—Sella had been sent to the United States to hone his mastery of the computer, which had become such a vital part of Israel's high-tech military.

The meeting that unusually cold day in December 1983 had been held in the sixth-floor conference room at Stern's securities office on Broadway, just off Wall Street. Present were a dozen hardened and skeptical New York Jewish stockbrokers and financial analysts who had come directly from their own offices at the end of the business day. Stern, who had visited Israel on several occasions and was fairly active in Jewish communal activities, served soft drinks and pretzels.

Stern had been asked by the Israel Bonds organization to arrange the session with the hope that bonds would be sold. Historically, New York brokers had shied away from Israel Bonds. Maybe Sella could spark some sales.

A lanky and handsome officer with an engaging smile, Sella had become a regular on the Israel Bonds lecture circuit. He was very popular, almost always well received by his audiences. Sella's English, though accented, was fluent. To the New York Jewish stockbrokers, he seemed straight out of Central Casting—the brilliant, tough Israeli fighter pilot.

Sella's address was breathtaking. He wound up spending over ninety minutes describing his role in Israel's spectacular bombing of the Iraqi nuclear reactor at Osirak in June 1981. He had been Chief of Air Force Operations, the lead pilot, and one of the chief planners of the operation, which was designed to smother Iraq's menacing nuclear development program. The audience, by all accounts, quickly became spellbound as Sella described how the Israeli Air Force had planned the operation, training its pilots to withstand enormous physical and psychological pressures as they flew 500 miles an hour at tree-top levels over enemy territory to avoid radar detection.

"The tension is incredible," he said. "A pilot can go berserk." At that low altitude and high speed a loss of concentration for even a second can be fatal. He had seen fellow pilots crash during intense, low-flying training exercises.

Sella was quite explicit in discussing details of the operation. He let the brokers know that they were receiving the real inside story, information they would not read in *The New York Times.* Thus, he said that the Israeli fighter aircraft took off from a desert air base just outside Eilat, Israel's southern port, and that in the weeks leading up to the Osirak raid, the air force had made certain that the same number of planes, in the same exact formation, had regularly taken off from the base on what were meant to appear to be routine training exercises. The U.S. and Soviet satellites monitoring the Israeli air base on the day of the raid would assume that the planes were merely embarking on just another exercise.

Born in Haifa in 1946, Aviem Sella was quite a remarkable man—one of the stars of the Israeli Air Force. What the stockbrokers could not have known that day is just how much of a star. A classified 1986 U.S. Defense Intelligence Agency (DIA) biographical sketch later obtained under the Freedom of Information Act reviewed his career this way:

> Colonel Sella entered the IAF in 1964, completing flight training in 1966. From 1965 to 1966 he was a pilot with an Ouragan jet squadron. From 1963 to 1969 he flew Mystere aircraft, participating in combat during the 1967 Six Day War. During and after the 1967 War he was an instructor at the IAF Flight School. He attended the Instrument Flying School in Yeovilton, UK, in 1968. From 1969 to 1971 he flew as junior deputy to an F-4 Phantom squadron commander, again participating in numerous combat missions during the 1970 War of Attrition against Egypt. In 1971 he earned a B.A. in economics from Jerusalem University. Sella made the transition to Mirage aircraft, flying with the 61st Squadron from Ramat David Airbase *circa* 1972. From 1972 to 1974 he was First Deputy to a Phantom squadron commander, and engaged in many combat missions during the 1973 War. From 1974 to 1976 he served at Air Force Headquarters as a staff officer in charge of developing advanced air combat methods. In 1976 he assumed command of the 201st Fighter-Bomber (F-4E) Squadron at Hatzor Airbase, remaining commander for an unusually long period of time. During his tenure, the 201st was the only squadron in the IAF not to lose an aircraft through accidents. He left in 1979 to pursue graduate studies, earning an M.A. in business administration from Tel Aviv

University. From 1980 to 1983, he was Chief of Air Force Operations. By 1984, he had almost completed requirements for a Ph.D. in computer science from New York University.

The report continued: "Sella possesses a good sense of humour, and is considered highly creative. . . . He has brown hair and eyes. He is a cigarette smoker. An energetic individual, he is a scuba diving enthusiast and avid tennis player." It also noted that he "drinks on social occasions and seems to enjoy it."

Sella was married in 1969 to Yehudit, an attorney in Tel Aviv. "Sella met his wife during the Six Day War while she was an officer in the IAF [Israel Air Force]." They have two sons, born in 1971 and 1978. Sella's mother died in 1960 when he was fourteen years old.

Even without knowing any of this, the group of New York stockbrokers were very impressed.

Yet Sella could easily have been sitting in their seats had his parents decided to come to the United States rather than to Palestine. His grandparents had been slaughtered in the Nazi death camps. He was named Aviem in their memory— *avi*, in Hebrew, means "my father," and *em* "mother." Sella, although a sabra, had what is commonly called a Holocaust mentality. Like so many other Jews of the postwar generation, he was deeply influenced by—even ashamed of—the impotence of the Jews during the war. With the creation of Israel, however, that kind of tragedy could never recur. Israel would forever defend Jews. Sella was personally committed to that proposition.

Not long after that meeting, an excited Stern told his friend Jonathan Jay Pollard all the details. It was, the wealthy New Yorker said, the most fascinating lecture he had ever heard in his life.

Pollard, who had been intrigued by Israel from an early age and had often fantasized about living there, told Stern he was keenly interested in meeting with Sella as soon as possible and would willingly come to New York to do so. Stern agreed to arrange it. He could see how anxious Pollard was to establish contact with the Israeli. Later, he would say that he had no knowledge that Pollard's real intention in meeting Sella was to volunteer as a spy for Israel.

The Stern and Pollard families were old friends. Stern's father, Gustav Stern, had been a generous financial contributor to Dr. Morris Pollard's research programs at Notre Dame. His picture still hangs on the stark cement-block wall of Dr. Pollard's modest office in South Bend, Indiana. As a boy growing up, Jonathan was quite familiar with it.*

Steven Stern used to see Jonathan Pollard at the annual scientific seminars which Dr. Pollard organized and chaired and Gustav Stern funded. And by the 1970s, Stern and Pollard had themselves developed a friendship. When Pollard began to work for Naval Intelligence in Washington, D.C., Stern would often discuss the international oil situation, the crisis in the Persian Gulf, and other matters that could affect the stock market on the phone with him. He found Pollard's analyses fascinating and rather informative. Indeed, like many others, he saw Pollard, who had a photographic mind, as a walking encyclopedia.

After that first meeting at the Israel Bonds reception, Sella would occasionally return to Stern's office to chat. They developed a modest friendship. And Stern, as requested, informed Sella of Pollard's very strong wish to meet him. He told Sella that Pollard was a Jew, employed by U.S. Naval Intelligence, and a strong supporter of Israel.

From the start, the pilot was intrigued. What exactly did Pollard have in mind?

The Israeli Air Force is basically a rather small, cohesive,

---

*Gustav Stern and his brother Max were German Jewish refugees who had escaped to the United States in the 1930s. There they founded the enormous Hartz Mountain pet-food empire. The business thrived although the two brothers eventually quarreled bitterly. In 1955, they decided to split. By literally losing a flip of the coin, Gustav's interests were bought out by Max. So Steven Stern's first cousin, Leonard Stern of New York, one of the richest men in the United States, runs the company today. Among other things, Leonard Stern also owns a great deal of property and *The Village Voice*.

and intimate operation, and extremely well disciplined. No senior pilot is going to meet with an American intelligence official on his own. Sella would get involved only if his commanding officers approved.

Sella therefore decided to go through channels. He had earlier met Yosef Yagur, the energetic science counselor at the Israeli Consulate in New York who had once worked for Israel Aircraft Industries. Yagur was an engineer by training. Among "official" Israelis stationed in New York, he was popular and well known.

Yagur, a short but intense man, reported directly to a special scientific intelligence-gathering unit of the Defense Ministry, the Office of Scientific Liaison, better known by its Hebrew acronym LAKAM *(Lishka Lekishrey Mada).* * Sella, who was well aware of LAKAM and its work, told Yagur about Stern's proposal. "Do you think I should meet him?" Sella asked.

Yagur responded that LAKAM would want to thoroughly check out Pollard before any meeting could be arranged. The Israelis had to make certain that Sella was not being set up.

At first, the Israelis were understandably very skeptical. "Walk-ins" are always suspect. Experienced agents fear that they might be blackmailed or compromised; they must be extremely cautious in dealing with these people. Still, walk-ins are not necessarily rejected automatically by any intelligence service. Occasionally, they can turn out to be very useful.

But there are strict precautions that have to be followed— precautions which the Israelis followed. Members of a Knesset investigatory committee and several other sources would eventually reveal that the Mossad—Israel's major external intelligence-gathering organization—was indeed contacted. A scan of its files showed that Pollard had quietly

---

*The acronym LAKAM has often been written LEKEM even though the correct Hebrew pronunciation is LAKAM.

passed some intelligence to Israel when he had officially participated in two formal intelligence exchanges with Israel in 1982. He felt that vital information—which actually had been authorized for release to Israel—should be shared, and became very upset when it was not. Other members of the U.S. delegation apparently thought that the information could be used as a bargaining chip to extract some parallel information from Israel during a subsequent session. That is the nature of such intelligence exchanges among friendly countries.

Pollard, however, was angry. He felt that Israel needed the information right away and was convinced it was not passed on because the other U.S. officials were anti-Israeli—if not anti-Semitic. He managed to inform a startled Israeli officer during a break in one of the meetings of the information.

"I'm Jewish," Pollard told the Israeli. "I want to help you."

The Mossad's files also showed that in 1981 Pollard had informally applied for a job with the American Israel Public Affairs Committee (AIPAC), the official pro-Israeli lobbying organization in Washington, but was turned down because he was considered "strange." He told a very detailed story of AIPAC's being watched by the Justice Department, maintaining that its phones were bugged. This information scared AIPAC officials even though they thought he must be a crackpot. They suspected that he might be involved in some sort of trap to set them up. They politely thanked Pollard for the information before getting rid of him; later they were amazed to learn that a Jonathan Jay Pollard did indeed work for Naval Intelligence.

The Mossad, after learning about Stern's approach to Sella, decided that it would have no dealings with Pollard. "We have no interest in meeting him," a Mossad report said.

There were good reasons for the Mossad to stay away from Pollard—beyond the AIPAC incident. The fact is that the Mossad itself has not undertaken covert operations *against*—as opposed to in—the United States for many years as a matter of sacred policy. Because of its very close and cooperative working relationship with the CIA, the Mossad does not actually run spies against the United States. Since the organization maintains very close formal liaison with the CIA in both Washington and Tel Aviv, routinely exchanging a great amount of information, it was felt too risky to violate that policy.

LAKAM, on the other hand, had no such specific prohibitions in its charter. Indeed, Israeli officials would later reveal that the unit was created some twenty years earlier specifically to collect scientific intelligence, largely behind friendly lines in the West. That's where the best scientific information happens to exist. One major and supersensitive objective was to strengthen Israel's nuclear development program. Much of that information comes from open sources—journals, seminars, meetings with scientists. Beginning in the 1960s, LAKAM had been involved in all sorts of operations in the United States and elsewhere. Some of the information is collected clandestinely.

It was LAKAM, in fact, that was partially responsible for the theft of the blueprints for the French-made Mirage jet fighter in 1968. LAKAM had been involved in the recruitment of a Swiss engineer named Alfred Frauenknecht to steal the documents. He was paid for the operation, which eventually was exposed. The engineer, who is not Jewish, spent five years in a Swiss prison before being released. But Israel successfully used the plans to help in the development of its own Kfir jet fighter.

Thus, any relationship with Pollard would by no means be the first time that LAKAM was involved in a covert operation.

Despite the Mossad's decision to stay away, Rafael "Rafi" Eitan, the politically well-connected and mysterious head of LAKAM and a legendary masterspy in his own right, decided that it might still be worthwhile to see what Pollard had in mind.

Eitan, who had been eased out of the Mossad years earlier after it became clear he was not destined to become its head, told Yagur to authorize Sella's introductory meeting with the U.S. Naval Intelligence analyst. Eitan, who had his own score to settle with the Mossad, was by no means prepared to reject an American Jewish "walk-in." He was convinced—based on his own actual experiences in the United States and elsewhere—that the parameters of LAKAM's mission authorized the establishment of contact with Pollard.

Eitan, a short, balding, and overweight man with very bad eyesight and hearing, had spent virtually his entire professional life spying for Israel. By all accounts, he had been involved in numerous incredible escapades, routinely risking his life. Born in 1926 just outside Tel Aviv, he joined the Palmach, the elite fighting army of the Jewish underground in Palestine, in 1944. He was severely wounded during Israel's War of Independence in 1948–49 but asked to join the Mossad in 1951, and was accepted. He remained in the intelligence community until 1972, working his way up to become deputy chief of operations.

In February 1960, the Mossad chief, Isser Harel, asked him to participate in a plot to capture Adolf Eichmann, the Nazi war criminal, who was then living in Argentina under the alias Rikardo Klement. Before leaving Israel, Eitan and his men practiced the operation by targeting a fellow Mossad agent for kidnapping in Tel Aviv. Israeli military and intelligence units always try to rehearse an action if at all possible. "We selected one of our own security men," Eitan would later tell an Israeli magazine, "whom we knew walked down Dizengoff Street to and from his house, the same route and at the same time, every day. One clear day we captured him [on the street] without anyone's being aware of it. He could have had a heart attack? Yes, but he didn't. That's why he's in the security services."

A few days later, they did the same thing on a street in Buenos Aires.

After leaving the Mossad, Eitan hoped that the Prime Minister would name him to head the domestic intelligence service, the Shin Beth. But that, too, was not to be. Eitan was considered an excellent and courageous field man; he was an operator. But he was seen as too undisciplined to head either the Mossad or the Shin Beth. He was not well organized, and physically and socially, he was unacceptable. His nickname, in fact, was "Rafi Hamasriach," or "Rafi the stinker," received in the army because he supposedly always wore the same socks.

As a result, an embittered and angry Eitan went into private business. But his associates would later quote him as saying that he would one day settle accounts with his former colleagues in the Mossad and elsewhere in the Israeli intelligence community. He would show them who was Israel's best masterspy after all.

One of his partners in an only modestly successful Sinai fishing enterprise during those lean years in the governmental wilderness was Gen. Ariel Sharon, himself then also temporarily out of government service. Sharon, one of Eitan's closest friends, would later play a major role in bringing Eitan back into the intelligence community.

After Menachem Begin and the Likud came to power in 1977, the burly Sharon was named Minister of Agriculture in the Cabinet. He strongly recommended that Eitan be named the new Prime Minister's adviser on counterterrorism—a position Sharon had himself held under Prime Minister Yitzhak Rabin. Begin agreed. A few years later, Sharon, after becoming Defense Minister, asked that Eitan simultaneously serve as head of LAKAM in the Defense Ministry. Again, Begin agreed. Sharon and Eitan—together with a handful of other Israeli intelligence and defense officials—would play the decisive roles in setting the stage for the Israeli invasion of Lebanon during the summer of 1982. Eitan, for example, was a key liaison to Bashir Gemayel, the Lebanese Phalangist leader.

But that war proved to be a disaster for Israel as well as for Sharon, who was forced to step down as Defense Minister after the 1983 Kahan Commission of Inquiry concluded that he was indirectly responsible for the September 1982 massacre of Palestinians by Lebanese Christians at the Sabra and Shatilla refugee camps outside Beirut. The new Defense

Minister was the untainted Moshe Arens, who returned from Washington where he was serving as Israel's ambassador to accept his new responsibility. Eitan survived—retained at LAKAM. Prime Minister Yitzhak Shamir had similarly retained Eitan as his counterterrorism adviser after succeeding Menachem Begin in September 1983.

Over the years, senior Israeli military officers had established a tradition of occasionally carrying out "special assignments" while on leave from their regular service. But any such extracurricular activity had to be carefully prescribed and formally authorized. Thus, Eitan recognized that Sella would first need the direct approval of the commander of the Air Force, Maj. Gen. Amos Lapidot, to meet—even informally—with an American intelligence official.

Several authoritative Israeli officials would later disclose that Sella received such written permission not only from Lapidot but from Lt. Gen. Moshe Levi, then IDF Chief of Staff, as well. Both Levi and Lapidot were told that Rafi Eitan had a special assignment for Sella. They agreed to let the pilot undertake it. At that point, the generals did not know exactly what Eitan had in mind; indeed, no one knew what was in store for Pollard. The generals assumed it was a one-shot, modest deal. They didn't ask questions. Eitan, they simply thought, must know what he is doing.

Eitan had known Sella personally. The Israeli masterspy had tried repeatedly in earlier years to win permission from Prime Minister Begin to undertake an Eichmann-type operation to kidnap Dr. Josef Mengele, the notorious Nazi "Angel of Death" who was believed to be hiding in Paraguay. Eitan, as Begin's counterterrorism adviser, had a detailed scheme to grab Mengele—one that would even use Sella as the get-away pilot. But his plans were vetoed by the Israeli leadership (including Begin) as too politically risky. Israel did not need another diplomatic crisis erupting if the operation failed. Eitan, it was said, would never forgive Begin for missing that chance to capture Mengele.

Shortly after receiving written permission from his commanding officers, Sella asked Stern to inform Pollard that a meeting could be arranged in Washington. Stern, constantly badgered by Pollard to make the match, had just called Sella a second time to press for the meeting.

Pollard was very excited. After years of hesitation and delay, he sensed that he was about to fulfill a life-long dream.

CHAPTER TWO

The "Hoosier Poet"

Jonathan Jay Pollard was born in Galveston, Texas, on August 7, 1954. His father, Dr. Morris Pollard, was then just starting a brilliant career in microbiology—a career that would quickly bring him to the vast and idyllic campus of Notre Dame University in South Bend, Indiana. His mother, Molly, was busy raising three very bright and active children—Harvey, the oldest, who would later become a doctor specializing in cancer research at the National Institutes of Health in Bethesda, Maryland; Carol, the middle sister, who would work in hospital administration in New Haven, Connecticut; and Jonathan, whom everyone simply called Jay.

"I loved the name Jonathan," his mother recalled. "He was named after an uncle of my mother's. He was a favorite uncle of my mother's." But within weeks of his birth, everyone began calling him Jay.

In South Bend, the family built a lovely ranch-style home at the end of a quiet cul de sac not far from the campus. It had a large, well-kept backyard where the children could play. The family quickly became an integral and active part of Notre Dame's academic community. They developed an especially warm relationship with Father Theodore Hesburgh, the university's beloved long-time president. Dr. Pollard said there had never been any problem because of his being Jewish. In fact, everyone seemed to go out of the way to befriend him and make his family feel comfortable on the Catholic campus.

From the start, Jay Pollard was a precocious and cute little boy, and he was pampered by his mother. "For all intents and purposes I grew up more or less as an only child, with all of the benefits and the problems of that," he would later say, noting that both his siblings were appreciably older.

His sister agreed. "Jay actually had two sets of parents," she recalled. "My older brother and I were one set, and my parents were another. He had the benefit of having people who were talking to him all the time—listening to him, taking him places. He was very privileged that way."

She said that her little brother, as a young boy, had "a group of little friends that he grew up with," but he spent a great deal of time either alone or with his family. She said she always loved him very much. "I would take him places, everywhere that I went. I enjoyed being with him. He was really a sweetheart." She felt very close to him. "Although there is eight years difference between us," she said, "we have some kind of very strong emotional connection, and I think it's because internally, we are very similar people."

That was not necessarily the case between the two brothers, whose age difference is eleven years. "Harvey went off to school by the time Jay was just beginning to blossom as a pre-teenager," said Carol. "That was kind of hard on Jay because he really idolized Harvey. He didn't want him to go to college. I remember we dropped Harvey off at college and Jay was crying."

Mrs. Pollard also remembered the special relationship that developed between Jay and Carol. "He responded to her," she said. "She would tell him to do things and he'd do them. She adored him."

Like almost everyone else, Carol remembered her younger brother as being "a very inquisitive, intellectually prone person." From a very early age, he was ready to reach out to the bigger world outside Galveston and South Bend. And Carol said that he was also "emotionally always ready to reach out." He was very warm and sensitive. "I always thought that any woman that got him for a husband was going to get a supreme catch."

Despite the age difference, she would later credit him with broadening her own horizons. "He's the one who got me into music," she said. In high school, he had indeed won several cello awards; the yellowed scrapbook newspaper clippings would years later still be displayed in the Pollard family living room. His mother rereads them with pride.

One picture of five students in the South Bend *Tribune* of May 16, 1968, shows Jay, almost fourteen, holding his cello and bow. Next to him are the other students rehearsing for a spring concert to be presented by the Stanley Clark School the following Sunday.

"He had such talent," his mother recalls. To this day, Jay's cello stands in the corner of the living room, a reminder of what once was.

In 1956, Dr. Pollard took the entire family to England for a year. He had been named a McLaughlin Faculty Fellow at Cambridge University. He recalled that Jay—only eighteen months old—had an Irish nanny "who had no children and thought of him as her child. When we left, she ran after the train crying."

Before he reached the age of five, Jay had already joined his parents in Paris, Stockholm, Mexico City, and elsewhere. Indeed, his fourth birthday was celebrated at the International Congress of Microbiology in Stockholm. "There were at least a dozen Nobel Prize winners at his birthday party, including Waxman and Sabin, and they were all singing 'Happy Birthday' to him," Dr. Pollard said. "He started crying. He didn't want all those old fuddy-duddies around. He wanted young people."

"I want children," Jay cried.

At that same conference, Dr. Pollard recalled with laughter, the four-year-old had a run-in with a scientist from the Soviet Union. "There was a common room to watch TV," Dr. Pollard said. "There was a small chair for children, where Jay sat. He had to go to the bathroom and when he came back, the chair was taken by a Russian delegate and brought to another room. Jay confronted the guy and said, 'I want my chair back.' It was almost an international incident."

At another conference in West Germany, Mrs. Pollard said, Jay looked directly into the eyes of the rector of a major German university and asked in a rather loud voice: "Are you a Nazi?"

Even at that young age, Jay was already aware of the Holocaust. "Are we in Germany?" Jay asked elsewhere during that visit. When Dr. Pollard said yes, Jay pointed his finger in the shape of a gun and shouted, "Bang, all dead, all dead."

Back at home in Indiana, Jay was a very bright student who developed interests in a wide range of fields. "He's the one who got me into archeology," Carol said. "He's the one who got me into history. It sounds kind of weird. He's eight years younger than I am but his intellectual curiosity really kind of sparked me into doing things with my life that I probably wouldn't have gotten into." They even went mountain climbing together.

Jay's bedroom walls were lined with books. He was totally fascinated by titles like *Characters and Events in Roman History, Pioneer Archeologists Tell Their Own Story, A Panorama of Life in the Second Millennium, B.C., Pictorial History of the Jewish People,* and many others. He had a special fascination with military history. But his ultimate passion was Israel. Indeed, there were numerous books about Israel and the Jewish people, with a heavy emphasis on the Holocaust. Jay's parents had often told him that the family had lost over seventy European relatives during the Holocaust.

"My parents are second-generation," Pollard said, carefully selecting his words. "They went through what I call the soft persecution of the pre–World War II days. They are both strongly pro-American to the depth of their souls— more so than I could ever imagine."

But he grew up with a different vision. For one thing, he very much wanted to live in Israel. But they did not share

his burning need to settle there. He wanted to personally
and directly strengthen the state. They certainly saw themselves as good Jews and committed Zionists, who loved Israel very much. They instilled a great feeling for the country
and their Jewish heritage in their youngest son. But for
them, America was home.

"My parents never ceased in their efforts to portray this
land as a Godsend for Jews, who throughout the course of
our long, often tortuous history in the Diaspora had never
experienced a country so full of opportunities.

"I was brought up with a fairly standard Jewish upbringing," Jay continued. "However, balanced with this notion of
civic responsibility was the centrality of Israel. It was with
me every waking moment since I can remember. The first
flag I remember was the Israeli flag. It was the first one I
could point out. I started learning Hebrew at a very early
age—*heder* and Hebrew school, both Conservative and Reform. My parents were not bigoted as far as that was concerned. When you have a small Jewish community, one
tends to try to support both institutions."

Slowly but steadily, Israel became Pollard's religion. "For
as long as I can remember," he affirmed, "Israel has figured
prominently in my life as an object of religious commitment
as well as a source of personal strength." He admitted that
he simply became obsessed with the country. It was always
on his mind. He spoke with pride of his family's personal
involvement in the struggle to create the state in 1948—six
years before his birth.

Thus, he recalled an uncle, Isidore Klein, who was a high-
ranking officer in the American military medical corps in
Paris in 1948. Klein, he said, found a way to divert significant
amounts of supplies—medicine, sheets, medical logistics—to
Israel. "For years our family took quiet pride in my late
uncle's decision to provide the fledgling Israeli Army in
1948 with military boots and medical supplies 'liberated'
from the American Hospital in Paris, which he commanded
at the time."

For Pollard, Klein became a personal hero. And there
were others as well. "All the time growing up, all I heard was

stories of individuals we knew—very close friends—who had performed what I call their racial obligation to Israel in 1948. This is a term which I grew up with."

Sometimes, he continued, it meant "shotgunning a trainload of illegal dynamite through San Antonio, stevedoring a covert Israeli arms shipment at night out of Galveston, spiriting a stripped-down aircraft out of an Air Force Reserve park in the desert—all of these things. I was brought up with the notion that this kind of service was not breaking the law but was the discharge, as I say, of a racial obligation. Certainly, it was made easier by the fact that as far as I was concerned—the way I was brought up—there was no difference between being a good American and a good Zionist. Even today, in my own mind, I still believe that to be the case. Both are founded on principles of pluralism and democracy.

"In addition," he went on, "many of the leading members of the local Jewish community I met while growing up in Texas were also known to have participated in other types of activities that were of critical importance to Israel during its War of Independence, which ranged from the organization of munitions shipments to the acquisition of surplus bombers." These escapades, he said, left a lasting and eventually fateful impression.

His family's friends were especially proud of Col. David "Mickey" Marcus, a much-decorated West Point graduate who was killed while fighting just outside Jerusalem with the fledgling Israeli Army in 1948. His example, Pollard said, "was emblematic of the lengths to which American Jews should hold themselves personally accountable for Israel's security." And Pollard was going to live up to the Marcus standard.

As a very bright and sensitive youngster, Pollard was not satisfied with the more traditional forms of expressing one's support for Israel "through such legal mechanisms as the donation of money, promotion of emigration, or participation in political lobbying efforts on behalf of the Jewish State in Washington." A real Zionist, he would later write in court documents, also recognized the possibility of being faced with a situation "in which something less overt and possibly of a confidential nature would be expected from him." But, just exactly what this might involve was never openly discussed.

> For example, Jewish homes were expected to be made available for visiting Israelis, who were not to be disturbed for days on end, while Jewish businessmen were routinely used to quietly broker the transfer of sensitive material or processes needed by the Israeli armaments industry. Despite the cloak and dagger impression left by these descriptions, American Jews were never encouraged or expected to betray the United States or to do anything which could possibly hurt this country. It was simply out of the question because American Jews were aware of the indisputable benefits conferred upon them by the vitality of America's pluralistic traditions and global military strength.

Politics aside, Jay was not a happy child. In 1961, his parents moved to South Bend, Indiana, and the effect would be devastating on the seven-year-old boy.

He was not popular in school. He was short and very smart and wore glasses. Some kids saw him as an egghead or a nerd; others regarded him as a smart aleck—a wiseguy.

Years later, in discussing this period in his life, his face would grimace with pain as he described his life in South Bend, through high school, as "a daily fight," characterized by "overt anti-Semitism." He always felt that the other kids considered him different because he was Jewish. This was in sharp contrast to his father's very positive experience on the Notre Dame campus.

"I was the only Jew in school," he said. "In high school, there were only two other Jews. And they made themselves scarce. In elementary school, there might have been one or two who barely kept their face above the surface. It was a daily fight, a daily one. If I had gone to other schools in the city, perhaps it wouldn't have been that bad because there would have been a larger Jewish population. But not where we lived, where I went to school."

South Bend had encountered a massive economic depression in the 1960s with the closing of a once-thriving Studebaker factory. "When you have an economic dislocation of that magnitude, there is a need on the part of the community for certain elements of that community to scapegoat. And there's always one around when you've got Jews—always."

The Ku Klux Klan, Pollard continued, "was well organized in my city, having found the climate and soil receptive to its extremist blandishments following a terrible regional economic depression in the early 1960s."

Overlooking the backyard of the Pollards' home was a hill. It was from atop that hill that the other kids would wait to taunt and then even physically assault the young Pollard. Often he was afraid to walk outside.

At the Marshall elementary school, Jay was constantly being beat up. In the fifth grade he asked to come home for lunch every day because the other boys were dividing up things that they stole. "I don't want to be a part of that," he told his mother. "I don't want to be near them."

But even when walking through his backyard to and from school, the other boys waited to taunt him. "How they did it was to simply walk up to him and punch him, and then say, 'I'm so sorry,' " Mrs. Pollard said.

On one occasion, he became absolutely terrified. "One lunchtime, four eighth graders linked arms and walked down that hill as a show of force against him." Pollard's teacher recommended that he transfer to another school. "Get him out of here," he advised. "They are playing with him."

The Pollards enrolled their son in a private school for seventh and eighth grades. There was instant improvement. "He started an orchestra there," Mrs. Pollard said. "He was already playing the cello." Jay also was active in cross-country running and soccer. And academically he began to excel, especially in English. He developed a real talent in writing. Indeed, whenever Jay returned to South Bend from one of the family's overseas trips, he would compose an essay.

He was a voracious reader. "Jay forbade us to break the back of any book," Dr. Pollard said. "He honored books."

Mrs. Pollard strongly encouraged him to read. "You know what I said to him? 'You may not have many friends. There are ugly children out there, but remember, you have a friend waiting for you when you get home. Your books wait.'"

But he then went on to Riley High School, a public school. Jay Pollard later described those awful days.

> Given the rather unwholesome characteristics of this environment, I was never able to establish friendships in my neighborhoods and was compelled to spend most of my time around the city's Hebrew Day School, where I felt at least physically safe and emotionally protected. This association lasted six days a week for ten years and involved a highly concentrated curriculum of religious and Zionist indoctrination that regularly stressed the advisability of *aliya,* or emigration to Israel.

"At the time, the only peace I really got was when I went to *heder,*" he added. "It was the only physical security I had."

Mrs. Pollard remembered how happy Jay was in Hebrew School. "He was completely relaxed there," and had "a beautiful teacher," who was "full of vim, vigor, and vitality. She made learning a joy." The teacher had visited Israel on several occasions and, according to Mrs. Pollard, she "filled the children with stories and with dancing. He loved every bit of it.

"I said to him, 'You are relaxed. Nobody will hit you. This is your religion and you will learn.' He loved it. He used to stand by the door and say, 'Mom, I'll be late.' I'm the one who drove him there. 'I'll be late. Please hurry.' Did you ever hear of a kid doing that?"

On one occasion, Jay had to make a presentation about something in Israel. He selected Masada, the mountaintop fortress in the Negev where Jewish zealots, two thousand years earlier, had committed mass suicide rather than surrender to the Romans. He had never visited Israel but wrote such a detailed paper that the teacher asked Mrs. Pollard when the family had visited the country. "We haven't been there," she replied.

"He gave one of the best talks I've ever heard—with such incredible details," the teacher said in amazement.

Carol, who was already in college when Jay was beginning high school, confirmed that he was constantly getting into fights. "I think the family unit saved him a lot," she said. "He used to have to walk to school through these kids who were just waiting. That area he grew up in was heavy Ku Klux Klan and heavy anti-black. In fact, the high school he went to had many riots. Blacks were rioting a lot. He had a very bad high school experience."

Pollard said that many other Jewish kids in South Bend also found themselves gravitating toward Israel. Of the fifty children he knew at the afternoon Jewish school, "roughly half left for Israel, which is a rate much higher than the national average but fully understandable within the context of a community that held us collectively responsible for an unemployment rate not of our making."

Pollard painted a very sad picture of his young Jewish friends. "Jewish children I saw grew up angry and alienated, wishing only to leave and never return. Whatever political conclusions I was forming at the time in terms of our dependence upon the State of Israel for racial survival tended to be confirmed and magnified by my own physical reliance on such local Jewish institutions and population that existed."

Simply going to public school was an ordeal. And the pain reinforced his connection to Israel.

Kids would beat him up constantly. "I mean I don't want to make this sound like a sad sack story, but if I had had kids I would have seriously considered getting them a gun—or as was advised by one of the principals of my school, giving him a guard dog, which they were willing to approve—or teaching him at home," he said.

"So along with this atavistic need I had to go to Israel," Pollard later said, "there were the physical surroundings that were tending to confirm in my own mind the fact that Jews had to rely on themselves in the final analysis."

The real change in his life—as far as Israel was concerned—occurred during the 1967 Six-Day War. At the time, Pollard was thirteen years old and very impressionable, preparing to celebrate his Bar Mitzvah in South Bend. "For me, it started in 1967. That was the turning point for me, as it was for many people."

His mother recalled how scared he was about the prospect of Israel's being destroyed. "Right before the Six-Day War," she said, "we arrived in Pittsfield, Massachusetts, where we were visiting my mother. Jay was crying. He said, 'They are going to kill Israel. I'll never get to see Israel.' And I said, 'Jay, take my word for it. Nothing is going to happen to Israel.' And he said, 'How do you know?' I said, 'I'm telling you, the good Lord will never let that happen.'

"So he went to sleep because I comforted him. The next day, I told him that the Israeli Air Force had knocked out the Arabs and the whole war was over. I can't tell you his reaction of unbelievable joy. 'Then, I'll get to see Israel!' "

It was the first time, he later recalled, that "a strong Jewish state" had successfully defended itself. Jews were not playing the role of victim once again.

> During the days preceding the onset of hostilities, though, our small community was in the grip of depression, fearful that this time Israel's luck, like that of so many other Diasporic groups, had finally run its course. Yet poised on the brink of annihilation, Israel had suddenly exploded across her threatened borders in what appeared to us to be a blinding flash of biblical decisiveness. The result of this absolutely astounded us all: the sight of Jewish tanks encamped on the banks of the Suez Canal and

our paratroopers praying at the newly liberated
Western Wall in Jerusalem was emotionally
intoxicating, especially for those of us who were
seriously considering emigration as a viable means of
asserting our self-worth.

Thus, Israel, during the war, began to completely domi-
nate Pollard's thinking. He read about the country vora-
ciously.

All of his misery tended to reinforce his fascination with
Israel: "When you have a small kid growing up in that kind
of environment, as I said, it tends to solidify the emotional
bonds one has with a distant, faraway, seemingly superhu-
man country that's larger than life, which in effect represents the self-respect—the physical security—which you
yourself were incapable of generating."

He admired in Israel many characteristics lacking in himself. "I got beaten up," he said, "but at least I knew the
Israelis would beat up a couple Arab countries and maybe
it would make me feel better." Israel's victory in 1967 further served "to emphasize in my mind the advisability of
leaving for Israel, where I could put all the humiliations of
my adolescence behind me.

"So there was this inner dilemma, I guess, that was building up in me slowly but relentlessly at the time. But how
could a thirteen-year-old boy emigrate to Israel alone?"

His parents recalled an incident just before his Bar Mitzvah that had a significant impact on Jay. The family had
belonged to the Reform Temple in South Bend. A new rabbi
had been brought to the congregation from Toledo, someone who was part of the so-called Classical Reform movement. "He grew up in the tradition of Sunday morning services for Jews," Dr. Pollard said.

Jay had been working for several weeks on his Bar Mitzvah speech. It was taken from Isaiah, with the message that
Israel will be a leader among nations. But the rabbi, who was
not a Zionist, did not want Jay to discuss that issue. "He
wanted Jay to rewrite the whole thing," Dr. Pollard said.
"And Jay went to Molly and said, 'I don't like that man.'"

The family switched to the Orthodox synagogue in town where Jay received his Bar Mitzvah.

In 1968, in the shadow of the Six-Day War, Pollard's parents took him to Europe, where six million Jews had been killed only twenty-five years earlier. "That really drove the last nail into the box as far as my attitude toward Israel was concerned," he said. At the time, Jay was fourteen years old.

By then, Dr. Pollard was emerging as a world-class scientist, named to head the prestigious Loband Laboratory at Notre Dame. He was cited in *Who's Who in America* and *Who's Who in the World,* and attended conferences all over the globe, often taking his young son along. "Let me put it this way," Jay later said. "I grew up in the house. My world was a library. And nine times out of ten I was overseas in Europe with my parents."

He described "an incredibly poignant" sidetrip to Dachau with his parents that summer. "I grew up in a family that I wouldn't say was obsessed with the Holocaust. But there was still the notion that one must never forget. I had more of an intellectual upbringing than a physical upbringing from my parents.

"In any case, this trip to Dachau was seminal because it gave palpable expression to the teachings of what could happen when Jews take their existence for granted. I guess it was really more of an intellectual awakening on my part than it was a visceral one. With me the mind always led the heart, and in this case it was the same phenomenon."

There was the barbed wire, the crematoria, the smoke stacks, the rows of wooden barracks, and the carefully detailed museum, complete with photographs of Nazi doctors performing "scientific" operations on Jewish inmates, including children.

"My parents let me walk around alone," he said. "Up until that point I had read Primo Levi, Andre Schwartzbart, Elie Wiesel. I had read a lot, including *Justice in Jerusalem* by Hannah Arendt. I had read everything, and I still thought at the time, in a sort of naive, childlike manner, that it couldn't happen again, not with the existence of Israel. But there it was. I really couldn't deny the fact that here was a German [Jewish] community that was politically potent and economically strong, and within the course of ten short years, they became *Luftsmenschen.* I guess it scared the hell out of me."

He began to wonder whether it could ever happen in the United States. The German Jews, after all, were "as culturally assimilated, politically influential, and financially secure as the American Jewish community appeared to be, but had still evaporated within the course of ten years. . . . As I stood in the ruins of the crematoria, it slowly dawned on me that every Jew had a responsibility, an obligation, if you will, to ensure that this nightmare would never happen again."

Pollard drew stark and depressing lessons from the visit to Dachau. "I was confused at that point as I walked out of the camp," he recalled. "I suddenly realized that if Israel went—disappeared—it would be the undoing, in the light of the Holocaust, of the Diasporic community, really in the spiritual sense, quite possibly in the physical sense. The Diaspora existed without Israel in the flesh for many thousands of years, but having become dependent on it since the Holocaust—both spiritually and physically as a refuge—I realized that we could, as a people, not really live past the experience. And a Holocaust, by the way, could be as much a spiritual one—which we are experiencing now in Russia, what I call forced assimilation, or a soft assimilation in the United States—as it could be a physical one, the gas chambers and the killing fields.

"From that point on, I suddenly realized what the expression of the American Zionist leadership—the centrality of Israel—meant for me as an individual. This was an easy concept for me to accept because of the way I grew up."

The combination of the 1967 war and Dachau had a powerful impact on Pollard. "I would have left the camp utterly confused and undecided about the future had I not come to at least one tentative conclusion concerning the contradictory lessons of Dachau and the Six-Day War," he said. "The only apparent way to prevent the former was to guarantee the latter."

That summer, his parents also took him to Czechoslovakia, shortly after the Soviet invasion, "and this was, as Arthur Clark would characterize it, the end of childhood for me. I actually saw for the first time what an occupied country looked like. I saw what military power could do in the hands of a country that was predisposed and free to utilize it to its fullest extent. That had a significant effect on me as far as my future career choice was concerned."

It underlined, he said, the real threat to Israel's security. "It wasn't any vague notion at the time. I actually saw tanks on the streets. I saw what it was like for a society to be completely overrun and occupied both spiritually and physically and I could draw my own conclusions as far as what would happen if there were an Arab victory in the Middle East."

He also concluded that "if the Russians ever succeeded in supplanting America as the premier world power, there would be no future for either Israel or our Diasporic communities. Once I had developed a more cosmopolitan and less racially myopic understanding of how the world worked, I clearly saw that Israel's ultimate security was a function of how effectively the United States could play the balance of power game with the Soviets."

In the summer of 1970, while still in high school, Pollard went to Israel for the first time. After all these years, his dream was beginning to come true. On the bulletin board at his Hebrew School in South Bend, there had been an announcement about a science camp for gifted students from around the world at the renowned Weizmann Institute of Science in Rehovot. "Do you think I could go?," he eagerly asked his parents.

Dr. Pollard, of course aware of Weizmann's reputation, immediately said yes. "We never dreamt that he would be able to get in," he added, "that they would accept him, because kids were fighting to get in. But the next thing we knew he was accepted. For $1,200, he could go."

It was the summer before his junior year in high school. "We were apprehensive," Mrs. Pollard recalled. That was one reason why they themselves later made their own first trip to Israel that same summer. They wanted to see how he was doing.

When they arrived, Jay was having a wonderful time. "He was in heaven," his mother said, "just in heaven." And Jay agreed. That experience "was one of the most liberating experiences I have ever had in my life," he said, noting that he began to see a more "normal" Jewish experience.

"I saw things like a Jewish prostitute," he would later recall. "I saw things that I had never seen before. And most importantly of all, I saw people who didn't have the Diasporic hangups. They didn't have the Diasporic stigma. They were wholistic people, I'll put it that way."

But even that summer, he found himself fighting with other kids. Indeed, a noted Weizmann scientist, Dr. Harry J. Lipkin, years later would write to *The Jerusalem Post* complaining about Pollard's behavior at the camp that summer. According to Lipkin, the young American "left behind him a reputation of being an unstable troublemaker, the worst case of this kind in the history of the summer camp. In one fracas, he was injured in a brawl and had to be taken to a hospital. This is the only time such a case has occurred at the camp."

His parents confirmed that there had been an incident. They said that a non-Jewish student from England had been taunting one of the other Jewish kids in the group. "Jay tried to protect this guy," Mrs. Pollard said. "It was no fight. The other boy, who played soccer, just kicked Jay in the stomach and ruptured his spleen." Jay wound up in an Israeli hospital for several days.

The parents had already returned to South Bend when they received the frightening phone call from the Weizmann Institute about Jay's condition. Mrs. Pollard said she had had a premonition. "Please take him with us," she recalled telling her husband before they actually left Israel.

"It's not good. The situation is not good." She said that she had "begged and pleaded but we left Jay in Israel."

Yet Jay had different recollections of that summer in Israel. He insisted that he had simply participated in a water-balloon war with some other kids. "It got a little too vigorous. I was the only casualty."

His most remarkable experience, he said, was seeing the walls of Jerusalem. "A lot of people say that when they see the [Western] Wall for the first time, they are overwhelmed. I won't diminish that. It was quite remarkable for me when I saw it."

But the walls surrounding the Old City had an even greater impact. "I guess that city has come to represent everything I hold dear as far as that country is concerned. You can see in those walls the course of our social history more than you can in the Western Wall. The Western Wall, I guess, represented the bond with God. The walls of that city represented our sociological ascendancy and decline at the same time."

Pollard returned from Israel more convinced than ever that he had no alternative but eventually to settle in that country. He wanted to join the Israeli Army and become a Jewish fighter. He was determined to become a "normal" Jew, living in a Jewish state. He was going to get rid of his Jewish ghetto hangups. Indeed, his parents recalled that he had simply wanted to stay in Israel after the Weizmann camp experience. "We had trouble getting him home," Dr. Pollard said. "He wanted to stay there and we told him to come home and finish his education and go back as a contributor."

The boy obeyed his parents. He came home refreshed and excited. He now had a game plan in mind, and it involved preparing himself for the move to Israel. But those heady plans were quickly thwarted upon his return to the real world of South Bend. The fighting with other high school students continued. "The white Fascists were really making life difficult for those who really wanted an education," Dr. Pollard said. "And there were militant blacks as well." According to Mrs. Pollard, "they would disrupt the classes. They would get up and walk out. It was frightening."

Yet despite that ordeal, Jay still received excellent grades, and he did very well on his SAT exams. He had good extracurricular activities and outstanding recommendations from his teachers and guidance counselors. And he also won a national award for a composition written during his senior year. Indeed, the South Bend *Tribune* carried another picture of him on Sunday, November 14, 1971, with the comment: "Jonathan Jay Pollard, center, Riley High School senior, has been chosen as one of the outstanding students of English in the country by the National Council of Teachers of English."

Ball State University in Muncie, Indiana, published his short prize-winning essay, entitled "Discipline in the Home," in March 1972. It was, his mother said, typical of his often-sarcastic writing style.

> Society's most important achievement must be, in the long run, the preservation of discipline in the home. It is not good merely for us just to nod our heads and say yes, it is true. Rather, we must all resolutely take a firm stand on this issue and when we are called upon to support it, uphold it most diligently. In some ways we might actually say that the future of our land lies in the palms of the parents.
>
> Down through the annals of history we have seen where obedience to a father or mother has been upheld by the child and as a result benefitted the child. Take, for example, William Tell's son Fritz at Bern. When William told him to stand still with an apple on his head, did he flinch? No, of course not! We can clearly see that as a direct result of this the present-day state of Switzerland was born, as well as Fritz becoming the chief target for every self-styled William Tell in the country.
>
> The terrible question is, though, would Fritz have stood still today? Unfortunately, the answer is no.

Fritz being a modern, average, teenager (although any boy who puts an apple on his head today to be shot off by his father who is blind in one eye would be considered a little different) would first have raised the question of the validity of the apple being on the head. After all, why couldn't it be on the father's head? Next, he would have had something to say about the apple. "It is too round and/or too red." (The latter statement can be excused since the color could bring bad thoughts into the mind of the child.) And, of course, we can't leave out the catchword of today's youth—relevance. "What in the world is it doing on my head in the first place?" Fritz would ask. "Why shouldn't it be back on the tree where it belongs?" As we can see, the formation of Switzerland would have been delayed by at least a year by the rudeness of a child towards a parent who was only trying to keep an eye on him.

Finally, we have the case of Julius Caesar in Rome. Thanks to a recent discovery by the noted Bronx Latin scholar Elephanto Candor, we have found out that the soothsayer was none other than Julius' long-lost father who had just come home from the religious wars in Northern Ireland (he was on the Roman side, of course). Julius, who had previously been a good son, passed off his aged father's prophecy with a curt "Non spectare limbo allat pater." (If there's one thing I can't stand it's a know-it-all father.) Tragically for Caesar, his father's words came true. Poor Caesar! No more wars! No more triumphs! Would that he could only have listened to his father. Even when his best friend Brutus took up his father's side, Caesar rudely snubbed him with a fierce, "Et tu Brute!" As a result of this, all Rome was thrown into a panic with runs on the banks (not on the Tiber) and general hysteria. Finally, Rome had to provide a massive pyre for Caesar's body around which they all had to pass weeping and wailing. There was one person who wasn't crying though—Caesar's father. He was huddled up in a corner laughing boisterously and saying something to the tune of "Io spectare torto! Io spectare torto!" (I told him so! I told him so!).

We can clearly see that following the orders of elders must be practiced by all children. Rebellion can lead only to disaster, as the above story reveals. Since Caesar got the point, perhaps there is still hope for today's youth.

Just before his graduation in the spring of 1972, Jay was named the outstanding senior Social Studies student at Riley High School; the class yearbook called him the "Hoosier Poet"; he made the National Honor Society; and as a result of his awards, test scores, grades, and extracurricular activities, he was accepted at Stanford University in Palo Alto, California. He could have attended Notre Dame for free as the son of a professor. But there was no way he was going to stay home—he had to escape. Jay had also been accepted at the University of Wisconsin and the University of Chicago but he and his parents, in the end, selected Stanford.

CHAPTER THREE

Education of a Spy

Pollard started his freshman year at Stanford taking courses in pre-medicine, planning to follow in the footsteps of his older brother, Harvey. He quickly changed his mind, however, and became a political science major. His mother recalled Jay's complaining about the cutthroat competition among pre-med students. "They were sabotaging to make sure that this one would get a zero or flunk something," she quoted her son as saying. "I don't want that sort of thing—I really don't. I don't want it that badly."

Pollard's childhood difficulties did not disappear when he went to college. Franklin Weinstein, Pollard's faculty adviser at Stanford, would years later tell *The Washington Post* that Pollard was a "very bright, extremely articulate" student, who "had a tendency to be overly aggressive and sometimes antagonize or alienate students in seminar discussions." Weinstein said Pollard "tended to overdo things. If you gave him an assignment to write a paper, it would come in elegantly but much longer" than required.

One of his roommates at Stanford, Steven LaPointe of Washington, D.C., recalled that Pollard's strong interest was in military history and intelligence operations. "Jay Pollard was definitely pro-Israel," he would tell the Stanford *Daily* shortly after Pollard's arrest. "He used to boast that he had a dual citizenship and that he was a colonel in the Israeli Army."

LaPointe described Pollard as a habitual practical joker. "He had a penchant for playing dirty jokes on people," he said, recalling that Pollard would wire room lights with fireworks so they would explode when turned on, and hide in people's closets and jump out at them when they walked into their rooms. "That's just scratching the surface of the dirty tricks he used to do," LaPointe said.

He also said that Pollard used to spend a great deal of time playing the games of "Diplomacy" and of "Panzer Blitz," which concentrates on German military strategy during World War II. Pollard captained food fights as if they were military campaigns. Indeed, his mother later recalled: "He had a friend and they used to stay up until two o'clock in the morning, sometimes, playing these war games."

Another student at Stanford, Jonathan Marshall of Oakland, California, recalled that he had heard stories about Pollard's bragging that he was on the Mossad payroll. In an interview with *The New York Times*, Marshall went on to say that Pollard "was unusually well informed and quite articulate, and made what might otherwise have been an outlandish series of claims quite convincing." He said Pollard was "a committed Zionist, but fairly liberal" on certain questions of Middle East politics. "In our discussions," Marshall added, "he described himself as part of an Israeli officers' group that favored more open channels of communication with Egypt."

Years later, in an article by Michael Satchell, *U.S. News and World Report* would also report that Pollard had posed as an Israeli spy during his college days, "had a background of heavy drug and alcohol use, and falsified his resume when he applied for his government intelligence job." The report quoted Marshall, now an editor at the Oakland *Tribune*, as saying: "I assumed after he left Stanford that Jay was going to continue working for Israel." Pollard was described as someone whose "rich imagination, keen intellect and barnyard braggadocio were convincing, and some of his college chums believed his tall tales. He didn't wear a cloak or carry a dagger, but he sometimes appeared on campus packing a large revolver, his Stanford senior yearbook photo listed him as 'Colonel' Pollard, and he convinced almost everyone that Mossad was paying his tuition."

"No, I was not a member of the Mossad," Pollard responded in prison. "I never minced words as far as my feelings about Israel were concerned, both in university and graduate school. If you had asked anybody at the time to characterize me, they would have said, 'an ardent Zionist.' Some people who didn't like me would have called me a knee-jerk Zionist, which, I guess, I am to a large extent. The security of Israel comes first. It must."

He recalled that he and his war game buddies had given themselves nicknames. His was "the Colonel"; another friend good-naturedly called himself a KGB major; a third was a captain. It was all "fun and games," Pollard said. "No one took it seriously."

After the *U.S. News and World Report* article was published, Pollard would again explain his college-day fascination with military affairs. Students like Marshall—not in his inner circle of friends—simply misunderstood what was going on. Sitting in jail, he increasingly became convinced that there was a conspiracy to get him. "Now," he said, "with respect to the *U.S. News* article, I was told rather explicitly during the course of my 'debriefing' that I would be 'smeared' beyond recognition for my refusal to implicate other Jews in what was held to be a conspiracy reaching up to the highest echelons of the American Zionist establishment. I had so many 'confessions' thrown at me by the NIS [Naval Investigative Service] regarding this it got to be a joke after a while. I repeatedly advised my lawyer about this but he felt it was insignificant."

The allegations in the article, Pollard continued, "are simply an example of 'creato ex nihilo.' How could I have been a drug addict given the battery of blood and urine tests we were periodically subjected to?

"As far as my purported alcoholism is concerned," he continued, "upon what is that based? Have I ever been admitted to AA or a detox clinic? Was I ever arrested for DWI, as several people in the office were, or cited for coming to work in a state of inebriation? Did anyone ever see me drink during lunch as many of my erstwhile colleagues did?

"Moreover, this so-called good friend of mine from Oakland, when confronted, is now claiming that he hardly knew me at all in school. . . . I admit to smoking pot in college and graduate school and have never tried to obscure this fact. I even noted it on my application for my first position in Naval Intelligence and it was obviously not held against me.

"The hardest thing to refute is a lie because if you don't say anything, it looks like you're confirming the allegation while if you overreact people assume that you're trying to hide something, i.e., 'protesting too loudly.' The only thing I can say, Wolf, is look at the record."

His parents say they were unaware of any fantasies he may have had during his years in college. "We don't know anything about that," Mrs. Pollard said. "He never did that in our presence." Yet Dr. Pollard confirmed that he had to fly to Stanford on one occasion in order to help his son get through a serious crisis. Jay, having smoked quite a bit of marijuana, sat alone in his room, convinced there was some sort of plot against him. Dr. Pollard blamed himself for Jay's imagination.

He recalled that his son had been aware of Dr. Pollard's own involvement with the CIA. "Of course," the father said, "Jay was witness to an awful lot of things that went on with me. I never worked for the CIA but I did tell the CIA anything to advance the cause of the United States that would be legitimate. I would do that. So I was debriefed, actually, on every trip I made."

Usually, the CIA would send agents to his Notre Dame office to interview him. "I knew what they wanted," he said. "Jay knew I was snooping around because he heard about this trip we made to East Germany, for instance. He was already in college. We were setting up a meeting on esopha-

gus diseases in New York, sponsored by the Stern Foundation at Hartz Mountain. This one was for foot and mouth
disease. I was the general chairman of the whole thing. We
had decided that we would invite people from all over the
world to discuss this problem. So I had contacted people in
East Germany and told them I would like to come there. I
would make some arrangements for them to come at our
expense to this meeting, which was sponsored by private
foundations. So we went to France. We went to Germany.
We went to Holland—places where they had active foot and
mouth diseases."

On another occasion, Dr. Pollard said a CIA official had
come to South Bend to inform him that the agency had been
investigating him for ten years. They were pleased by what
they had discovered. The official asked if Dr. Pollard would
go to a scientific conference in the Soviet Union to discuss
some militarily related problems. The official noted that Dr.
Pollard was still a lieutenant colonel in the U.S. Army Reserves. During World War II, in fact, Dr. Pollard had served
at the U.S. Army's Brooke Medical Center Laboratory in
Fort Sam Houston, Texas. He pioneered research in immu-
nology for the tropical diseases that American soldiers in the
Pacific were routinely coming down with. For those scientific studies, he received the Army Commendation Medal
and a Presidential Citation. But he turned down the request
to travel to Moscow, largely because Mrs. Pollard was
scared. "I said no," she recalled. "We are not going to
Russia."

Dr. Pollard said that "Jay was witness to this. He was filled
with romanticism from the time of his birth."

Indeed, Dr. Pollard said his son had witnessed one encounter which he had with a CIA official—"Maybe it influenced him." Dr. Pollard recalled that the CIA official had
asked if he would be willing to question Russian delegates
at an international scientific conference on diseases of military importance. They handed him a list of names of Soviet
scientists and the research they were undertaking. "They
said, 'Read it and burn it,'" Dr. Pollard said. "So I took it

back to the room and I looked at the names there—big long names. So I kept the list in my breast pocket and when I came to someone, I looked at the nameplate. 'Oh, yes, Dr. Schmolkoff,' and I assumed that they looked at their list, too. It was very funny."

Gail Landau, a lawyer in Rockville, Maryland, who also studied with Pollard at Stanford, said he had "trashed" his midterm exams in the fall of 1973 when the Yom Kippur War broke out. "He told us he was going to Israel to serve in the army," she said, insisting that Pollard had boasted of being a member of the Golani Brigade, an elite infantry unit.

Pollard described those days during the war as a real crisis in his life. "It was one of the most frustrating experiences for me because I just basically wanted to pick up and leave at that point and go there," he said. "I was a sophomore. I felt guilty over not being there." But he managed to get only as far as the Los Angeles airport. "Unlike the experiences of 1967," he said, "all we kept hearing on the news was how precarious the margin of Israeli success was and that the casualty lists were growing to alarming heights. A call for volunteers went out to permit ablebodied men to be transferred from kibbutzim to the fronts, but the group I was in spent five frustrating days waiting for an El Al flight in Los Angeles before we were told the need for us had passed with [Gen. Ariel] Sharon's crossing of the Suez. Although we had won after all, the price had been appalling and I had spent the whole time sitting in an airport terminal 15,000 miles from Israel unable to do anything more than think.

"It was during that vigil," he added, "that I decided the intelligence field would provide me with a skill which would be well received in Israel once I emigrated. Like Colonel Marcus, I was ready to serve the United States faithfully and then, once I had contributed something to the national defense effort, leave for Israel.

"The problem with long-range plans is that they very often are overtaken and invalidated by unanticipated events. In my case, I quite simply began to enjoy living in the United States and could almost admit that perhaps I would stay here after all."

During the summer between his freshman and sophomore years, Pollard was home in South Bend. His mother recalled that he enrolled in a daily course at Notre Dame in African history. "At least I'm doing something constructive," she remembered him as saying. That interest in Africa would continue over the coming years.

Peter Walshe, a professor at Notre Dame, later recalled in an interview with *The Washington Post* that he had taught that summer course. He described Pollard as one of his best students, who "had a drive to understand the inner working of politics in all their Machiavellian dimensions," and was "fascinated by the exercise of power." Pollard, he added, was especially intrigued with intelligence-gathering and security services. "He was interested in the security network in South Africa, he was interested in the way the CIA operated in this country, he was interested in Israel's capacity to defend itself in that way."

During another summer, Jay went with his parents to Japan where Dr. Pollard was invited to a scientific conference. "He went to the Foreign Office while he was there," Dr. Pollard said. "He introduced himself, and some fellow came out and said to him, 'Come with me, I'm a Stanford graduate.' Later during that visit, we met with a Japanese newspaper editor. We met him through friends. Jay was talking about Russia and the threat to civilization as we knew it. The editor, a man in his eighties, looked at Jay and said, 'What are you talking about? They're scared to death of you. You act as though you are afraid of them.' That was a revelation to Jay because he had the perception that Russia was going to destroy us. The editor and Jay later had a long discussion on the early history of the Japanese naval forces and how they destroyed the Russian fleet. Jay named all the ships, and recalled how they went down, and where they went down. This guy looked at him and asked in amazement, 'How did you know all that?' "

On another occasion, the State Department asked Dr. Pollard to host a visiting Soviet scientist to the United States. Jay was home from school. During dinner, Mrs. Pollard said, the Russian and Jay had a lengthy discussion on the Battle of Stalingrad. "Jay went into the various sides, what was happening." The Russian (who was about 5′3″) was very impressed. "How could you know all of that?" he asked. Mrs. Pollard told me the answer: "He was, of course, playing those war games at night. And that little Russian was so amazed."

Pollard's interest in international affairs was further stimulated when he went to Paris during the summer between his junior and senior years at Stanford. He worked as an intern at the Atlantic Institute, a private think tank which he later described to me as "a CIA front."* Among the professors with whom he was associated were Dr. Benjamin Cohen of the Fletcher School of Law and Diplomacy and Dr. François Sauzey of the Trilateral Commission in New York. When his parents later asked him what kind of work he did there, he replied by asking them whether they had seen the movie *Three Days of the Condor*—a spy thriller about a CIA intelligence-gathering unit that analyzed espionage novels looking for new counterintelligence techniques. "That's where I was," his mother quoted him as saying. "I was upstairs in the library."

That, of course, was an exaggeration. His father said Jay actually went around Paris interviewing foreign diplomats. "And he learned how to read and speak Afrikaans." That was not all that difficult because Jay had earlier studied German in South Bend, during high school. He also met and befriended some white South Africans that summer in Paris, and that sparked his interest in the apartheid regime. Indeed, years later, when Pollard was already working in

*While many former U.S. military and intelligence officials are affiliated with the Atlantic Institute, I could find no evidence to support Pollard's claim.

Naval Intelligence, his interest in South Africa would get him into some very serious trouble.

Back in California, he studied a wide range of political science subjects. Military strategy was his favorite. The February 1976 issue of the Stanford *Observer* published a photograph of a dozen students in a classroom with the caption: "Undergraduates participate in simulated arms limitation negotiations." Pollard, clean-shaven, wearing a jacket and tie like the other male students in the picture, sits in the corner glancing at documents. The accompanying article notes that the "professional training program, which provides some fellowships for graduate study and includes internships with government agencies, aims to develop a 'new generation' of professionals to deal with arms control problems."

Curiously, during his four years at Stanford, Pollard was not active in Jewish organizations. He was not a member of Hillel, the Jewish students' group, for example. He also did not have many friends. "There were Jewish organizations. But I guess I've always been a loner. I've never felt comfortable in organizations." He said that the reason for this was "more complex than we have time to go into."

He probably would have been better off joining some of those organizations, as he later acknowledged. "I guess I was burning more energy with this inner debate I had than I had time to spend on organizations. Perhaps if I had joined organizations I would have been able to rationalize this Diasporic existence, but I guess I just didn't see any need to do so. What I saw as being most important for me was helping the state directly some way. Personal involvement was always something that I was brought up to believe was the mark of a responsible individual." Organizations, he felt, simply could not satisfy that need.

"After that," he added, "this miasma set in as far as where I would go."

Despite a rich fantasy life, Pollard was becoming increasingly more bogged down about his commitment to Israel.

Yet he also continued to come up with further rationalizations to stay put. "Intellectually, at least, I realized that the same effort I expended to fight the Russians would also indirectly assist Israel."

Still, he was very much aware of his inner torment. "I was utterly lost emotionally since I had prepared myself for so long to emigrate that the thought of remaining and never committing myself physically to the state was incredibly traumatic. So, I continued to be in a moral dilemma as to what I should do to help Israel directly."

His parents continued to discourage him from making *aliya*. " 'Don't,' " he quoted them as having said. " 'You'll be worth more to the state if you get your education, get a career started here, and then come to the state with something useful'—which, by the way, was on the one hand very responsible. On the other hand, it was a little selfish in keeping me here. But it was certainly motivated by what I consider to be good sound advice both for Israel and for myself."

He reluctantly accepted their advice. "I guess it was just a materialistic rejection on my part. You know, it's very easy for people who come from totalitarian societies to make *aliya*. They have no alternative. But for those of us who live in the West, it's a voluntary act which is very difficult. The bonds of materialism can be very addictive—more so perhaps than we Jews would like to admit. Never really being all that materialistic—the stereotypes notwithstanding—this emotionalism, this very need to go on *aliya* started picking at me."

Carol, his sister, thought that he also could not leave because he was simply too attached to his family. "He may have wanted to go, but remember, you're talking about someone who is very close to his family and to have your whole family over here and he's over there. . . ."

He constantly tried to encourage her to visit Israel. "Carol," she quoted him as saying, "you'll love it there. You'll come over there. You'll see what it's like."

With hindsight, Carol added sadly, she could see that Jay would have been better off moving to Israel after finishing Stanford. "I think a lot about that."

In June 1976, Pollard graduated from Stanford with a B.A. in political science and returned to South Bend to attend law school at Notre Dame—at the strong urging of his father. Carol remembered that he quit after only a few months, even though the professors found him "very interesting" in the classes. "He couldn't take it," she said; he would complain of his fellow students, "They all are just interested in making money. They are not interested in changing anything."

His parents recalled that he was disappointed by the lack of professors in international law at Notre Dame. "I don't want to be a corporation lawyer," he told them.

After dropping out, he spent a semester studying political science at Indiana University in Bloomington before winning admission to the Fletcher School of Law and Diplomacy at Tufts University in Boston. Before leaving Indiana, he was offered a full scholarship to do a Ph.D. in African Studies, but he chose Fletcher.

Beginning in the fall of 1977, he studied there for two years but never completed his degree. "It's something I regret and would still like to do, obviously," he would say in 1986.

During his second year at Fletcher, Pollard said he worked as "an unpaid research assistant" to Professor Robert Pfaltzgraff at the Institute for Foreign Policy Analysis in Cambridge, Massachusetts, "although he may be rather hesitant to openly admit this since he derives most of the Institute's funding from the DOD [Department of Defense]." Pfaltzgraff has repeatedly denied that Pollard was ever employed there in any capacity.

In general, Pollard said that he found the environment at Fletcher very anti-Jewish. Asked years later whether he too shunned Jewish organizations at Fletcher, he replied: "A Jewish organization at Fletcher is as unlikely as a branch of the NAACP is at a Ku Klux Klan meeting. The school is barely assimilated in the post–World War II social experience."

Still, for one semester, he did have a Jewish roommate named Richard Feen—someone who would play a complicating role in Pollard's troubles years later.

There also was one Jewish professor at the school whom Pollard greatly admired. Indeed, he said that Professor Uri Ra'anan, a well-known Sovietologist, had a profound influence on him. Ra'anan was "a real asset for the Jewish community as well as for the United States." Ra'anan, Pollard added, was "my Jewish experience at Fletcher."

Ra'anan, a former Israeli journalist and diplomat, had left Israel to pursue an academic career in the United States. In Israel, he was considered a *yored,* a disparaging term for an émigré. The word *yored* suggests someone who has gone down—as opposed to an *oleh,* an immigrant to Israel who has gone up.

"He may have gone down physically but he brought me up intellectually as far as fine-tuning my understanding of the real political issues that are facing Israel—internally as well as externally," Pollard commented. "American Jews tend to look at Israel as a monolith. There are good Israelis and there are bad Israelis. The bad Israelis want to talk to the Arabs—the bad Israelis recognize that there are Arabs; the good Israelis spend most of their time chasing them all over the map."

But Ra'anan "showed me that you can shoot and talk at the same time. And peace is a continuation of war by other means. I guess that was the big lesson I learned—not that you have to take risks for peace, but you have to be smart enough to use peace to improve your military position. You mustn't sacrifice anything through the peace process. It formed a useful arrow in the quiver of policy options. It stripped away the naivete as far as the illusion of a possible true peace coming into the picture—following the alleged Arab victories in '73—the Egyptian victory in '73, I don't think there was any question about what happened on the Golan."

Ra'anan, he continued, "polished both my political and my strategic awareness of what it took to keep that state alive. He also was very good at unraveling the complexities of the Palestinian issue, which are more complex than a Diasporic appreciation of that phenomenon would lead you to believe. That too is not monolithic. This is not to give it any concrete [form] but to recognize the fissures of differences within the Palestinian movement are things to be recognized and exploited—much as the differences in the Communist world are, from an East-West standpoint. So that's basically what he gave me. It was very important. It polished off what I would call my purely emotional attachment to the country."

After Pollard's arrest, Ra'anan telephoned Dr. Pollard seeking some information about a new treatment that possibly could be used by his son, who was dying of cancer. Dr. Pollard recalled that he gave Ra'anan the information but was very upset at the end of the long conversation because Ra'anan had not asked about Jay.

During the summer between his first and second years at Fletcher, Pollard had an internship at the Naval War College in Newport, Rhode Island. "Apparently," his father recalled, "he had a very exciting experience there. He enjoyed it tremendously."

But while he felt he was growing intellectually, he was still an emotional wreck because of his decision to remain in the United States. "As time passed," he said, "I just continued to sink ever deeper into a spiritual no-man's-land. And as with all borders, be they physical or cerebral, it is the sense of conflicting allegiances that causes the most confusion for an individual who feels he might be living under the burden of a double standard."

By now, he said, he was fully tormented by his conflicting emotions. "The psychological hallmarks of divided loyalties were certainly there for all to see: the uneasy conscience, the sense of personal failure. I was becoming a weak man with good intentions and doomed by pride, which was a condition that perhaps had more in common with classical tragedy than with Jewish melodrama."

He still tried not to feel sorry for himself. Self-pity was

"something I don't think I ever knowingly cultivated at that time because it denied the possibility of a solution to my crisis. Despair, though, was the price I paid for setting myself an impossible aim. It is, I was once told, the unforgivable sin; but it is a sin, I believe, that the corrupt or evil man never practices. He either has hope or a very short memory."

But Pollard also stressed his commitment to the United States. "They are not incompatible goals as far as I am concerned. One cannot exist without the other. Israel grows—basks in the sunlight—cast by the American sun. That sounds like a hack expression but in physical and practical terms it's true. I don't think anybody who looks at the military balance or the economic balance could debate that point."

At Fletcher, Pollard was also exposed to a different student environment. "There were a lot of Third Worlders," he said, "a lot of pro-Arabs, a lot of people who really still question the United Nations Partition vote [that called for the creation of a Jewish state in Palestine] in 1947. In that kind of environment, one tends to take extreme positions—more out of a need to be heard and to confront these people with their own inconsistencies than perhaps out of conviction."

Pollard had been to Israel only once—during high school. "However, the amount of time I spent involved with Israel academically and emotionally was very heavy. You can't lose sight of that." He was still constantly reading about Israel.

And he was still deeply troubled by his decision to remain in the United States. "Merely recognizing that a contiguity of interests existed between our homeland and the United States was not sufficient to quiet the doubts in my mind about the propriety of living safely in the materialistically affluent West while the Israelis were sacrificing their hard-won economic gains on the altar of Mars," he said. "I still harbored desires to emigrate immediately, but did not want to callously abandon my parents, who had tried so desperately to provide me with an alternative perspective on the Diaspora. My dilemma took on the characteristics of an obsession and the harder I tried to resolve it the more elusive a solution became. This inner turmoil intruded into my social and academic life to such an extent that at times I just wanted to pack my bags and move to Israel."

Indeed, he did almost that on several occasions. "But the thought of what this would do to my parents eventually stopped me. The net results of this unstable situation were incomplete studies, fantasies, a failed engagement, and a totally unjustified belief that my parents bore some of the responsibility for my problems, since they didn't encourage emigration. I seemed to be stuck between my passion for Israel and my very real love for this country, which suddenly appeared as two mutually exclusive beliefs."

The engagement was to a fellow Fletcher student from Wilmington, Delaware. "She was a doctor's daughter," Mrs. Pollard recalled. "She was Jewish." They came to South Bend on one occasion to meet the Pollards. "She was a beautiful girl, but there was something very immature about her, and we got a little scared." The relationship was serious enough to the point that the two sets of parents spoke to each other. "They were delighted about the whole thing," Mrs. Pollard said, referring to the perspective in-laws. "They were nice Jewish people." But the engagement fizzled shortly thereafter.

The Pollards recalled that Jay, on an earlier occasion, had brought another girl home from Stanford. "She really liked him," Mrs. Pollard said, noting that that young woman had later come to Washington while he was already working for Naval Intelligence and living with Anne. By then, the girlfriend from Stanford was an executive for Xerox. "I think she came to see how things were," Mrs. Pollard said, referring to the relationship between Jay and Anne.

It was at Fletcher, Pollard recalled, that he first became directly involved with the world of intelligence. In his words, he became "a free-lancer" for the Central Intelligence Agency, regularly reporting to someone, he said, about the activities of various Third World students. Several other American students at Fletcher were also involved in some sort of informal covert CIA program. According to

Pollard, these students thought that their cooperation with the CIA, while in graduate school, would later help them win internships and even real jobs in the Agency. Thus, Pollard said he routinely reported to the CIA on the activities of several Arab students at Fletcher, including one whom he described as a Saudi prince.

But his subsequent application for a position at the CIA was rejected—a major disappointment in his life. "He did apply to the CIA," his father confirmed. Following Pollard's arrest, CIA officials said that Pollard had been turned down for the job because of his occasional drug use during college—something that was spotted during a polygraph examination.

Yet he remained in a state of perpetual torment. The idea of moving to Israel had "by no means" been resolved in his mind even as he swore allegiance to the U.S. government. He had not come to grips with the notion of remaining forever in the United States. "Again," he said, "it was a question of delay. You know it was like a Talmudic question—well, let me ask another question. Why don't I go? Well, why don't I stay?"

He could easily have made the move. He was not married; he knew some Hebrew; upon arrival in Israel, he could have received instant citizenship under the Law of Return. He could have lived out his fantasy by simply enlisting in the Israeli Army. Yet deep down, he probably feared what would be in store for him in Israel. Was he actually cut out to be an Israeli soldier? Would he be able to really master Hebrew? What if he proved to be a failure in Israel? Instead of dwelling on those questions, he preferred to blame his parents for his decision to remain in the United States. And he came up with other reasons as well.

"I could have picked up and gone," he said. "But I felt at the time that this, too, would be a good experience. Certainly, it was very practical and could be of service to the state when I went on *aliya.*" He noted that the national security intelligence field was indeed "useful" to the Israeli State. "It was a good, practical profession. That was the most important thing—that I could make a contribution."

CHAPTER FOUR

The Patrician Bigot

On September 19, 1979, a rather hot and muggy day in Washington, an eager Jonathan Jay Pollard was hired as an Intelligence Research Specialist by the Field Operational Intelligence Office of the U.S. Navy in Suitland, Maryland, a middle-class southern suburb of the nation's capital. He came to Washington without his master's degree from the Fletcher School of Law and Diplomacy at Tufts University, but confident that he eventually would complete the requirements. During his second year at Fletcher, Pollard had, by his own admission, become somewhat lazy in terms of his academic discipline. His grades had slipped. He failed to finish some required course papers, already preoccupied with thoughts about his future career.

He had tried to get into the CIA but was turned down, so he settled for Naval Intelligence. The CIA was said to have been concerned about his occasional use of drugs in college. But officials there, for whatever bureaucratic reason, did not share their concerns with the Navy.* It was a classic example of the left hand of the U.S. government not knowing what

---

*A Defense Investigative Service official later said that DIS investigators had interviewed Pollard's father and eleven other people who knew him at Fletcher and elsewhere as part of their routine background screening.

the right hand was up to. "The CIA rarely shares its information with us," a former Naval Intelligence official said.

Having just turned twenty-five, Pollard proudly received his U.S. government identification pass, which included a picture of him wearing a sleeveless green sweater and navy and red striped tie. He would often remove it from his wallet and simply stare at it; quite impressive, he thought. There was no mustache or beard in those days. The card identified him as having brown hair and eyes. He was 5 feet 8 inches tall and weighed 165 pounds. By the time of his arrest six years later, he would weigh nearly 220 pounds.

One of his first assignments was to study surface ship systems of non-Communist countries. Over the years, he had read numerous books on the subject. His "war games" experience in college would also be useful. He felt he was well prepared with the necessary background.

His sister Carol was not happy at all about his career move. "Stay away from it," she recalled pleading with him. "I don't like government anyway." But he was determined.

"I really want to do this," he said one night as they chatted in her New Haven apartment. He asked for her support.

"I can give you emotional support, but we're not going to talk anything about politics because I think it's going to screw your mind over," she said.

Little did she know how prophetic her comments would be.

As he had on so many other occasions in his still rather young life, Pollard came to encounter what he described as very serious anti-Semitism in the Navy. "Although I had been cautioned by many of my Jewish friends about the unhealthy atmosphere which reportedly permeated the office, I was totally unprepared for the level and extent of the anti-Semitism that was tolerated within the organization. I tried many times to understand what was behind the deprecating comments and the biased stereotypes but, in the end, I came to the conclusion that the U.S. Navy, like many other naval establishments around the world, was the last refuge of the patrician bigot."

On the job, he said, "people were routinely expressing attitudes toward Israel which were barely distinguishable from those I had heard about Jews while growing up in Indiana, without being reprimanded or even cautioned."

Anne Pollard would later remember that among her husband's colleagues, he did not widely advertise the fact that he was Jewish. She, too, insisted that there was widespread anti-Semitism in Pollard's office. "I would go with Jay to parties with people in his office, and I would constantly hear all sorts of anti-Semitic comments."

She said that many of the naval officers often brought up the matter of Israel's sinking of the U.S.S. *Liberty* during the 1967 Six-Day War. That American intelligence-gathering ship was in international waters, just off Israel's Mediterranean coast, when Israeli warplanes attacked it on June 8. Thirty-four U.S. sailors were killed. Israel insisted that the attack was a mistake; Israeli pilots thought they were bombing an Egyptian vessel. The U.S. government officially accepted Israel's apology and explanation. Israel paid compensation to the victims' families. But many U.S. naval officers have not accepted Israel's version of what had occurred.

The Navy, moreover, has historically always been the least friendly of the U.S. armed services toward Israel; the Air Force and Army had a much closer working relationship with their counterparts in Israel. But the Navy was understandably more interested in winning favorable port facilities throughout the Arab world and in the Persian Gulf. Israel, over the years, had little to offer, and its own navy was modest in size and capability.

However, that attitude in the Navy clearly changed during the Reagan administration, especially during the tenure of John Lehman as Secretary of the Navy. The Israeli ports of Haifa and Ashdod on the Mediterranean have increasingly become important facilities for the U.S. Sixth Fleet; more than thirty thousand American sailors had shore leave in Israel in 1986 alone. The Navy began to purchase Israeli-made pilotless reconnaissance "drone" aircraft and other Israeli-made equipment. And a squadron of Israeli-made Kfir jet fighters was leased to the U.S. Navy, which has used them to simulate Soviet-made MiGs in training exercises.

Indeed, the same was true in terms of the overall U.S.-Israeli relationship. The CIA, under director William Casey, was sharing previously restricted intelligence with Israel almost routinely.

But Pollard did not see that bigger picture. He focused only on what the Navy was not giving Israel. And in the course of his work, Pollard came across what he later described as "horrifying" threats facing Israel. He said there was "a veritable flood" of Soviet military equipment "quietly entering the region unnoticed by the Israelis, who were depending upon the U.S. intelligence community for warning of such activity."

By 1981, frustrated by his job in Naval Intelligence, he began to look for work elsewhere. During the angry confrontation that year between the Reagan administration and Congress over the sale of AWACS reconnaissance aircraft to Saudi Arabia, Pollard actually went to the offices of the American Israel Public Affairs Committee (AIPAC), the official pro-Israeli lobbying organization in Washington, asking to be a defense analyst for the group.

"He came to our office, identified himself as working for Navy Intelligence, and proceeded to give a bizarre presentation," an AIPAC official later recalled. Pollard had warned that the American intelligence community was listening in on AIPAC. "After Pollard left," the official said, "we laughed because this guy seemed to be off the wall." Another AIPAC official said that Pollard seemed "very strange." Pollard, according to this second official, had told an alarming story of grave dangers facing Israel. "He also spoke of his incredible access to TOP SECRET information," the official said. "I thought that AIPAC was being set up as part of a 'sting' operation. His story simply sounded too incredible to be real. So I got rid of him."

Pollard later bitterly complained about AIPAC's decision. "I couldn't believe how stupid they were," he said.

In August 1981, Pollard met Anne Henderson, a pretty twenty-one-year-old redhead with large blue eyes, then working as a secretary at the American Institute of Architects and attending the University of Maryland at night.

They had been introduced by one of her roommates and quickly fell in love.

"Oh, we were the best friends immediately," she would later recall. "It was love at first sight."

They started dating exclusively right away. "We were inseparable from that day on—until the ordeal occurred."

Her lawyer, James Hibey, would later say that the young couple became interdependent, "each fulfilling the needs of the other." Others who knew them agreed; they seemed made for each other.

"She was struck by Jay's gentleness, but also by his intelligence, and the two shared many hours of intellectual conversation about current national and world events," Bernard Henderson, Anne's father, said. "In addition, Jay offered Anne a deeper pride in and understanding of her Jewish ancestry."

For her part, Anne knew from the start that Jay, in her words, was "an ardent Zionist." She said he was very open to her about his commitment to Israel. "He never hid that. I knew of his deep love of Israel." And as they discussed the issue, she slowly came to share his feelings and commitment. "I felt similarly to him," she said. "Jay was an excellent teacher."

The relationship blossomed. They decided to live together the following year. In June of 1982, when her lease expired, Anne moved into Pollard's apartment in Arlington, Virginia, across the Potomac River from the District of Columbia. By then, she had already met his parents, who visited Washington frequently. She was pleased to discover how quickly they became good friends. Because her parents had divorced when she was a teenager, Anne was deeply moved by the very close, loving family environment of the Pollards. He clearly had the family that she would have wanted.

The two eventually moved to a modest two-bedroom apartment at 1733 20th Street N.W., near Dupont Circle, right in the middle of Washington. The gray-brick building, named the Nelson, was just a block off Connecticut Avenue, around the corner from the huge Washington Hilton Hotel.

They paid $750 a month in rent. The most distinctive feature of the apartment was the walls: they were lined with shelves for the hundreds of books Jay had collected over the years.

They loved the neighborhood, with its cafés, bookstores, and other shops within easy walking distance. There was only one major problem—parking. But they were willing to pay that price in order to live there. They often strolled around the streets in the evenings.

"With combined salaries of some $50,000 per year," her father said, "the young couple could afford a reasonable middle-class lifestyle. This was especially true since my mother had given Anne most of the money for an automobile and Jay's father picked up most of the gasoline bills off of a credit card."

Henderson recalled that he first met Pollard during a business trip to Washington. "I was struck by his intelligence and ability to converse on a wide variety of subjects," he said. "I also liked Jay's sense of humor."

Henderson was bothered somewhat about Pollard's job, thinking it involved "some danger." But he quickly concluded that "his was a desk job removed from field intelligence gathering."

His greatest concern, as he recalled, was Anne's deteriorating health. She was already suffering sharp and mysterious abdominal pains. "She had gone through a series of treatments from different doctors and had been hospitalized on three occasions," he said. It was only in 1984 that a Washington physician, Dr. Herbert A. Moscovitz, discovered that she was suffering from a rare stomach disorder. The doctor would later write that she had "a motor abnormality of the stomach," meaning that she couldn't digest food properly. As a result, he said, "undigested food residues accumulate and coagulate with mucus and bile to form soft masses, which are known as bezoars. These have to be removed or broken up endoscopically so that they can pass through the digestive system." He said she required "the continuous use of drugs which stimulate the stomach to empty."

Anne underwent all kinds of treatments; but while the pains periodically went away, the overall problem persisted.

Still, she was able to advance her career, moving from secretarial to editorial and press relations jobs. In September of 1979, for example, she worked for the Chemical Specialties Manufacturers Association, a trade association, where she developed her public relations skills. "Despite her youth at the time, Anne proved to be a very qualified, conscientious, and efficient secretary," her supervisor, Joan Gerson of Rockville, Maryland, would later write. "Her outstanding qualities were her ability to communicate well with our members, and her good public relations skills. . . ."

In 1982, she began working in the public relations department of the National Rifle Association (NRA) in Washington. According to her associates there, she demonstrated a keen talent for the job. She had learned some of the skills from her father, who himself had worked in public relations for much of his professional career.

At the NRA, in fact, she honed her professional skills. "Although Anne's background was primarily clerical, her desire to move into project management coupled with her enthusiasm, sincerity and creative ideas was very persuasive," her boss, Laura W. Stroup, of Silver Spring, Maryland, later said, adding that Anne became "one of my most dependable and capable staff members."

But Anne, despite her own health problems, was concerned about her husband's frustrations. Even then, she already knew that he was considering a decision to share classified information with the Israelis. "Anne felt that Jay was in a work environment which was causing him great personal anguish and urged him to quit," her father explained. "She encouraged his often-stated speculation that he would be better off working or lobbying for a defense firm or for someone involved in the Israeli armaments industry. She suggested he might want to become a consultant to an Israeli firm."

That was one reason why he had earlier turned to AIPAC. But that career switch was not in the cards.

Pollard stayed in Naval Intelligence where, ironically, he continued to move up the ladder despite a major crisis in

1981 that temporarily lost him his security clearances and almost lost him his job.

In the course of his graduate studies, Pollard recalled, he had developed a close personal friendship with a South African naval officer who later returned to South Africa. "We were just friends. That was the extent of it," he said.

During the final year of the Carter administration, U.S.–South African intelligence cooperation was severely strained. The South Africans had expelled an American Air Force colonel for spying. The United States retaliated. The scaled-back level of cooperation hurt both countries' intelligence communities.

"We had a problem with intelligence collection in the South Atlantic," Pollard said. This was crucial for the United States, he explained, because so many U.S. ships—with Russian submarines and ships crawling around them—were going around the South African Cape on their way to and from the Indian Ocean and the Persian Gulf. Americans at that time were still being held hostage in Iran. Pollard then worked on the Atlantic Desk in the Naval Ocean Surveillance Information Center.

Around the same time, Lt. Gen. P. W. van der Westhuizen, South Africa's chief of military intelligence, came to the United States secretly with a five-member military delegation. Their presence in Washington leaked—to the embarrassment of the State Department and others in the administration.

Pollard, although still relatively fresh in Naval Intelligence, said that he approached his supervisor and told him that he had a personal contact with the South Africans—going back to his days at Fletcher. He had a friend, he said, who was now deputy head of the Bureau of State Security in South Africa. "I asked if I could establish a back channel to him," Pollard said.

According to Pollard, he received permission to do so after a lengthy debriefing from the CIA. "A very productive relationship was started," he insisted. "South Africa provided locating data and photographs of Soviet warships, including the first photo of a particular short-range Soviet naval SAM."

Pollard claimed that as a result of his behind-the-scenes involvement, U.S. and South African naval officials began to talk to each other "for the first time in two years." The relationship was good "until the NIS got involved."

But as the operation unfolded, questions involving its legality were raised. That, he claimed, was because he was asked to plant some incriminating documents on one of the South Africans—a request he said he had refused on moral grounds, considering it unethical. This supposedly angered his naval supervisors.

Pollard claimed that he also got caught in a power struggle between NIS and the CIA. The CIA, he insisted, had actually wanted him transferred to its control. As things disintegrated with the turf battle, it became evident that NIS wanted Pollard to resign. Some officials charged he was unstable. His credentials were suspended.

Naval officials said that they had indeed originally believed Pollard's boasting about his personal relationship with van der Westhuizen and others in South African intelligence. In fact, they saw an opportunity to take advantage of that relationship by embarrassing van der Westhuizen. "The thought on the South African was: 'Let's get the S.O.B. and burn him,'" a Navy source was later quoted by reporter Michael Satchell in *U.S. News and World Report* as saying.

But as the Navy pressed Pollard for more details of his relationship with the South Africans, his story began to unravel. According to the account in *U.S. News and World Report,* Pollard told naval investigators "fantastic tales about having lived in South Africa and his father's being [CIA] station chief there." One senior Naval Intelligence official said: "It became obvious the guy had to be unstable. . . . He wasn't on anybody else's wavelength. And that's when the system got nervous about him."

Pollard would later confirm that he was told to get psychiatric help after his credentials were lifted. His father recommended that he meet with Dr. Neil Parker, who was then affiliated with the Johns Hopkins University Hospital in Baltimore. Dr. Parker subsequently concluded that Pollard was not mentally ill—at which point Pollard filed a formal grievance to get his credentials and his job back. Rr. Adm. John L. Butts restored his credentials "in accordance with established procedures."*

Already personally paranoid about anti-Semitism in the Navy, Pollard would later recall that he had decided to become a spy for Israel as early as 1982, following two authorized meetings with Israeli military representatives visiting Washington. He had attended those sessions together with other U.S. intelligence analysts, and—according to government documents—he concluded that the United States was not providing Israel with enough classified information to enable it to strengthen its own military capability.

"What I knew was that there was information vital to the security of the state and ultimately to the United States as well which was not getting through," Pollard said later, in prison. "When the other side is pleading for information, it's fairly evident that they are not getting it one way or another because in any kind of exchange there's a quid pro quo. You never voluntarily give anything, even amongst friends. You never voluntarily give something if you wouldn't have to under the circumstances. So if you have this information at your disposal, why yield valuable quids for acquiring the information from another source?"

The United States shares a great deal of information with Israel—and vice versa. But they do not share everything. The United States, for example, does not offer Israel its sensitive intelligence on "friendly" Arab countries, notably Jordan, Saudi Arabia, and Egypt. That is a matter of policy. And other extremely sensitive intelligence is not shared out of fear that Israel could take some countermeasure that might tip off the Soviet Union or some hostile Arab country that it has been penetrated. There is also fear that Israel's intelligence community may have been penetrated by the Soviets. Protecting the sources and methods of intelligence collection is rule number one in the spy business.

---

*But the story would not end there. Shortly after Pollard's arrest in 1985, Dr. Parker went through his patient files. He discovered that the Pollard file was gone—the only patient's file missing from all his records. Pollard suspected that Naval Intelligence had stolen the document, a charge I could not confirm.

Pollard was well aware of the restrictions on the disclosure of this kind of classified information to foreign governments, including allies. He had been fully briefed on this matter and had signed many forms swearing that he would not make any unauthorized disclosures. One standard clause had said:

> I have been advised that direct or indirect disclosure, unauthorized retention, or negligent handling of SCI [SENSITIVE COMPARTMENTED INFORMATION] by me could cause irreparable injury to the United States or be used to advantage by a foreign nation. I hereby agree that I will never divulge such information to anyone who is not authorized to receive it without prior written authorization from the United States Government department or agency that last authorized my access to SCI. I further understand that I am obligated by law and regulation not to disclose any classified information in an unauthorized fashion.

But Pollard felt that he was responsible to a higher authority. Citing moral grounds, he eventually concluded that those restrictions were inappropriate for Israel. He kept his views to himself but began to think very seriously about approaching Israel. He had often fantasized about helping Israel; now, after all these years, he was about to live out his fantasy.

Years later, he would dramatically describe his deep concern over what he was convinced was the deliberate U.S. decision not to provide Israel with enough intelligence. He said the U.S. Navy was holding back vital details from Israel: "Despite the commonly held belief that the U.S. provides 'everything' to the Israelis, the intelligence exchange from the Navy, at any rate, is anything but equitable."

Pollard recalled his own participation in the two formal intelligence exchanges with the Israelis. "I participated in two official intelligence conferences with the Israelis and was amazed to see how high-level directives about releasing certain types of information to Jerusalem were routinely shelved by the men in the trenches, who felt that the 'Jews' didn't need to know anything."

He recalled that during one such exchange, a U.S. analyst, when asked for "releasable" information on Soviet chemical warfare agents, "turned to me laughing and said that he thought the Jews were overly sensitive about gas due to their experiences during the Second World War and suggested that they should just calm down a bit."

According to Pollard, the underlying attitude of "many of the American participants in these meetings was overtly racist, which produced a corresponding degree of anger and distrust on the part of the Israelis, most of whom felt that their country's security concerns were being totally overlooked."

Pollard became increasingly angry as he witnessed these trends. "The principal instruction I received from my supervisor was that we should only be prepared to give the Israelis enough information to get them paranoid but not enough, say, to let them figure out a countermeasure to a newly identified Soviet weapon system. When I carefully asked how they were expected to cope with all the state-of-the-art Russian equipment pouring into the region, the response was that all they had to do was lose a few planes and then they'd know what radar frequencies to jam."

This attitude was completely unacceptable to Pollard. "As can be imagined," he said, "it was very difficult for me to work in this kind of atmosphere and not become frustrated at what I thought was an unbelievably cynical view toward Israel's survival."

The Israelis, he said, were providing the United States with "everything they had acquired, at great personal risk to many of their agents, and the Navy bureaucrats couldn't care less about reciprocating in an equally open-handed manner, as per their instructions.

"In retrospect," Pollard concluded, "if I had only reported what I'd seen to the Navy's Inspector General, this anomalous situation might have been rectified through channels, without me feeling compelled to take matters into my own hands. Instead, I watched the threats to Israel's existence grow and gradually came to the conclusion that I had to do something."

Another turning point for Pollard came in 1983 when the U.S. Marine headquarters in Beirut were bombed by fundamentalist Shi'ite terrorists. The tragedy, he said, had an enormous impact on his ultimate decision to spy for Israel. "As I stood in the back of the National Cathedral [in Washington] listening to the memorial service for the fallen soldiers, it all seemed so senseless—over two hundred dead men and all the U.S. government could do was respond with an ineffectual air raid in which more Americans were killed."

The incident, in Pollard's mind, had very direct ramifications for Israel. "The thought struck me that if the government were unwilling to defend its own interests in the Middle East against a type of threat which could be targeted with public support, then it would be unreasonable to assume that the Israelis could be assured of adequate assistance in the event the tide of battle turned against them," he said. "I had already seen how one branch of the intelligence community was consistently undermining Israel's ability to prepare for war, while the various Arab powers were receiving what seemed to be a constant stream of Soviet bloc and Western European military equipment and intelligence information about Israel. The situation had all the characteristics of a sellout in which Israel would face the combined power of its numerous opponents alone, without the benefit of even one reliable ally."

He walked out of the memorial service "committed to do something that would guarantee Israel's security, even though it might involve a degree of potential risk and personal sacrifice. I knew what I was contemplating was wrong but at the same time all I could see was that the ends justified the means. As with many cases of situational ethics, the individual's most difficult hurdle is to accept the fact that the contemplated action, while apparently 'compelled' by a power beyond his control, was still a matter for which he would be held personally accountable. There could never be any excuse which would absolve him of guilt, only explanations which might provide a motivational guide to his crime."

This decision to spy for Israel helped to resolve Pollard's continuing crisis about not moving there. He also came up with a sophisticated rationale about espionage on behalf of a friendly country. The United States, he assured himself, would not be hurt. In fact, it might even be helped since a close ally—one that shared America's concerns about the Soviet Union—would be strengthened in the process.

"Having made this decision I could admit to its blatant dishonesty, but never its disloyalty," he said. "What I thought I'd done was resolve my dilemma in a way which would permit me to work in the Diaspora against the Russian menace while helping Israel at the same time."

CHAPTER FIVE

The Walk-In

In June 1984 Jonathan Pollard was transferred to the newly created Anti-Terrorist Alert Center (ATAC) of the Naval Investigative Service's Threat Analysis Division to serve as a watch officer. He saw this as a plum assignment. He would be right in the midst of the action, well positioned to collect vital information for the Israelis.

The commander of the unit was Jerry Agee, a hard-nosed career naval officer with twenty years of intelligence experience. Agee, a tall and balding man with only hints of red hair atop his head, had been named head of ATAC a month earlier. He had come directly from sea duty, where he had served on an admiral's executive staff aboard a ship attached to the U.S. Sixth Fleet in the eastern Mediterranean and off the coast of Lebanon during the U.S. bombing raids against terrorist targets in 1983. "That was one reason why I had been chosen to take over that anti-terrorist function," Agee would later say. "Certain other duties I had in my past fitted in well, plus my recent experience in the Middle East. I was asked if I would take that job and I said yes."

The ATAC had been formed in December 1983. When Agee stepped in, the unit was still in the early formation stage. There had been many temporary assignments to its staff, but it was clear that the Navy wanted ATAC to become a permanent intelligence organization. Its mission would be to deal with terrorism issues that threatened the U.S. Navy and Marine Corps. "It was a new element of the Naval Intelligence system," Agee said. "It had just been created. There were very few permanently assigned personnel actually there."

The temporary people who were assigned to ATAC had been pulled from other Navy commands. Agee was the first permanent officer attached to ATAC. "So when I got there in May," he said, "the majority of the people working there were temporaries, and it was, more or less, up to me to move the temporaries to permanent status. I could use temporary personnel as long as necessary but preferably as short as possible."

Each individual naval command in Suitland, Maryland, had been instructed to detail a certain number of civilian and military officers to ATAC. "Jay was part of that second group of people to come into ATAC," Agee recalled. "They rolled in around May and June."

When a new unit like ATAC is created and other established units are instructed to detail personnel to it, they will very often ask those people who are considered troublemakers or nonproducers to make the switch. At ATAC, Pollard was initially received skeptically because of his earlier run-ins with his superiors at the Naval Intelligence Support Center, a separate command in Suitland.

At that point, Agee did not know anything about Pollard or his background. "He just appeared on the doorstep one morning and said, 'I'm your new guy.'"

Pollard's first assignment at ATAC was to work on the twenty-four-hour-a-day watch. Two people work on the desk at a time. They are responsible for receiving all of the intelligence coming into ATAC. Their specific mission is to sort through the reams of information and try to determine what it may mean for the Navy and the Marine Corps. "Pollard was assigned to stand that watch," Agee said. "He initially underwent a few weeks of training at the command. It was a kind of on-the-job training. I would guess by late June he had qualified to start standing the watch along with someone else who was more experienced. His job was then to basically go through all of the intelligence information and also the public press reporting—Reuters, AP, or whatever—as it came in, and then to sort of do a quick analysis. Is this a threat to a Navy unit someplace? And if so, is it an immediate threat? If it is, warn them of it. If not, pass it on to someone who was working in the daytime so that he could do more analysis of it."

In this new position, Pollard was assigned duties that included research and analysis of intelligence data pertaining to potential terrorist threats. He initially was responsible for monitoring the daily classified message traffic received in the ATAC for information pertaining to terrorist activities, and passing the information along to the analyst responsible for the geographic area in which the activity was occurring. Pollard, drinking many cups of coffee and smoking packs of cigarettes, worked on twelve-hour shifts—either from 6:00 P.M. until 6:00 A.M. or from 6:00 A.M. to 6:00 P.M.

Agee said that Pollard "initially looked like just another analyst," but proved competent in his performance. "He was just there and he looked like he was doing a decent job," he said. "He was able to do some fairly quick analysis and be, I thought, above average in his analysis of things, what it meant as a threat. He was able to write short articles very well and very quickly. And that was all that was required in that job. You had to do a lot of things. You had to do them quickly and relatively well. It didn't require any sense of mental discipline or personal discipline—to stick with something for a long period of time. So in dealing with short-term issues in intelligence problems, he did very well."

Pollard held security clearances to obtain, receive, and use CONFIDENTIAL, SECRET, TOP SECRET, and SPECIAL COMPARTMENTED INFORMATION (SCI).

According to U.S. government regulations, information is classified CONFIDENTIAL if its unauthorized disclosure could reasonably be expected to cause "damage" to the national security; SECRET if its unauthorized disclosure could reasonably be expected to cause "serious damage" to the national security; and TOP SECRET if its unauthorized disclosure could reasonably be expected to cause "exceptionally grave damage" to the national security. SCI is a designation reserved for especially sensitive classified information, "the dissemination of which is strictly controlled and limited to selected individuals within the military and intelligence community who have special security clearances."

SCI data, according to court documents, principally involves information about sophisticated technical systems for collecting intelligence, as well as the intelligence product collected by the systems. Conventional intelligence activities employ human sources; SCI intelligence collection primarily employs technical systems. Communications intelligence is the classic example of SCI as it is normally derived through a technical system which intercepts communications.

Because of the extremely fragile nature of SCI—compromise of a technical system is much like the loss of a network of agents—strict security criteria have been established for its access. In its subsequent presentation to the court, the government prosecutors said that only a relatively small percentage of the individuals who have been granted TOP SECRET clearances are also approved for SCI access. "Access to SCI information is limited to persons who have a clearly established need for SCI information and who meet more rigorous personnel security criteria."

Information classified TOP SECRET and/or SCI is maintained in several secure libraries and repositories throughout the Washington area. Certain of this information, the government said, is contained in a secure computer system which is accessible through terminals located in such restricted locations as the ATAC work space in Suitland, Maryland. Pollard, as well as other ATAC analysts with TOP SECRET/SCI clearances and appropriate access codes, could readily access these libraries, repositories, and computer terminals to obtain data in order to perform their specific duties.

But ATAC analysts operated on what the government said was "an honor system." They were supposed to limit their access only to that information for which they had an official "need to know." Still, once an ATAC analyst who had appropriate access codes was on these secure premises, he or she also had the capability to access and obtain highly classified information unrelated to their duties.

Pollard, for example, was assigned to the Caribbean/Continental United States Desk of ATAC, and his "need to know" classified information was limited to data that concerned terrorist activities or developments in those areas. Yet according to government papers, he could—and as early as June 1984 did—routinely access and obtain classified data relating to the Middle East and other geographic areas remote from his assigned area of responsibility.

Agee recalled that Pollard was very knowledgeable about the Middle East and South Africa. Pollard, however, kept his pro-Israeli political views to himself. "For a long time," Agee said, "I didn't even know he was Jewish. . . . He never said he was Jewish. A few people knew, people who knew him on a more personal level than I did. He never indicated that he was Jewish. He never indicated that he was a practicing Jew. It just never came up at all. . . . He never came out and said, 'I am Jewish,' but after a period of time, I put two and two together, and I assumed he was. I never asked him if he was. It really didn't make any difference to me whether he was or he wasn't."

Agee said that Pollard, while assigned to the Naval Intelligence Support Center, had "made comments that he had worked for Israeli intelligence." But in that office, Pollard also came to be known as "a bullshitter. He was always telling tall tales. It was more or less a joke in the office, 'Did you hear the story about Pollard?' There were a lot of Pollard stories."

Agee said that no one ever officially reported Pollard's alleged statement about working for Israeli intelligence. "It was never, to my knowledge, indicated officially that he had made that statement. It was never reported. And I think his reputation as a teller of tall tales made anything he said in a conversational tone very suspect."

But Agee acknowledged that "in all his bullshit stories, all his tall tales, somewhere in there was a kernel of truth. So this story about working for the Mossad—whether it was true or not—maybe he was thinking about it."

What Agee didn't know was that Pollard was already compromising U.S. security, first by smuggling out documents to impress his friends and then by attempting to recruit another friend into a spy ring that was taking shape in his mind.

Court documents later released by the government in fact showed that already by 1982 Pollard had earlier provided "to certain of his social acquaintances U.S. classified documents." Two of these friends were professional investment advisers. The documents, the court papers said, contained "classified economic and political analyses" which Pollard believed would help his friends in giving advice to their clients. On a third occasion, according to the government's affidavit, Pollard gave classified documents to another "social acquaintance" he knew could utilize the information to further his career.

Pollard told U.S. investigators that although he was not paid for the information, he hoped to be rewarded ultimately through business opportunities that these individuals could arrange for him when he left Naval Intelligence. "In fact," the government's pre-sentencing memorandum stated, "defendant was involved in an ongoing business venture with two of these acquaintances at the time he provided the classified information to them." Pollard admitted that his actions "reflected an unfortunate desire" to impress his friends with the importance of his work and his knowledge of areas of interest to them. His insecurity, in effect, made him show off to his friends.*

---

*The identities of these three people were later disclosed in court documents as Kurt Lohbeck, Joe Harmon, and Laura Caro. None possessed security clearances. They reported their dealings with Pollard after his arrest.

The idea of recruiting a friend to help him pass documents to the Israelis originated shortly after Pollard received the long-awaited phone call from Steven Stern, the stockbroker in New York who had met Sella earlier. Finally, Pollard was going to be introduced to Sella, the war hero. In the process of leaking documents to his friends, Pollard had discovered that he could easily smuggle files out of his office. Now he would undertake some serious work for Israel. A plan for a spy ring began to emerge in his mind. He would need some help.

Even before his first meetings with Sella, according to government documents, Pollard had sought to recruit an old friend and roommate from Fletcher, Richard Feen, as a possible courier in taking documents to the Israelis in New York. U.S. prosecutors (without naming Feen) said that after Pollard's arrest, "a friend of defendant's reported to the FBI that, at one time, defendant had sought to recruit the friend in an ill-defined effort to aid Israel."

Pollard, accompanied by Anne, visited Feen, who was told that he could make some money by helping Pollard deliver certain unspecified information to the Israelis.

"In a clumsy effort to interest the friend in this endeavor, defendant and Anne Henderson Pollard were critical of the friend's lifestyle, and stated that it could be substantially improved by additional income," the government would later say. "The friend was aware of the nature of defendant's employment, and assumed that defendant was proposing the delivery of classified information to Israel. The friend firmly rejected defendant's proposal and the subject was never raised thereafter. However, at about the same time, in the summer of 1984, defendant informed his friend that he [the defendant] was going to be meeting with the Israeli pilot who led the 1981 air raid on the Iraqi nuclear facility."

Both Pollards later acknowledged that Pollard attempted to solicit his friend's participation in whatever might come of the contact with Sella. But they insisted they were not certain at that point exactly what would in fact unfold. Pollard had thought that Feen might be in a position to travel to New York if necessary. But, according to Pollard, there

was no discussion of payment. Pollard simply assumed that
Feen would be reimbursed by Israel for his travel expenses.*

Aviem Sella had received formal authorization from his superiors to meet with Pollard in Washington. Rafi Eitan had
concluded that Pollard was in fact who he said he was. Sella,
however, was still advised to be very careful.

Within a few days, he found himself aboard a packed
Eastern air shuttle to Washington. Sella, himself a top-notch
fighter pilot, was forced to sit in a middle seat between two
rather bulky, sweaty, and tired businessmen. This was no
way to travel, he said to himself, as the plane circled, await-

---

*The government later released sections of Anne's post–plea-bargaining poly-
graph session of July 29, 1986, with FBI Special Agent Barry D. Colvert, during
which she described in detail the evening she and her husband attempted to
"pitch" Feen as a backup to the espionage operation:

Anne Henderson Pollard stated that the Washington friend had grown up
in Detroit in a predominantly black neighborhood and that his "Jewishness"
had been an impediment to him while growing up and in later life in seeking
employment. Defendant Anne Henderson Pollard described the Washington
friend as being very "Jewish" and in her mind initially was as much a propo-
nent of "Zionism" as was her husband, Jonathan Jay Pollard. She described the
Washington friend as being violently "anti-Arab" and espousing, at least in
private, the same views with regard to the need for the security of the state
of Israel as her husband Jonathan Jay Pollard.

Anne Henderson Pollard stated that during the Spring of 1984 a number of
terrorist incidents had occurred throughout the world that were directed at
Israeli citizens and American Jews. Those escalating incidents greatly dis-
turbed both Jonathan Jay Pollard and Anne Henderson Pollard. Jonathan Jay
Pollard became upset with the fact that he was unable to provide any assistance to the state of Israel.

Jonathan Jay Pollard knew that a New York friend had been quite active in
working with the Israelis and knew that the New York friend was dedicated
to helping the Israelis. Anne Henderson Pollard stated that she had learned
that the New York friend, in addition to helping in fund raising for the state
of Israel, was also instrumental in obtaining high technology transfers to the
state of Israel.

In conversations with the New York friend, Jonathan Jay Pollard had offered
his abilities in analytical research. Jonathan Jay Pollard informed her [Anne]
that during these conversations with the New York friend he had learned that
someone would be "in touch" with him in the near future. Jonathan Jay Pollard
apparently had not been given a name or an exact date of this contact. Anne
Henderson Pollard thought that any assistance he would give would necessi-
tate him having to travel to New York to get assignments or some type of

ing permission to land at National Airport. He, of course, preferred the cockpit of an F-16 jet fighter.

The timing of the long-awaited meeting worked out excellently for Sella. By coincidence, he had been invited to deliver an Israel Bonds lecture in the U.S. capital. But he had another purpose as well.

A Knesset investigatory report, chaired by Abba Eban, would later conclude that Generals Moshe Levi and Amos Lapidot "applied faulty judgement in this affair. They acceded to Colonel Aviem Sella's request without carrying out a comprehensive check of their own so as to verify that a senior officer was not being used for a mission that would

---

"tasking" and that in the event he was unable to make these trips he would need someone to go in his place. He felt that it was extremely important that this person be as committed to the state of Israel as he, Jonathan Jay Pollard, was. It was in this vein that he thought that the Washington friend would be an excellent candidate for this "backup." Both Jonathan Jay Pollard and Anne Henderson Pollard considered this Washington friend to be reliable, intelligent, a "quick study," and felt that he was as completely "pro-Zionist" as they were.

Anne Henderson Pollard stated that she thought their contact with regard to this proposal or "pitch" occurred in April or early May of 1984. She stated that she had gone to the Washington friend's apartment during the evening to ask the Washington friend for his assistance. Anne Henderson Pollard stated that during a discussion with regard to the situation in Israel and the mounting acts of terrorism, Jonathan Jay Pollard began asking questions of the Washington friend in an effort to determine his "Jewishness." When Jonathan Jay Pollard ultimately asked the Washington friend for his assistance, he was unable to provide any exact details as to the nature of this assistance, only that he would need his help. The Washington friend's response, according to Anne Henderson Pollard, was one in which he did not say "yes" or did not say "no." Anne Henderson Pollard stated that she felt very negative "vibes" about this conversation as the Washington friend did not show any enthusiasm for the idea presented by Jonathan Jay Pollard. She noted no expression of sympathy and felt immediately that Jonathan Jay Pollard should never have brought this subject up with the Washington friend.

At the end of the evening as they were driving home, Anne Henderson Pollard stated that she can recall saying in effect, "This was a bad idea. I think you should just forget that you had this conversation." Anne Henderson Pollard stated that she could not recall Jonathan Jay Pollard's exact response but felt he must have reiterated what she had said. . . .

Anne Henderson Pollard stated she could think of nothing else relating to the evening in which the Washington friend was "pitched."

Feen later refused to discuss the incident with me, merely confirming that he was Pollard's roommate for one semester at Fletcher.

exceed his domain of command." The report recommended that in the future approval "should not be given for using a career army officer within an intelligence framework outside the IDF without the advance permission of the Defense Minister. It is to be regretted that former Chief of Staff Moshe Levi did not act accordingly in this affair." But that was 20/20 hindsight.

A Likud member of the Eban Committee, David Magen, would later insist in the official report that Eitan, for his part, had acted with authority in pressing for the initial connection with Pollard. "By the nature of things," Magen said, "the committee was unable to specify in this report—due to its being published—numerous details which would have attested to the nature of the unit Eitan headed. The clear conclusion stemming from these details is that the recruitment of Pollard and his handling were done with authority, and committee members agree that Rafael Eitan did not exceed the authority invested in him."

"This is Avi Sella," the pilot said matter-of-factly in an authoritative but friendly voice.

"Shalom," Pollard replied, jumping up from his chair, literally standing at attention as he held the phone. He couldn't believe how excited he became simply hearing Sella's low but pleasant voice.

"How about lunch?" Sella asked.

"Sure," Pollard replied. "What's your schedule?"

They arranged to meet at the recently refurbished coffeeshop of the Washington Hilton Hotel on May 29, 1984— five months after Sella had first met Stern. Sella was staying at the Hilton, which was filled with conventioneers. It was only a two-block walk up 20th Street to Florida Avenue from Pollard's apartment.

There was very good chemistry during that first meeting. They sat in a corner booth, away from other diners. Both men were concerned about being overheard. On their mind was an incident a few years earlier when Stephen Bryen, then a senior staff member of the Senate Foreign Relations

Committee, was having breakfast at the Madison Hotel cof-feeshop with three Israeli officials. David Saad of the Na-tional Association of Arab Americans later filed an affidavit with the FBI charging that he saw Bryen transfer classified documents to the Israelis—a charge Bryen denied. After a lengthy investigation, no charges were ever made against Bryen, who eventually received a high-level appointment in the Pentagon during the Reagan administration—his TOP SECRET security clearances intact.

Pollard took an instant liking to the pilot. He was every-thing that Stern had said—smart, sincere, sensitive, and savvy. Pollard was quickly convinced that he could trust Sella completely. He began to pour out incredible informa-tion, in part to impress Sella.

Pollard, that day, was rather blunt—so blunt, in fact, that Sella was a bit scared. He informed Sella in no uncertain terms that he wanted to work as an agent for the Israeli government. "I know I can help you," he gushed. "You have no idea how much vital information the United States is denying Israel."

He said he wanted to provide classified documents and information. He described the position which he held and the nature of the classified intelligence information and doc-uments he could provide, including "signal intelligence and technical information which could be used by Israel to strengthen its defense capability."

Sella could hardly believe what he heard. He was nervous. Was he being set up? Was Pollard wired?

But the more he listened to Pollard, the more he gained confidence in him.

Pollard said that while he ultimately intended to emigrate to Israel, he was willing to remain in his present position to exploit, on behalf of Israel, the "holes" in the U.S. intelli-gence system. But he did not bring any actual documents to that first meeting.

Sella, well briefed in advance of that session, was prepared to give Pollard a cautious go-ahead, but only if he was abso-lutely convinced that the American was sincere. According to subsequently released government papers, Sella said that while he did not want information on U.S. military capabilities per se, he was very much interested in acquiring information that the United States had collected about Arab and Soviet capabilities. This, Sella said, would help strengthen Israel's own defense capability without hurting the United States.

The Israelis, Pollard was flatly told by Sella, wanted to differentiate between spying "in" the United States and spying "against" the United States. The former was okay; the latter was not. That certainly eased Pollard's conscience, as the Israelis knew it would.

Pollard later maintained the same position. "From the start of this affair," he said, "I never intended or agreed to spy against the United States. A review of the documents collected, as well as the results of FBI polygraphs bear out this statement. . . . The notion that I was a traitor or working on something which would harm the United States never arose since the agreed-upon ground rules of the operation clearly stipulated that I would never be asked to provide material which would put my loyalty to this country in question."

Pollard and Sella had a lengthy lunch at that first meeting at the Washington Hilton. The pilot, while still nervous about possibly being set up as part of a "sting" operation, asked that Pollard provide a sample of the information he could obtain, and proposed another meeting for this purpose.

In order to facilitate subsequent clandestine meetings, Sella also requested that Pollard provide a list of numbers of pay telephones near his apartment. Once Pollard provided the list, Sella would assign a Hebrew letter—*Aleph, Bet, Gimmel, Daled, Hay, Vuv, Zion,* etc.—to each number. Sella then explained that he would call Pollard at home, mention a Hebrew letter, and thereby direct him to a particular pay telephone to await Sella's call. It was a classic method of clandestine communication. Pollard was pleased that he had mastered the Hebrew alphabet during his years in Hebrew School in South Bend.

Both Pollard and Sella felt that a good relationship had

been established between the two of them. They were both pleased.

Sella returned to New York and told Yagur about the meeting. Yagur immediately drafted a full report to his anxious boss in Tel Aviv.

Eitan, after receiving Yagur's report, immediately flew to New York from Tel Aviv. He wanted to meet personally with both Yagur and Sella to make certain that Pollard would be properly handled. He knew that neither Israeli had any serious experience as field agents; that was Eitan's specialty. And in any case, Eitan always enjoyed traveling to New York, where the shopping and food are good.

On June 18, he told Yagur that Sella should arrange a second meeting with Pollard. The next day, Eitan and Yagur met with Sella to prepare him for that second meeting. The air force pilot was still, after all, rather inexperienced in the murky ways of espionage. But he was eager and willing to learn because he felt the information provided would strengthen Israel's defense. He proved to be a quick study.

A few days later, Sella contacted Pollard to arrange another Washington meeting for July 7. This one was to be held in a secluded outdoor location at Dumbarton Oaks, the beautiful old park in Georgetown where the public can stroll at leisure. It was at Dumbarton Oaks that the Allies conceived of the United Nations during World War II. The chances of conversations being recorded while outside, Eitan had told Sella, were certainly less than inside a room.

It was very hot and muggy at that second meeting—a typical July day in the nation's capital. Pollard parked his Mustang on 32nd Street, around the corner from the main R Street entrance to the estate, surrounded by a red-brick wall. He read the statement inscribed in concrete on one wall, attributed to Mildred Bliss, who donated the estate to Harvard University in 1940:

> Those responsible for scholarship should remember that the humanities can not be fostered by confusing

instruction with education, that it was my husband's as well as it is my wish that the Mediterranean interpretation of the humanist disciplines shall predominate, that gardens have their place in the humanist order of life, that trees are noble elements to be protected by successive generations, and are not to be neglected or lightly destroyed.

The young American arrived early. He strolled on the cracked brick sidewalk around the park, reading up on the impressive history of Dumbarton Oaks. In 1702, for example, Queen Anne granted the Rock of Dumbarton to Colonel Ninian Beall. In 1717, his son, Col. George Beall, bought additional land for the estate. His son, Thomas Beall, sold the estate in 1780 to William Dorsey. And the title continued to be changed—until 1940.

The trees and gardens were lush; there was a clean smell to them. Pollard walked past the gold-painted tips of the main gate, up a crushed rock and dirt driveway to the main house on the hill overlooking the park. He waited anxiously for the pilot. Sella, he said to himself, was not going to be disappointed.

Pollard brought with him that day a brown leather briefcase full of highly classified documents to demonstrate his ability and willingness to assist Israel. Among the forty-eight documents were formal intelligence publications and satellite photographs.

One of the most impressive was an incredibly detailed aerial photograph of the destroyed Iraqi nuclear reactor at Osirak—a picture taken only hours after the Israeli air strike that Sella had commanded three years earlier. It was the first time Sella would see that picture.

Finally, Pollard spotted Sella walking up the driveway. The pilot had arrived in an ancient taxi, without air conditioning. He wore a short-sleeved shirt—no tie for this Israeli—and was still sweating.

Before exchanging greetings, both men glanced all around to make sure they had not been followed. It was,

Pollard thought, a sort of spy's minuet. They finally established contact, walking to a far corner of the estate.

"I thought this might interest you," Pollard said dryly. He watched Sella's face light up upon seeing the pictures of the Iraqi reactor. But the pilot quickly became angry that the United States had not officially shared that picture with Israel. "Why didn't the U.S. show us this picture?" he asked Pollard.

"There's a ton of information which the U.S. does not show Israel," Pollard replied. "Take a look at this."

They began to examine the other documents.

Sella still refused actually to take delivery of the documents. He had been strongly warned by Eitan and Yagur not to accept any documents, as they still suspected a possible trap. But Sella, following instructions, did describe other particular technical information that would be of primary interest to Israel and stressed that Pollard should obtain TOP SECRET material. In so doing, Sella specifically informed Pollard that Israel did not need information relating to terrorism; it already had sufficient information on that subject. It was also imperative that Pollard not risk possible detection by collecting too many documents, especially unimportant ones.

Sella had earlier been informed by Eitan that once they were convinced that Pollard was the real thing, they should follow standard operating procedures to make sure that the walk-in did not walk out. The most important step, traditionally, is to get the prospective spy to accept money; then he would forever be compromised. He could never leave. Yes, his colleagues would be grateful for the information. And yes, they would want to show appreciation. But they would also need to corrupt him. They would want him to like the extra cash, trips, and presents. They would want him to get used to a more comfortable lifestyle. This was how all intelligence services deal with agents around the world, and it was how the Israelis would deal with Pollard.

So Sella, as instructed, raised the issue of money that hot day at Dumbarton Oaks. He said he would arrange for Pollard to be paid for providing any such additional classified information to Israel, and discussed a possible "cover" story to explain his possession of large sums of money beyond his U.S. government salary. At that meeting, he also discussed some alternative methods by which Pollard could be compensated.

But Pollard made clear that he was not getting involved in espionage for the money. "When I first made contact with Colonel Sella and offered my services to the Israelis," he would later say, "I never intended to establish a business relationship with them. My sole objective was to provide the Israeli Defense Forces with enough information to prepare for the next generation of Soviet military technology which had been scheduled for export to the Middle East."

He said he was "content" to work for the Israelis without any financial compensation "until the issue of salary was raised by Colonel Sella." At first, Pollard said, he did not know how to respond, "since I hadn't planned on being paid for my assistance."

At most, Pollard hoped that if the operation were successful, "the transfer of intelligence data to the Israelis would permit me to work for one of their defense industries in the United States or Europe, such as Israel Military Industries, Tadiran, or Israel Aircraft Industries—where I could continue to aid the state as an armaments marketing strategist."

But according to Pollard, Sella said that Rafi Eitan was determined to find a way to reward the U.S. analyst for his efforts. Pollard, again, did not know how to respond. "Some ridiculous amounts were initially discussed until I understood that Eitan intended to pay me as if I were a regular agent operating in 'friendly' territory."

Sella explained Eitan's thinking to Pollard this way: "Nobody would question a CIA operative living off two salaries when he's employed overseas by an unknowing firm as deep cover."

Pollard later said: "The same logic applied for me as an Israeli operative."

Pollard's lawyer, Richard Hibey, would state afterward that Pollard and Sella "discussed compensation because

Sella stated that standard practice dictated that all 'agents' receive compensation for their activities. This policy probably reflected the Israelis' conviction that one who provided information for ideological reasons was less likely to stay the course than one who acted for money."

Pollard, for his part, may have been very intelligent; he may have read a lot of spy novels. But he was fundamentally naive about the world of real espionage, which can be ugly. Spying is a rough business, and Israeli agents can be as ruthless as any in the world.

Thus, with Sella insisting at that meeting in the park that money change hands, the two men began to discuss a variety of options. After Pollard said he was considering a move to New York in order to advance Anne's public relations career, Sella quickly became concerned because such a move would deprive Israel of Pollard's access to vital information. Sella, on his own initiative, then offered to help Anne get a good job in the Washington area.

"The problem with such an approach was that it could force Mr. Pollard indirectly to involve his wife in his activities, which neither he nor the Israelis desired," Pollard's lawyer later wrote.

Still, Sella then offered to pay Pollard a sum that would compensate him for the income lost by his wife's remaining in Washington. That seemed to make some sense. But no final decisions about money were made that day.

Sella, cautious and nervous, was constantly on the lookout for strangers. He was suspicious of everyone, including women pushing baby strollers.

"It's amazing how clean they keep this place," he said to Pollard as their encounter was coming to an end.

At the conclusion of this second meeting, the two men made plans to meet again. Pollard, as earlier instructed, provided Sella with a list of pay telephone numbers near his apartment. Each was assigned a Hebrew letter. At their third meeting, Sella said, Pollard could begin to deliver documents.

CHAPTER SIX

The Corruption of Jonathan Jay Pollard

The call came a few days later. Using the Hebrew alphabet code, Sella directed Pollard to a pay telephone near the corner of Florida and Connecticut Avenues. Very excited, Pollard literally ran out of the apartment building. He then had to wait patiently for the phone to ring. It seemed that it took forever. He read the graffiti scratched around the phone to pass the time.

Eventually the ring came. The receiver was lifted within a split second—Pollard's hand was already on it. His heart was pumping very rapidly. He calmed down only when he heard the friendly, reassuring, and authoritative voice on the other end. Sella, his commanding officer, was clearly in a good mood.

Pollard, during the conversation, was asked to bring certain documents on July 19 to an address in Potomac, Maryland, an affluent Washington suburb. Only much later would he discover that the address was actually the residence of Ilan Ravid, the Israeli Embassy's science counselor in Washington. Pollard was not told by Sella that Ravid lived there nor even who he was. But Eitan and Yagur, both excited about the prospects of working with Pollard, knew that

Ravid's home would be a suitable "safe house" for the initial transfer of documents. Because the house was secluded, it would be very easy to check out whether it was under surveillance. By then, in any case, they were absolutely certain that Pollard was not part of any trap.

And on that occasion, Pollard did indeed provide Sella with numerous classified documents and information, including the actual documents he had shown him at the second meeting in Dumbarton Oaks. He also brought highly classified message traffic and intelligence summaries on the latest batch of Soviet weaponry arriving in Syria. He was quite proud of himself.

After Sella and Pollard reviewed the documents, the material was taken by an Israeli—unknown to Pollard—to the second floor of the secluded suburban home for copying. They sat in the modestly furnished living room, on a sofa, both leaning over a large glass coffee table. There were several very good pieces of modern Israeli art on the walls. Both men were nervous, although they tried not to show it. Pollard chain-smoked.

While waiting for the originals, which Pollard would have to return, Sella casually dropped a bombshell. He said that Pollard would have to travel abroad to meet "the old man"—a reference to Rafi Eitan. But Sella, as instructed, did not reveal Eitan's identity. That would come later. At that point, Pollard still had no need to know the names of the other Israelis involved.

It would be too dangerous, the pilot explained, for Pollard to meet "the old man" in the United States. Someone in the United States might recognize Eitan or Pollard. Why take that risk, even if slight? In Paris, Sella added, the legendary Israeli spymaster would outline collection priorities and determine the exact amount of compensation for Pollard.

The mystery, of course, reinforced Pollard's already inflated sense of self-importance. He was very excited and prepared to take the next step.

Sella, as instructed, also raised all sorts of possible ways for Pollard to explain his newly found money. It was agreed, for example, that Pollard would explain his ability to pay for a trip abroad by stating that it was an engagement gift from a rich, but fictitious, uncle in Paris—"Uncle Joe Fisher." Under any serious counterintelligence scrutiny, the story would quickly crumble. But Pollard liked that idea very much. To him, it seemed like a very good cover.

Sella, speaking softly and looking directly into Pollard's eyes, told him to make reservations to travel to the French capital, along with Anne, in November 1984. Sella said the government of Israel would pay for this trip. He instructed Pollard to choose first-class accommodations at the Paris Hilton. Staying at luxurious hotels was important. The reason was that other U.S. government bureaucrats—Pollard's colleagues—would supposedly be less likely to accidentally bump into him at an expensive hotel. Pollard was told that he would receive $10,000 to pay for the hotel, the flights, the meals, the rental car, and the other expenses of the Paris trip.

It was also agreed that prior to the trip, Sella would come to Washington to meet with Pollard and Anne Henderson for dinner. Sella said he was to be introduced simply as a potential business partner.

Even at their very first meeting at the Washington Hilton, Sella had told Pollard that the true nature of their relationship should not be revealed to Anne. But Pollard disobeyed that order. Anne knew all about his actions from the very start.

Sella, who had been in the United States since February 1983, informed Pollard that he would soon be returning to Israel to take command of the brand-new, U.S.–built and –financed Ramon Air Base in the Negev. As a result, Pollard would be meeting his new "handler" in Paris. Sella would also come to Paris to make the introductions.

Eitan thought it was critical for Sella to serve as the "icebreaker" at that upcoming meeting. Pollard had to feel comfortable and confident. He did not know Yagur and Eitan; he did know and like Sella. In fact, he trusted him completely.

"Congratulations on the new assignment," Pollard said. "But I'm going to miss you."

Sella, as instructed, also went over some elementary procedures with Pollard in case the operation was compromised. He gave him an emergency phone number. Pollard
was assured that he would be rescued if he were in trouble.
"Don't worry," Sella stressed. "We'll take care of everything."

Eitan was certain that he had the built-in authority to run
Pollard. But he did not want to take any chances, so he did
not formally raise the matter with either the Prime Minister
or the Defense Minister. There are some things, he understood, that are best left undiscussed.

And in any case, he probably had his own agenda in ap-
proving the Pollard operation. It would certainly make him
look good. Obtaining TOP SECRET documents from the
United States was no simple matter. He and his small staff
would carefully "sanitize" those documents before distributing them throughout the defense establishment in Israel. He
wanted as few people as possible to know that he had an
agent working deep inside the U.S. intelligence community.
Protecting sources and methods in any intelligence operation, after all, is rule number one. The fewer Israelis who
knew about Pollard, the better. And Eitan would understandably have preferred to let everyone inside the Israeli
government assume that he had numerous sources all over
the place—not just one man.*

Sella, joined by his wife Yehudit, returned to Washington
on July 21 to have dinner with Pollard and Anne at the Four
Ways, an expensive French restaurant only half a block from
their apartment. He told Anne that he was an old friend and

---

*The U.S. government would later allege that shortly after the meeting in Poto-
mac, Sella and an unknown "accomplice" met with someone described only as "an
associate" of Pollard. They asked him to "facilitate the payment of monies" to
Pollard "in consideration of valuable assistance Pollard had provided to Israel."
Sella and the associate said that "it would be advantageous to pay these monies"
to Pollard "through an intermediary so as to disguise the true source of the monies." But this scheme never materialized because Pollard's "associate," an American Jew, backed out.

a potential business contact. Anne went along with the pretext.

"I liked him," Anne would later say. "I thought he was bright, articulate, a gentleman, extremely kind." She said she felt an instant attraction for both Sella and his stylishly dressed wife, whom the Americans simply called Judy.

At the dinner, Anne recalled, "it was all pleasure. We never spoke business."

Sella picked up the check, for which he was later reimbursed by Yagur.

Four days later, Pollard and Sella met alone in Pollard's apartment. It was during this meeting, Israeli officials would later tell two separate Israeli investigatory committees, that Sella slipped Pollard an envelope containing $2,000 in cash. Pollard, for his part, steadfastly denied receiving any money until he arrived in Paris.

On July 28, 1984, Pollard returned to Ravid's suburban home in Potomac to deliver a second batch of classified documents—as requested. He had carefully collected the material, making certain that no one grew suspicious. Sella, coming from New York, arrived late; the Eastern shuttle was again behind schedule. Pollard sat in the living room on the sofa, talking to some Israelis whose names he did not know.

Finally, Sella arrived and Pollard handed over the documents. The Israelis were deeply impressed by the quality and quantity of the material Pollard had brought. It was quickly sent to Eitan and his LAKAM unit in Israel for processing.

Israeli investigatory committees later heard testimony that it was during this meeting that Pollard received from Sella a second envelope containing $2,000 in cash. But Pollard would again steadfastly continue to insist this was simply not true; his first payment came only in Paris—some five months after his initial meeting with Sella.

In September, the new national unity government took office in Jerusalem. The Labor leader, Shimon Peres, began a two-year term as Prime Minister, while the Likud leader,

Yitzhak Shamir, would serve as Foreign Minister. During the second two years of the government, the two men would switch jobs. Yitzhak Rabin of Labor, a former Prime Minister, Ambassador to Washington, and IDF Chief of Staff, was to serve as Defense Minister for the entire four years, succeeding Moshe Arens.

Arens would later acknowledge that he was Defense Minister when Pollard began to pass documents to Israel, but he maintained that he exercised no supervision over Eitan since he was then preoccupied with the war in Lebanon. Arens insisted that Eitan's involvement in the Pollard intelligence operation had come as a complete surprise; his meetings with Eitan were devoted to the problem of Shi'ite terror in Lebanon. Arens said he had not been briefed about LAKAM's activities upon becoming Defense Minister, although he of course knew that the unit existed.

Eitan, during his own appearance before the committee, would have a different version. In August, shortly before Rabin became Defense Minister, Eitan cryptically said, Arens heard a report "which should have led him to increase his alertness." Arens later maintained that he had no idea what Eitan was referring to.

Peres, the new Prime Minister, asked Eitan to give up his counterterrorism responsibility. He was replaced in the Prime Minister's Office by Amiram Nir, a former Israel Television military affairs correspondent who had been active in supporting Peres's political campaign that year. It would be Nir who would later join Lt. Col. Oliver North, the National Security Council staffer, on that ill-fated May 1986 journey to Teheran in an effort to free the American hostages in Lebanon.

Rabin did not ask Eitan to leave LAKAM. They had known each other for over forty years, going back to their joint service in the Palmach. This was a case of Israel's old-boy network at work.

One of Eitan's supporters on the Eban Committee, David Magen, would later say: "During this period in which Eitan headed LAKAM, it reached the peak of its achievements." A security official testified before the committee that until

Eitan arrived at LAKAM, the unit was always called LAKAM. "But since Rafi arrived, we simply called it 'Rafi.' The material Rafi Eitan was made of was more than once described by the highest echelon as 'priceless.' "

Magen noted that Eitan, during the early period of Pollard's recruitment, had indeed "understood the particular sensitivity of the issue and took the trouble to define the potential hazards of running Pollard in a detailed document. In the document, he issued instructions on special rules and caution. In retrospect, it emerges that Rafi Eitan's instructions were not fulfilled." Eitan, moreover, received permission from the Israeli Air Force to use Sella in the operation. Magen pointed out that the air force, "in a letter to Col. Sella, gave approval for his cooperation with LAKAM."

In October 1984, a daytime position at ATAC for an analyst with some terrorism experience opened up. This was exactly what Pollard was waiting for. He hated the night shift; so did Anne. Pollard quickly indicated that he was interested in applying for the job.

There was another reason why Pollard wanted to make the switch. He suspected that it would better facilitate his collection of documents for Israel. An analyst, it seemed, could request all kinds of sensitive information needed for researching a project.

"He applied and based on what we had seen during his four or five months there, it looked like he would be a good candidate, and so he was interviewed and ultimately selected," Agee, his commander, later said.

Thus, Pollard began a daytime job (8:00 A.M.–5:00 P.M.) as an Intelligence Research Specialist within ATAC. Like all daytime analysts, he also was given certain NIS counterintelligence responsibilities. The job that was open involved terrorism threats to the continental United States and the Caribbean region. It was the one for which Pollard had applied and was accepted, although he made it clear to everyone concerned that in the long run he hoped to use it as a stepping stone to the Middle East Desk. "He was willing to settle for it in the short term," Agee recalled. "He wanted the Middle East. My comments and those of his supervisor were, 'Do this job well and when we have an opening on the Middle East Desk, then we'll consider transferring you over there.' " Agee stressed that the promise to Pollard was only that they would "consider" moving him. There was never any firm commitment, despite Pollard's subsequent assertions that he had received a flat promise of the transfer. Indeed, Pollard maintained that he was being groomed to take over the Middle East.

In November 1984, as instructed, Pollard flew to Paris with his girlfriend, Anne Henderson. They held hands during much of the flight. Anne, who was not much of a traveler, was especially thrilled. She was seeing the world with the man she loved. And what could be more romantic than a vacation in Paris? They had a fabulous time during their week in a suite at the Paris Hilton.

In that week, Sella escorted Pollard to a safe house in central Paris, where they met with Eitan and Yagur several times for "business." Eitan was formally introduced to Pollard as the head of the operation; Yagur was then the science counselor at the Israeli Consulate in New York—a position he had held from July 1980. Eitan wanted Sella to bring Pollard himself as he suspected that Pollard would feel more comfortable in Paris with someone present whom he knew and trusted.

Throughout these meetings in Paris Pollard was again repeatedly told that he would be "taken care of" if apprehended by U.S. authorities. Eitan, like Sella in Potomac, assured Pollard that any action against him could be contained. "Don't worry," Eitan said.

Eitan also flatly told Pollard that he already was an Israeli and asked Pollard to provide some passport photos. It was a classic ploy of the spymaster—make the agent feel secure and comfortable. The first afternoon, Pollard and Anne went to a coin-operated passport machine outside the hotel for the necessary pictures.

During the meetings, Sella, Eitan, and Yagur provided Pollard with detailed "tasking" of specific requests for classified documents and information that Pollard was to obtain. Eitan said that Israel needed this information to identify and assess threats to its security. In particular, Yagur described in detail the specific weapons systems and other subjects on which Pollard was to obtain classified documents. The Israelis again expressed little interest in information on terrorism or counterterrorist activities, explaining that they already had sufficient information on the subject. Pollard was asked to deliver the documents to Ravid's house in Potomac, Maryland.

Money was also discussed. Pollard was promised a flat $1,500 monthly salary for his espionage. And, in fact, at the conclusion of the trip to France, Pollard was paid $10,000 in cash by Yagur as reimbursement for his expenses. Again, they discussed all sorts of cover stories regarding the extra income.

"I still didn't like the situation that was developing and discussed alternative forms of compensation with Sella, Yagur, and Eitan while in Paris," Pollard later said. "I suspect that the best way of characterizing the way I felt at the time was extremely dirty, which was not how I envisioned feeling as a result of helping the Israelis. This was an ideological operation that was slowly being turned into a banking expedition by Eitan."

Pollard said that Yagur and Sella agreed with him that "the payments would be misinterpreted and look terrible if I were arrested, and [they] suggested to Eitan that Anne be employed by a sympathetic public relations firm instead." But Eitan, according to Pollard, "predictably" and "adamantly" refused to consider anything other than a salary, and "emphasized that, as an Israeli working for him, I was expected to follow orders and proceed with my collection activity."

Up to a point, Pollard did exactly that. He did accept the money, but when Eitan, in Paris, requested information which he "considered to be incompatible with my objectives and intentions, I simply did not provide the material."

Pollard later recalled that Eitan did press him for "information pertaining to the activity of the National Security

Agency in Israel and the names of the Israelis who were providing classified material to the United States." Eitan, like Ariel Sharon, was in fact obsessed with the notion of American spies in Israel. He was convinced that the U.S. Embassy in Tel Aviv had a large network of Israeli moles feeding it information. Eitan hoped Pollard would help uncover those moles.

According to Pollard, it was at one of the sessions in Paris that Eitan also specifically asked him to collect "political blackmail on members of the [Israeli] Cabinet" as part of an effort "to leak such inflammatory information" to discredit them. But Pollard insisted that he had disobeyed Eitan's order. "I never provided this type of information and was later told by my chief handler, Yosef Yagur, that the material Eitan wanted was totally off limits, outside the scope of the operation, and if provided would be grounds for immediately terminating our relationship."

During one angry exchange with Eitan in Paris, Pollard recalled, Yagur was standing directly behind Eitan shaking his head, signaling silently to Pollard not to agree to provide that kind of information.

Pollard continued: "I had absolutely no intention of spying on the United States or to provide any critical national defense information to a belligerent. At no time did I ever compromise the names of any U.S. agents operating overseas, nor did I ever reveal any U.S. ciphers, codes, encipherment devices, classified military technology, the disposition and orders of U.S. forces, war fighting plans, secret diplomatic initiatives and obligations, classified organizational writing diagrams or phone books, vulnerabilities of nuclear stockpiles, or communications security procedures."

Pollard said that he did not put "any U.S. covert activity in jeopardy which might, if compromised, either be used to embarrass the administration or cause a rupture in relations with a foreign government. One has to keep in mind the fact that my sole objective in this affair was to provide Israel with information concerning threats to its existence, of which the United States is clearly not one. The collection effort was clearly directed against the Soviets and those Arab states which pose a clear and present danger to Israel's security."

Pollard has maintained that throughout the operation, he remained "true to my ideological convictions—as imperfect and flawed as they might have been in retrospect." In his mind, he said, "assisting the Israelis did not involve or require betraying the United States. I never thought for a second that Israel's gain would necessarily result in America's loss. How could it? Both states are on the same side of the geopolitical barricade."

Sella, for his part, treated Pollard and Anne to expensive meals and entertainment throughout their stay in Paris. It was Sella who also took note of Anne's interest in a particular diamond and sapphire ring which she spotted in a jewelry store—Mappin and Webb on the Place Vendôme—and saw to it that the ring was purchased. It would be delivered to Pollard on December 8 in Washington when he was scheduled to resume his delivery of documents to the Israelis.

Anne would later recall that the ring had a $10,000 price tag on it but she was able to bring the jeweler down to $7,000. She was told by her husband that the Israelis purchased the ring in cash. Pollard later said that the ring was part of the cover story designed to convince Anne about the rich uncle.

During their stay in Paris, Anne joined the other wives—Yehudit Sella, Varda Yagur, and Miriam Eitan—in sightseeing and shopping. "You see," Anne explained, "I was never supposed to know what was going on."

But she, of course, knew almost everything her husband was doing. He discussed the operation with her from start to finish. As the government later charged in a pre-sentencing memorandum:

> From Jonathan Jay Pollard's arrangement with the
> New York friend for the first meeting with Aviem
> Sella; to Jonathan Jay Pollard's discussions with his

new handler, Yossi Yagur, and the head of the
operation, Rafi Eitan, in Paris; to her awareness of
the regularity and location of his drops; to his illegal
use of their apartment as an illegal, top-secret,
classified information depository—Defendant Anne
Henderson Pollard was right in the middle of it, a
knowing wife and the willing recipient of Jonathan
Jay Pollard's espionage proceeds.

From Paris, Pollard and Anne traveled to a number of
places, including Marseilles, Saint-Tropez, Cannes, Nice,
Monte Carlo, Pisa, Florence, Rome, Venice, Innsbruck, and
Munich. They paid cash for almost everything.

After the Pollards returned to the United States, Pollard met
with Yagur at Ravid's home on December 8 and was given
the diamond and sapphire ring. At that meeting, which was
also attended by another Israeli identified only as "Uzi,"
Pollard delivered literally suitcases full of classified documents that he had been collecting. Yagur provided Pollard
with a plain business envelope containing fifteen $100 bills.
And another meeting was scheduled for Ravid's house for
December 26. More documents would be brought—and
Pollard would receive another envelope containing cash.

"Every time Yagur passed money to me," Pollard later
recalled, "a silence would descend over our discussions and
a rather pained look would appear on his face."

Pollard cited one occasion when "I did refuse to accept
the money, but Yagur pointed out that it was not up to me
to lecture a man like Eitan on ethics—what we were involved with was a matter of critical importance for our
homeland, and insubordination in the field would not be
tolerated. There was no denying the fact, though, that neither one of us fully enjoyed the salary aspect of our operation, which conveniently hung like a sword of Damocles
over my head."

Pollard was briefed on various procedures to be followed
thereafter for the routine delivery of classified documents to

the apartment of Irit Erb, Ravid's young and attractive secretary. Pollard was also told of emergency procedures to be used in the event of unexpected developments in, or detection of, the espionage operation. Government documents later said that Pollard was provided with an emergency telephone number and code words to be used "to alert the Israelis to unexpected occurrences or in the event the espionage operation was detected." Pollard was told that if he were ever picked up for questioning, he should always delay for as long as possible any polygraph examinations, which would almost certainly show that he was lying. Unlike many Americans, the Israelis basically believe in lie detectors; they are convinced that the tests are almost always accurate. Pollard was also tasked on specific documents to obtain.

On January 3, 1985, Pollard passed another routine security clearance examination which did not include a polygraph. He signed a security agreement that stated: "I will not discuss or reveal any classified information except in the performance of my official duties. I take this obligation freely, without any mental reservation or purpose of evasion." And he was granted access to SENSITIVE COMPARTMENTED INFORMATION, which "involves or derives from intelligence sources and methods . . . I understand and accept that by being granted access to SCI, special confidence and trust shall be placed in me by the United States Government."

But in the months that followed, Pollard, about three times a week, removed classified documents from his office. He took these materials to his car, drove to a car wash on upper Connecticut Avenue, then transferred them to a briefcase. Approximately every two weeks, he delivered a suitcase containing the documents to Irit Erb's apartment at the Van Ness complex just off Connecticut Avenue.

Pollard delivered the documents on a Friday evening. Ravid's secretary copied those for which Pollard was accountable so that he could return them within a few days (usually the following Sunday evening) to their classified repositories. Those materials for which Pollard was not accountable were left with Irit Erb.

The operation was moving along smoothly, much better than Eitan and Yagur had imagined. They were extremely pleased.

By March 1985, Yagur and Eitan decided that they needed another safe house in Washington where Pollard and Yagur could routinely meet on the last Saturday of each month, and where sophisticated photocopying equipment could be installed.

Eitan, through the Defense Ministry, made the arrangements to obtain this second apartment in the same building where Irit Erb lived. Harold Katz, an American-Israeli lawyer who has lived in Israel since 1972 and had worked for the Israeli Defense Ministry for several years as a legal adviser, was asked to purchase this second condo for $82,500 in cash, according to District of Columbia real estate records. The eighth-floor apartment at 2939 Van Ness Street, N.W., was obviously convenient for Irit, who had to do the actual copying.

"I did not take part in the Pollard operation," Katz later said in a carefully drafted statement. "I passed no monies to the Pollards or anyone on their behalf. I neither received nor handled any documents." He stated that while his Washington apartment "was unoccupied, I am told certain persons made use of that apartment in connection with the Pollard operation. If such use was made, it was without my permission or knowledge."

Yagur and Pollard, meeting in Katz's apartment, would review in detail those documents that Pollard had brought the previous month. It was also at these monthly meetings that Yagur paid Pollard in cash. In the spring of 1985, Pollard's monthly salary was raised from $1,500 to $2,500.

By then, Pollard later said, "Eitan felt that it was time to recognize the quality of the material being collected and awarded me a salary increase which I received without any discussion: Yagur handed me an envelope, we shook hands, he apologized, and I felt like a prostitute.

"In spite of this disquieting aspect of my case," Pollard

continued, "I never considered myself to be a mercenary, no matter how corrosive the payments were on my sense of personal integrity. Luckily, my ideology prevented me from descending to a level where I would reflexively respond to Eitan's commands, like some type of Pavlovian dog."

The documents obtained by Pollard were forwarded to Rafi Eitan, who had assembled a three-member team of experts in Tel Aviv to analyze and distribute the documents to the relevant offices in the Israeli military. The documents were thoroughly "sanitized" to make certain that LAKAM's sources and methods of obtaining them were not revealed. Eitan was careful not to reveal Pollard's identity. Indeed, only two of the three members of the LAKAM team were actually aware of him—and one of those two consistently urged Eitan to drop him because the operation was too dangerous. Eitan, for his part, recognized the dangers but became obsessed with getting as much information as possible. "He was like an alcoholic," an Israeli official later said. "He needed just one more drink—and then he would quit."

LAKAM, in addition to distributing the documents to the army, air force, and naval intelligence officials, also received specific requests for more information from them. If, for example, the United States had officially provided Israel with an intelligence handbook on certain Soviet-made weapons systems but had blacked out various paragraphs and pages for whatever reason, LAKAM was asked to obtain the original. And that turned out to be a major assignment for Pollard.

The various Israeli military intelligence chiefs knew that LAKAM had some excellent sources; they did not know about Pollard per se, and they did not ask Eitan how he was collecting this material. There was no "need to know"—and Eitan would not have told them in any case. He was anxious for other Israeli intelligence officials to believe that he had many different sources for his information. He did not want anyone to know that all of that valuable data was actually coming only from one spy.

Some Israeli intelligence officials, of course, suspected that Eitan had a spy or spies in Washington; but others were not so certain. In any case, even those who were privy to some of the original documents obtained by Pollard did not ask questions. Indeed, Defense Minister Yitzhak Rabin would later tell an Israeli investigatory panel that he simply assumed Eitan could be getting the information from a source in Britain or another of America's NATO allies who, unlike Israel, would have been in a position to receive some of those kinds of documents officially from the United States.

In Washington, meanwhile, Pollard was encouraged to gather as many vital documents as possible. During the monthly review, according to the U.S. government, Yagur would also advise Pollard of specific instances in which the information had been utilized by various branches of the Israeli military. And at each meeting, Yagur continued to specifically task Pollard to obtain certain classified documents.

"The tasking was often done by Yagur according to particular needs," government documents said. "With one exception, Yagur's detailed tasking did not include requests for information on terrorism. Indeed, Pollard, on his own initiative, brought certain classified information relating to terrorism to one of the monthly meetings with Yagur, who then specifically informed him that no further delivery of such information should occur." Why risk possible detection for marginal information.

In the summer of 1985, Pollard was told by Yagur that Eitan wanted to meet with him again and that the expenses for a trip to Israel for this purpose would be paid as part of Pollard's compensation. Pollard readily accepted this offer since an Israeli-financed trip enabled him and Anne to be married that summer in Europe, instead of in Washington as originally planned. Pollard had initially hoped to marry Anne in Israel, but Eitan rejected that proposal. He did not want any record of Pollard's getting married in Israel; it would be too risky.

Pollard notified his superiors at the office that he was

going to get married in Europe. "To me," Agee would later recall, "it sounded like another one of his stories. At the time, I said to myself, Who goes to Venice to get married? You can do that here in Washington."

But by then Agee was already convinced that Pollard was basically strange, so the fact that he was going to Europe did not raise any other particularly significant question marks in Agee's mind. Pollard did not tell his boss that he would be visiting Israel too. "He said he was going to France and Italy to get married," Agee recalled. "There had never been any mention that he would be going to Israel. There never was any mention that he was there when he came back."

But Pollard did indeed speak about his rich uncle in Paris who was paying for the honeymoon in Europe.

The thought of going to Israel was thrilling for Pollard. Anne had never been there, and he longed to show her around the country. Pollard himself had not been there since his summer experience at the Weizmann Institute while still in high school.

When they arrived in late July, Pollard and Anne were entertained at a dinner held at Uzi's house in a Tel Aviv suburb. By then, Pollard had learned that Uzi was being groomed to replace Yagur as his handler. He was told that Uzi was an international arms dealer who specialized in sales to Iran. Pollard still did not know Uzi's last name.

The dinner was also attended by Yagur, Sella, and their wives. Pollard later said that as a result of this dinner, as well as his subsequent meetings with Eitan a few days afterward, he was encouraged to redouble his espionage efforts for Israel.

"When I walked through Yad Vashem, the memorial to the Holocaust in Jerusalem," he recalled, "I was able to look into those countless lost faces staring out of the faded pictures and know, for once, that I had kept faith with them. Nobody will convince me that I had to become a traitor in order to feel this way."

During his two meetings with Eitan, who was hospitalized in Tel Aviv for eye surgery at the time, Pollard was again reassured that he would be protected by the Israelis if the operation were detected. Yagur also attended those meetings at Eitan's bedside at the Beilinson Hospital.

Later, Eitan would testify before the Eban Committee that he was beginning around that same time to have some serious reservations about the entire operation. But because of his eye problems and his hospitalization, he let the matter slip. Member of the Knesset David Magen said: "I assume that in regular conditions he would have succeeded in ascertaining that his orders to halt the link with Pollard were being fulfilled; he was prevented from carrying out this action due to his illness. Here it should be recalled that even with his return to work in October, his sight was still physically limited."

A top LAKAM official who knew about Pollard again warned that he should be dropped because of the extremely risky nature of the operation. But his advice was ignored as well. Eitan was hooked on Pollard. His instincts certainly told him to drop him; the prospect of exposure grew with every transfer. But he simply could not order the operation shut. Someone does not spend a lifetime in intelligence gathering and then simply walk away from such a goldmine.

Indeed, while Pollard was in Israel, Eitan and Yagur requested that he provide even greater quantities of classified documents. When Pollard expressed some reluctance, pointing to the risk of detection, Eitan and Yagur offered him an additional $30,000 to be paid into a Swiss bank account each of the following ten years. Eitan also instructed Yagur to give Pollard an additional $2,000 in cash, over and above the more than $10,000 Pollard had already received to cover the expenses of this trip to Israel and Europe. Pollard agreed to get the documents.

During their stay in Israel, Pollard relished taking Anne around the country. The most emotional part of the trip was their time in Jerusalem. "It's strange," Pollard said later, "because when I was standing on the balcony of the King David Hotel during the summer of 1985 with my wife, I looked at those walls and I had a very strange feeling. I felt as if my wife and I were two stones apart; that's the way I put it then. Those walls represented in some way, I guess, the strength and resiliency of our people. The Western Wall was the religious strength. Those beautiful sandstone walls around the city are the military, physical, and security strength. Here we were: two stones apart from that wall but still distinct."

During the three-week trip to Israel and then Europe, Pollard and Anne stayed in first-class hotels in Tel Aviv, Jerusalem, Vienna, Venice, Zurich, Paris, and London. A subsequent U.S. government investigation showed that the charges for the hotel rooms alone came to $4,500—all paid for in cash. Their meals were also paid for in cash.

They were married on August 9 in a civil ceremony in Venice.

In August 1985, Yagur flew to Switzerland to establish a bank account for Pollard. And later that fall, Yagur showed Pollard an Israeli passport, bearing Pollard's photograph taken in Paris, in the name of Danny Cohen. According to Yagur, Danny Cohen was to be Pollard's new name when he eventually moved to Israel. The passport was a demonstration of gratitude for services rendered in that it identified Pollard as a citizen of Israel. Pollard would assume that name upon his eventual immigration.

Pollard later revealed the story behind the selection of the fictitious name. During the November 1984 talks in Paris, the subject of Eli Cohen came up. Cohen was the legendary Israeli spy in Damascus in the 1960s who managed to penetrate the highest echelons of the Syrian regime before being exposed and eventually hanged in the city square in 1966. Pollard, as a teenager, had read a popular book on Cohen entitled *Our Man in Damascus.* He clearly admired the Israeli spy and what he had accomplished for Israel.

But both Pollard and Yagur, while in Paris, were stunned to hear Eitan begin to ridicule Cohen and his achievements. According to Pollard, Eitan—who had been in the Mossad at the time of the Cohen operation and knew Cohen well— claimed that Cohen was actually a very poor spy, not highly regarded by the Mossad. Cohen, he charged, had behaved stupidly in Damascus. He should never have been captured. Eitan also spoke derogatorily of Cohen's Sephardic ancestry.

Pollard said he couldn't believe that Eitan would speak so derisively about a genuine Israeli hero—someone who had sacrificed his life for his country. Later, Pollard confided his outrage to Yagur, who concurred. "It was Yagur's idea to give me the name of Cohen," Pollard said, the implication being that Israel once had an Eli Cohen in Damascus and it now had a Danny Cohen in Washington. "Yagur also knew it would rub Eitan the wrong way."

In addition to the passport, Pollard was given the number of the Swiss bank account which had been opened for him in the name of Danny Cohen. He signed signature cards. Pollard was told by Yagur that $30,000 would be deposited in the account each year for the next nine years—ten years being the projected life of the espionage operation. This amount was to be in addition to the direct cash payments that Pollard received for a total of nearly $50,000—a big chunk of which covered his travel expenses.

Once back in the United States, Pollard increased the volume of documents he was providing Israel.

"Everything I seemed to show them was like adding stones on top of a man desperately trying to remain afloat in shark-infested waters, and as each new revelation confronted them with seemingly insurmountable problems, another one arose to replace it," as Pollard later described it. "At times, it seemed as if I were becoming the traditional messenger of bad tidings, sowing the intelligence equivalents of the proverbial dragon's teeth.

"But their needs were understandably insatiable and as the urgency of their requests took on an almost infectious quality, my whole life seemed to be driven by a fear of overlooking something that might ultimately prove catastrophic. Literally everything I showed them set off alarm bells, particularly those things pertaining to nuclear and chemical warfare advances in the Arab world."

Pollard found himself spending increasingly larger amounts of money at restaurants. Between November 1984 and November 1985, according to a subsequent FBI audit, Pollard and Anne made cash payments on their American Express credit card bills of almost $20,000. The charges to their American Express card during this period included almost daily lunches, dinners, or drinks at various Washington restaurants; airline tickets for the two trips abroad, in November 1984 and July 1985; and $2,300 in jewelry purchased in Israel in July and August 1985.

He bought Anne jewelry in Washington as well—in March 1985, a gold necklace and earrings for $1,800; and in June, a gold bracelet at the same Georgetown store for $300.

Jonathan Jay Pollard, while spying for Israel, had become corrupted.

At the same time, Anne was losing interest in her job at the National Rifle Association. She had honed her public relations skills during her three and a half years there, but she wanted to strike out on her own. In the summer of 1985, she resigned from the NRA. She had learned that one of her father's contacts, Karen Berg, formerly with the public relations firm of Hill & Knowlton, was establishing her own company, CommCore, in New York. Berg hired Anne to represent her in Washington on a freelance commission basis.

CommCore, aware of China's effort to improve its image in the West, was interested in winning a media training contract. Berg asked Anne to try to get an appointment with officials at the Chinese Embassy in Washington. Using Dr. Pollard's contacts—he had previously met the Chinese ambassador—Anne succeeded. Together with Berg and other associates, they made a formal presentation on September 30, 1985. They explained how the Chinese would benefit from a more sophisticated use of the U.S. news media.

"In her effort to secure the embassy as a client," her lawyers later wrote, "Mrs. Pollard determined to learn as much as possible about the PRC [People's Republic of China] and its business, cultural and diplomatic relationships with the United States, including, of course, the embassy in Washington. To that end, she asked Mr. Pollard if he could bring home from work some articles containing general background information on China."

Pollard, who by then was easily removing classified papers for Israel, brought home five separate documents—each marked SECRET—about China. They described Chinese diplomatic personnel and operations in the United States, including Chinese intelligence-gathering capabilities. The five documents were: (1) People's Republic of China, Embassy—Washington, D.C., 1984 (73 pages); (2) People's Republic of China, Mission to the United Nations—New York, 1984 (35 pages); (3) People's Republic of China, Consulate—San Francisco, 1984 (47 pages); (4) People's Republic of China, Consulate—New York, 1984 (46 pages); and (5) People's Republic of China, Consulate—Houston, 1984 (62 pages).

Anne read the documents, taking careful notes. She then returned them to her husband.

On the morning of the presentation, she briefed her associates about the Chinese Embassy without revealing where she had learned some of the background. Ultimately, however, CommCore did not win the contract. A subsequent government investigation confirmed that Anne did not disclose any classified documents or information to the Chinese.

CHAPTER SEVEN

Suspicion

Jonathan Jay Pollard, by all accounts, was not very well liked at ATAC. His colleagues recognized that he was talented. They accepted the fact that he had a wealth of detailed military and political-related information stored in his head. But they resented his arrogance, his bragging, his know-it-all attitude. He was not a typical Navy bureaucrat. They came to regard him as obnoxious. This was especially true of his boss, Jerry Agee, who on two separate occasions suspected that he had caught Pollard lying.

The first incident occurred in the spring of 1985. According to Agee, it was a totally insignificant event "that meant nothing to anybody, but he told me something that I subsequently checked and tried to clarify, and it wasn't even close to the truth. It was just a flat lie." The incident involved ATAC's dealings with another governmental agency. "It was an internal thing in which he had dealt with another agency and he came back with a story which did not make sense to me, and I followed up and found that it wasn't what happened at all. The thought in my mind at the time was, 'Why? Why would he lie about something that was so insignificant and was so easy to check out?'

"I thought, that's bullshit," Agee said. "That's just a lie."

Agee thought that Pollard, by lying, was simply trying to

make himself into a more important person than he was. But other than that, he had no real explanation for the incident. He did not file a formal complaint in Pollard's record. "I thought it was unusual," he would later recall. "I thought it was childish. I thought it displayed a certain amount of untrustworthiness but you can't fire him because of that."

A second incident occurred a few weeks later when Pollard told Agee a story about Kurt Lohbeck, a freelance journalist who had made some trips into Afghanistan to write about the freedom fighters. Pollard had befriended Lohbeck. He would later acknowledge that he had even leaked some classified documents to him to impress him. Pollard told Agee that Lohbeck was involved in a supercovert operation that was being run directly out of the National Security Council in the White House. National Security Adviser Robert McFarlane was supposedly handling Lohbeck personally.

"I thought that, too, was all bullshit," Agee said. "And I thought, Another lie."

Agee said that it was like "a tick in the back of your brain—'I wonder why he would make up these stories?' It was just something that went into the back of my memory. It just lodged back there and did not go beyond that."

Lohbeck's name would surface again later in Pollard's life.

Around the same time, Agee started to complain about what he described as Pollard's lack of production. Pollard had been assigned several long-term research projects. One involved East German intelligence activities in the Caribbean; another focused on domestic American terrorist threats, including what were regarded as violently anti-nuclear groups; a third was on terrorist threats to the U.S. Navy in Central America. Pollard was asked to prepare a list of domestic American organizations opposed to the U.S. involvement in Central America that might have some connections to hostile powers. Some were later targeted for surveillance and penetration by the Justice Department even though no charges were ever leveled. The investigation was eventually dropped.

"These were things that required some personal discipline to go out and to do the research with other agencies," Agee said. "It required a lot of work, but it was not an impossible thing to do. It certainly was not something that he should have pushed off as long as he did."

An increasingly frustrated Agee repeatedly contacted Pollard's immediate supervisor, Tom Filkens, another civilian analyst, to ask about Pollard's papers. "What's the status?" Agee asked. Filkens, a meticulous bureaucrat, checked with Pollard, who insisted that he was still working on the projects.

But Agee felt that it was still taking much too long. "This thing was going on and on and on," he said. "As long as we gave him something short to do—it had to be done by the afternoon or the next morning—he would do it. You would get a quick product. It was good. It met the need and it was over with. But if you asked him to do something that took two weeks or a month and required a little discipline and doggedness, forget it. He was never going to come up with it."

And this deeply bothered Agee. "I began to see no production. I began to see that he was spending more and more time out of the office. These are things that occurred over a period of weeks and months. At the same time he was out doing more research, I was also saying, 'If he's doing all this research, where's the products? What are we getting from this?' There was nothing. All he was ever able to give me was an outline of what he was doing, but no actual written product."

It was not long after Pollard returned to work in August that Agee noticed some more strange things going on at the ATAC headquarters. One day, for instance, he casually walked past the brown metal desk of a low-level clerk who was responsible for receiving classified material and logging it in.

"As I walked by," Agee recalled, "I picked up some envelopes and looked at the documents just to see them; there was a big stack of them there. I asked him why it was taking so long to get the job done. I picked them up and they dealt with a lot of the subjects which we, as an organization, had absolutely no interest in—or should have had no interest in."

The TOP SECRET documents had to do with the most advanced Soviet military equipment being supplied to the Arab world.

"What the hell does this have to do with anything we're dealing with?" he angrily asked the clerk. "Why did we get this?"

The clerk responded that Pollard had ordered the documents. "What does he need those documents for?" Agee asked. The clerk simply shrugged his shoulders and said: "I don't know."

Agee immediately walked over to Filkens's office to ask why the documents had been requested. "I don't know," Filkens replied. "Jay got them."

"Well, find out why," Agee ordered, "and then get rid of them. Let me know why he got them. Destroy them or send them back. We are not going to keep them here."

Filkens confronted Pollard, asking about the sensitive documents. But Pollard, fast on his feet, came up with an excuse which his boss thought was actually reasonable. "They're background for a project I'm doing on terrorist threats in the Caribbean," Pollard said.

And with that, the matter was dropped.

Alarm bells, of course, should have immediately gone off in Pollard's head. With hindsight, the questioning by his boss about the classified documents should have ended—at least temporarily—the entire operation. At a minimum, it should have been dramatically scaled back. But it did not. The collection continued unabated.

The reason was that by then Pollard had already decided to quit Naval Intelligence by the end of the year. He was frustrated and nervous. In his mind, he was going to undertake another assignment for Israel. He knew that his espionage in Washington was becoming increasingly more dangerous. But instead of reducing his activity, he actually accelerated it. He would scoop up as many vital documents as he could before quitting. In fact, again in his mind, he already was gearing up for a new mission for Israel—this one involving Saudi Arabia.

Pollard had befriended some Saudis during his days at Fletcher. He had maintained and expanded those contacts ever since. One of those contacts was a well-connected Saudi whose identity has never been revealed. "I recruited and was then obliged to 'subsidize' a Saudi bureaucrat who soaked up tons of money in the process of assuaging his guilt," Pollard would later say. Indeed, Pollard maintained, much of the money that he received from the Israelis went into this Saudi operation.

"Perhaps the most significant impact my additional funds had on our life was that it provided me with the resources to co-opt a Saudi bureaucrat," Pollard went on. "His potential utility for my eventual plan to leave the Navy and initiate a covert penetration of the Saudi Ministry of Foreign Affairs was incalculable. A great deal of money was spent on the project, which would have resulted in a tremendous opportunity for me to work as this bureaucrat's private representative in London and Brussels. Beyond the evident intelligence value of this relationship, it would have allowed me to end my operation in this country, which Yagur told me in October of 1985 had already provided the Israeli armed forces with enough information to probably win the next Middle East war. Ironically, it was money taken from a commission I earned brokering an oil contract on behalf of the Saudi with which I intended to repay the Israelis for all the funds I had received from them."

Pollard maintained that the act of repaying the Israelis "would not have totally erased the stigma I felt by having accepted their money in the first place, but it would have constituted the first step on the road to my personal redemption."

The notion of his spying for Israel because of money, he said, was totally unacceptable. "My Lord, if I were a mercenary, I should have sold Israeli secrets to the Arabs, who would have been only too happy to pay a fortune for them. What a lot of people don't understand is that this was a rather sophisticated affair, logistically speaking, and that I was responsible for paying certain recurrent bills which were generated as a direct result of my involvement with the Israelis."

As far as Agee was concerned, the situation continued to get worse. Pollard was totally unreliable. He was simply not producing; he was not part of the team. His mind seemed focused on something else.

Late in September 1985, Agee told Filkens to warn Pollard formally that if he did not produce one especially long-awaited report, he would receive an official notice that he was not complying with his duties. "That's the first step in firing somebody," Agee would later recall. "You've got to document very carefully what a person is supposed to do, what they don't do, that you have warned them of that, told them what they have to do to improve their performance, and so forth. If they then don't do that, then you have grounds for firing."

Around the same time, Agee received a notice from the administrative department that Pollard had been asked four months earlier to fill out a routine form involving his personal history for an updated background and security clearance investigation. Pollard had been reminded twice about the form, but it was still not completed. Agee, upon learning of this, sent Pollard a sharply worded notice informing him that he had two weeks to complete it. Pollard assured Agee that he was in the process of completing all the questions, but because of his extensive foreign travel over the years he was having a difficult time recalling all the details.

For Agee, that was yet another source of irritation:

"He wasn't doing his work. Now he wasn't doing some other work he was supposed to be doing. He was spending a lot of time out of the office doing research but we never saw any of the product from it. He had all this crap around there which meant to me at the time that he was doing research in areas that he wanted to be interested in, but he was not doing anything that he was asked to do."

But Agee still did not conceive of the notion that anything

more sinister was going on. "He was a pain in the ass," Agee said. "He was a nonperformer, however intelligent he was. And if he couldn't do the simple task, I wasn't going to keep him around forever. He was going to be gone."

Pollard made a very bad mistake one unusually beautiful and crisp day in mid-September. He left the office early in the morning and did not return until late in the afternoon. Agee, for whatever reason, had Pollard on his mind that day. He wound up spending most of the day looking for him.

Eventually Pollard returned to the office. It was very late in the afternoon. Agee, visibly angry, asked where he had been all day. Pollard said he had been doing some research at another intelligence library, but Agee suspected that he was lying. He decided that he was going to challenge Pollard.

"That's not true," he said matter-of-factly. Agee was merely bluffing.

In response—to Agee's utter surprise—Pollard conceded that he had in fact lied. "Okay," Pollard said. "You caught me."

Pollard said he had gone on a job interview with a nongovernmental firm in Washington involved in foreign policy consultancy work. He said he had lied because he did not want Agee to think that he was job hunting, thinking about quitting Naval Intelligence, especially on government time.

That made some sense to Agee, who in fact was only too happy to learn that Pollard was thinking of leaving on his own. Firing a civil servant, especially someone as crafty as Pollard, can be quite difficult, if not impossible. Agee, quietly, was relieved.

What Agee did not know was that Pollard had spent the day at another secure intelligence library, collecting some specific information ordered by Yagur only a few days earlier.

The information involved everything the United States knew about the Libyan, Tunisian, and Algerian air defense systems. Israel was already then thinking about an air strike against the PLO headquarters in Tunisia. It was only a contingency plan—a retaliatory attack for a terrorist incident against Israel. Israel would be prepared.

Pollard also had been asked to start collecting information about Soviet, French, and U.S. ship movements in the Mediterranean. Israeli planes would not want to be detected on their way to Tunis.

On September 25, 1985, which happened to be Yom Kippur, three Israelis slept aboard their modest yacht, docked at the Larnaca, Cyprus, marina. They were not religious. Reuven and Esther Paltzur of Haifa, and Avraham Avneri of Arad, all in their fifties, had taken advantage of the holiday weekend in Israel to get away and make the brief journey to the neighboring Mediterranean island. The Paltzurs were veteran members of the Carmel Yacht Club in Haifa. Mr. Paltzur had been active in the Haifa Sea Scouts for many years, teaching youngsters to sail. Avneri, a founder of Arad in the Negev, was a tour guide.

But what was supposed to be pleasure turned into horror when three terrorists early that morning boarded the yacht. They were members of Yasser Arafat's elite Force 17 commando unit. Two were twenty-four-year-old Palestinians: Elias Nassif and Mahmoud Khaled Abdullah. The third was British: Ian Michael Davison, a twenty-seven-year-old former carpenter who had joined the PLO after seeing pictures of the 1982 massacre of Palestinians at Beirut's Sabra and Shatilla refugee camps. "It changed my life," he would later recall.

They immediately shot and killed Mrs. Paltzur. They then held the two men hostage, informing arriving Cypriot authorities that Israel would have to release twenty Palestinian prisoners. There were nine hours of intense negotiations. The terrorists grew impatient and scared. They eventually surrendered, but only after shooting the two men—their hands and feet bound by ropes—in the head.

An Israeli government communiqué stated that Israel

would use all means to protect its citizens and that "the murders would not go unpunished." Israel was going to retaliate. Pollard thought that he knew what they had in mind.

October 1, 1985, was one of the happiest days in Pollard's life. It was on that day that eight single-engine Israeli Air Force F-16 fighters flew 4,800 kilometers—roundtrip—undetected across the Mediterranean to bomb PLO headquarters in Tunisia. The planes were refueled in midair. It was the furthest the Israeli Air Force had ever flown on a bombing raid.

Several PLO buildings were destroyed, and about sixty people were killed. Mohammed Natour, the commander of Force 17, and several of his men were among those who died. Arafat's secret residence was demolished but he escaped uninjured. He was not in the area when the Israeli planes swooped down over the Tunisian coast. Prime Minister Shimon Peres later said he was "not sure" that Israel had a special interest in killing Arafat. Israel's war, he said, is "against a terror organization—not this or that individual leader."

The air strike had been planned before the three Israelis were murdered at Larnaca. Indeed, the Israeli military planners had a whole series of other retaliatory options before them. The Cabinet, in the end, made the decision which contingency to accept.

Pollard was simply delighted that Israel had used one in which he played a significant role. He had, in fact, provided Yagur with a large stack of documents pinpointing the exact location of Arafat's headquarters at Hammam Plage, a beach in the suburban outskirts of Tunis. Pollard had collected U.S. intelligence on Tunisia's air defense system. He also obtained similar information about Libya's capabilities. How far out into the Mediterranean, for example, could the Libyan radars go? Israeli jet fighters, of course, had to pass Libya on the way to and from Tunisia.

And Pollard, as instructed, had obtained related intelligence about U.S., Soviet, French, and other naval vessels in the region. The Israelis wanted to avoid any encounter with them.

When he learned on October 1 that the operation had succeeded in destroying the headquarters, Pollard decided to step up his collection before quitting Naval Intelligence by the end of the year to pursue another covert operation for Israel.

"I stayed all night in the office monitoring information on the raid," he later confided. "I had a wonderful feeling as I stared at the Reuters terminal and watched the reports flow in. I prayed that Arafat had been killed. The scene of the murdered Israelis in Larnaca was still fresh in my mind. I saw the raid as a simple act of retributive justice."

A few days earlier, some of his colleagues at ATAC had circulated a wire service photo of the slain Israeli yachtsmen with a handwritten caption: "Force 17: 3—Mossad: 0." Pollard, knowing that many of the Force 17 terrorists had been killed during the Israeli air strike, smiled to himself. "I felt an incredible amount of satisfaction that the perpetrators of this outrage in Larnaca against our people were finally being brought to justice," he said.

His colleagues later got into a big argument about the Israeli raid. Some of them accused Israel of practicing "state-sponsored terrorism"—a charge rejected by Pollard. But he did not want to show too much of his own feelings. "I left and went home to bed at that point," he said. "I chuckled to myself."

In the meantime, he again vowed to gather as many vital documents as possible before leaving Naval Intelligence.

But his luck was beginning to run out.

Increasingly more concerned that Pollard was not going to quit on his own, Agee, with each day, became even more determined than ever to dismiss Pollard, but he needed additional grounds.

On Friday, October 25, one of Pollard's co-workers—another civilian analyst—coincidentally spotted him leaving the ATAC offices with what appeared to be TOP SECRET classified documents. Agee was still in his office when this co-worker, who also did not like Pollard and was anxious to score some points with his boss, called from his home.

"I just got home," he told Agee, "and something has been bothering me. I thought I should call and tell you."

"What is it?" Agee asked.

"I don't know what it means but at about four-fifteen I saw Jay leave the building, and his wife was outside waiting for him. He came out and had a package under his arm which looked like it came from the Communications Center."

The wrappings from the Center are very distinctive, designed to underscore the classified nature of the documents. They have a big red stripe across them. The fact that Anne was there waiting for Pollard did not necessarily bother Agee. What aroused his concern, he later recalled, was that Pollard had the package outside the building. On a Friday afternoon, at four-fifteen, he had no need to take that kind of sensitive material out of the building. "There's no place to go with it," Agee said to himself. "And it's forbidden to take classified material like that to your home."

So even if Pollard was simply taking some classified documents home, it was wrong. He was going to get Pollard after all.

Agee knew that in theory Pollard could have been going down the street in Suitland to another building in the compound to give the documents to an authorized official. But that was rather unlikely because most of the staff went home around that same time. "If he was taking it home," Agee thought, "that was a serious violation." Maybe this was exactly what Agee needed to fire Pollard.

Agee, excited but angry, went downstairs one flight to the Communications Center to check if Pollard had in fact picked up a package that day. He learned that Pollard had indeed picked one up and signed for it. The package involved very sensitive SCI messages. Agee went to the guard and asked whether Pollard, who had a courier pass, had taken the package out of the building. The guard answered yes.

Agee went back upstairs to Pollard's compact cubicle work space, which was surrounded by the high cloth walls. He wanted to see if he could locate any other sensitive documents.

Pollard's work space consisted of some standard semi-modern government desk furniture, including a computer terminal. Agee looked around the desk and the shelftops. He looked in the tin trash can and the beige burn bag. There was nothing there to reflect that he had brought the package upstairs. Pollard's safe was locked, and Agee did not have its combination. His desk was also locked. And in any case, Agee thought to himself, he did not have authority to search it. Looking around for anything visible, he could not find anything suspicious.

Agee, his palms sweating, was now very worried, but he did not want to look like an idiot; maybe there was some simple explanation for Pollard's behavior. He decided to wait another week to see if Pollard was picking up these kinds of classified documents regularly. He discovered, to his mounting concern, that there was indeed a pattern. The following Friday, November 1, Pollard again picked up a package of TOP SECRET documents on Soviet weapons systems.

Agee resolved to get to the bottom of the whole thing.

But he was not yet prepared to challenge Pollard head on. "I wasn't willing to confront him directly because if it was that serious," he explained later, "I wanted to make sure that it was done the right way." He wanted to be certain that Pollard would be in no position to cover up his actions. He wanted that man fired.

Agee also knew that any serious infraction would first require NIS's formally opening up an investigation. "So I wasn't going to blow the investigation by confronting him directly."

On Monday, November 4, a clear fall day, Agee went to the Communications Center and started to go through all of the records. He did not inform anyone there what he was looking for.

"I want to see certain records," he told the clerk.

Agee, sitting alone in a corner, went through a stack of papers. He wanted to learn which people were logging in and out documents—and what they consisted of.

The clerk gave him the documents.

Agee was thunderstruck by what he discovered. Pollard, it seemed, was routinely taking out numerous highly classified documents that had absolutely nothing whatsoever to do with his work; and all the documents basically involved the same subjects—Soviet weapons systems and Arab military capabilities.

"What I found was that he was picking up packages periodically," Agee later recalled. "It looked like he was picking them up every Friday, and maybe sometimes twice a week, but at least once a week on Fridays. That caused me to say, 'Why on Fridays?' And that right there told me that something was up. There was a pattern. He was doing it on Fridays, late in the afternoon. 'Something is not right here,' I said to myself."

Agee knew that the Suitland complex pretty much emptied early on Fridays. If Pollard was removing documents from his building late in the afternoon, he was almost certainly taking them home, which was forbidden. It would be highly unusual to take documents to other intelligence analysts that late in the day on Fridays.

With that, Agee began a more intensive investigation into the type of information Pollard was picking up. He told the clerk in charge of security at the Communications Center that he thought he had a serious problem involving Pollard. But he was not certain unless he could dig into it some more. He asked for the clerk's cooperation. "Don't say anything to anyone," Agee said sternly.

"I want to monitor everything that he does," Agee went on. "If he comes down here and picks up something, I want to know about it. I want to know about it the minute he walks into the door down here. And I don't want him to pick up anything else unless I know about it. And I want to go back and try to re-create everything that he has picked up—all the old messages. Go back, go into the computer, and dig them out, and see what they are."

The two of them, in the next few days, did exactly that.

"Again," Agee would later comment, "we found that there was a pattern about the type of information that was asked for—the subject matter—and the times that he was picking it up. When I began to see the pattern, then all the other little things started clicking in."

The information involved extremely sensitive intelligence on the Middle East—information that Pollard had absolutely no "need to know" in his current assignment.

"So now," Agee recalled, "I am looking at this, plus the fact that Pollard was spending a lot of time out of the office. There was a lot of classified material in and around his work space that he had no need to have access to, and he was accumulating it by the barrelful. There was also his strange departure from the building on Friday afternoon with what I believed to be very sensitive information."

On that same Monday morning, November 4, Agee made certain that he was very close to Pollard's work area in order to see what he brought back to work with him. He knew Pollard had taken classified documents home the previous Friday; he also knew that Pollard had not been in the office over the weekend. Agee wanted to see whether Pollard brought back the package with him. But Agee, his guts in turmoil, did not spot any package.

Throughout the day, Agee saw no evidence that Pollard had brought it back. After Pollard went home, he took a closer look through Pollard's garbage can and burn bag. He checked to see if Pollard had returned the documents to the Communications Center. He had not. So Agee was now absolutely convinced that Pollard had left the building with the documents that Friday and had not returned with them on Monday. Pollard, at a minimum, was violating basic security procedures. But what else was going on?

"I've got a serious problem here," Agee said to himself.

But he still had only circumstantial evidence of wrongdoing. Agee did not know whether Pollard was taking the documents home simply to work on them or whether there was something more sinister. "Jay was arrogant enough to take them home to work on them," he recalled, "just to read up on them."

But while Agee was convinced that Pollard was involved in something very wrong, espionage still was not considered. Thus, Agee had still not informed Lanny McCullah about his suspicions. McCullah, a tough-minded and experienced counterspy, was in charge of counterintelligence at the Naval Security and Investigative Command in Suitland.

"I was getting a little bit dicey because I had accumulated a lot of evidence and I still had not told him about it," Agee said. "And it was getting bad very quickly."

On Friday, November 8, Agee again ordered the Communications Center to be on the alert for any documents requested by Pollard. And Pollard did once again order a package of TOP SECRET papers. Agee was asked whether Pollard should be allowed to receive them. Agee said yes because this time, the documents had a remote connection to his regular work. And in any case, he did not want Pollard to become suspicious that he was now onto him.

It was 3:00 P.M. when a smiling Pollard took the documents. He came back up to his office, where he remained until about four-thirty. Agee was waiting nearby, secretly watching. "Thank God," Agee said to himself. "He brought it back up to the office. He didn't take it out of the building."

After Pollard left the building to go home, Agee walked over to Pollard's work area to look for the package. "I didn't find it," he said. "I went through his trash cans, his burn bag. I went through all the stuff on his desk, under his desk."

During the search, Agee found another stack of very sensitive documents on Middle Eastern arms shipments and Soviet weapons hidden under Pollard's desk. He also discovered that Pollard's safe was open. But Agee did not find anything inside.

"I knew what I was looking for," Agee explained, noting that the officer at the Communications Center had told him the nature of the documents Pollard had taken that day. "I knew what it looked like, the kind of paper it was on. I couldn't find any evidence of it in or around his desk."

Agee literally turned Pollard's work area upside down looking for the documents. He then put it all back together very neatly.

"Maybe," Agee thought, "he gave it to the Middle Eastern analyst."

So he went over to that analyst's work space and turned it upside down. "I went through drawers. I went through desks. I went through safes, file cabinets. You name it. I went through it."

But by eight o'clock that evening, Agee had not found the documents. "By this time," he recalled, "I was scared shitless. I knew we had something. You just don't think every day that somebody is spying. You are always looking for other reasons—'Something's wrong. I can't figure it out. I can't find what I'm looking for.'"

Agee drove to his home in Annapolis—about a thirty-minute drive. His mind was reeling and his head was pounding. He looked haggard. He collapsed into a chair and his startled wife, Karen, immediately asked: "What's wrong with you?"

"I don't know," he said softly. "I think I've got a very serious problem."

"What do you mean?"

"It has to do with Jay Pollard," he said. Karen had met Pollard on a few occasions.

"I wouldn't be a bit surprised if he's spying," Agee blurted out.

"What?" she asked, startled. "What are you talking about?"

"You heard me."

"What are you going to do about it?"

"I don't know. I'm not sure if I'm right or wrong. I'd sure hate to charge him with that or accuse him of that if it's not right."

Agee did not tell his wife that he thought Pollard was spying for Israel. "At that point, by looking at the material, I started to think that Israel might be involved. But that was not my concern. My concern was that he was doing it. He was going out of the building with it, and I knew it was going someplace. And where it was going, it wasn't authorized to be."

Agee was a nervous wreck.

"You better not wait until Monday," his wife wisely advised.

He agreed. He did not sleep at all that night.

It was still very dark and cold at about 5:00 A.M. Saturday morning, November 9, when Agee drove back to his office. There was almost no traffic on the John Hansen Highway heading toward the Washington Beltway. He stopped at a 7-Eleven for coffee and a doughnut.

The guards and the two watch officers were surprised to see him at the office so early on a Saturday morning.

Agee went into his own office and hung up his coat. He then walked outside into the main room, toward Pollard's area.

Once again he searched through Pollard's work space looking for the documents that had been taken out of the Communications Center the day before. "I wanted to make absolutely sure that I had not missed anything—a hiding place—a secret cache of notes that he may have hidden which might explain where all of this stuff was going. I couldn't find it."

After several hours in the office, he stopped searching. It was already late in the morning. Agee was exhausted. He paused and said to himself, "I've got a fuckin' spy here."

His hands shaking, he called McCullah, the Navy's senior counterintelligence officer, who was at home raking his lawn.

"Are you gonna be home for a while?" Agee asked.

"Yes."

"I need to come over and talk to you. I think we've got a serious problem."

"Okay. Come on over."

Agee drove from the naval complex in Suitland, Maryland, to McCullah's home in Springfield, Virginia, another Washington suburb. It took thirty minutes, although it seemed much longer.

They sat down in McCullah's den in front of the television set, watching a college football game. McCullah brought out a few cans of beer. Bit by bit, Agee started to relay his incredible suspicions. Although nervous and excited, he spoke slowly and methodically, reviewing the subject matter and the quantity of information involved. For a long time, McCullah simply listened.

"The guy's a god-damned spy," McCullah—who of course knew Pollard—said finally.

They also agreed that the information was almost certainly going to Israel. Looking at the pattern of material, the two Naval Intelligence agents concluded that it was not something the Soviets would be interested in. "It didn't take a fool to find out that the Soviets were not buying back all their own information," Agee said.

When they wondered who else might be interested in this kind of information, they both responded: "Israel."

They also knew that Pollard was Jewish.

"Are they really that stupid or arrogant?" McCullah asked Agee, referring to the Israelis. "My God, we're giving them all this stuff. Are they really that stupid that they would hire Jay, of all people?"

McCullah and Agee agreed that a full-scale investigation of Pollard was essential. But because Pollard was a civilian employee of the Navy, NIS could not investigate without at least advising or seeking cooperation from the FBI. That was the next step.

On Monday morning, November 11, Agee, McCullah, and two other NIS counterintelligence agents met in McCullah's office to plan their strategy. They reviewed their evidence. Later in the morning, an FBI agent joined them. They presented their assumptions, but the agent was initially skeptical of their conclusions.

"There's got to be some other explanation," he said.

"We think we're legitimate in our belief," Agee said. "We think we have enough evidence to at least warrant an investigation."

Agee and McCullah proposed a full-blown investigation, including around-the-clock surveillance. They wanted to see where Pollard was taking the documents.

But the FBI agent—to their horror—insisted that the agency did not have enough people to undertake that kind of investigation. The FBI's resources were already fully tied up. The Washington field office was deeply involved in two other espionage investigations then under way. Full-time surveillance requires a tremendous effort, including a minimum of twenty agents. The logistics, manpower, money, overtime, and other things involved are mind-boggling.

"It's probably not what you think it is," the FBI agent said. "There's probably a simple explanation to all of this. Why don't you just go down the hall and bring him up here and we'll talk to him?"

But McCullah completely rejected that proposal. He wanted to make certain that if their assumptions were right—if Pollard was in fact a spy—they would be in a position to find out who was receiving the information. If they simply confronted Pollard with their suspicions, Agee thought, Pollard would of course deny it and immediately stop what he was doing. They would never know the truth.

McCullah, over the next few days, was firm in demanding a full-scale investigation and eventually the FBI agents agreed. They asked if it could begin the following Monday, November 18, so they could finish another investigation. In the meantime, the NIS could conduct their own probe.

NIS agents began to make preparations that week to question Pollard after his next pickup and his exit from the building. Then, they would have reason to question him. But they wanted to delay that pickup until the FBI was ready—meaning the following Monday, November 18.

On Wednesday, November 13, Agee discovered that Pollard had in fact requested that more classified messages be printed out in the computer center. The documents were ready that same day but Pollard made no effort to pick them up. Agee, of course, knew of Pollard's previous pattern of picking up documents on Fridays.

Late that Wednesday night, after the day shift had gone home, Agee emptied the ATAC office of the two watch officers and everyone else. He told them to go to another office under a pretext in order to enable McCullah and his NIS counterintelligence agents to install two hidden pinhole lens video surveillance cameras in the ceiling which could film everything going on around Pollard's desk. Agee was the only person in ATAC who knew about the cameras. McCullah and his agents, of course, also knew.

On Thursday, November 14, Agee went to the computer center to retrieve the package of classified documents requested by Pollard. He locked it in a safe where no one would be able to find it. Agee was assuming that Pollard would go down on Friday as usual to fetch the package—but there would be no package. That would give the NIS and FBI agents time to get into a position to pick him up for questioning the following Monday. Agee's goal was to delay the Friday pickup until the following week when the FBI would be ready to assist.

Pollard did in fact go to the computer center late on Friday afternoon—to be told that the package was not there.

"What do you mean, it's not here?" he angrily asked the clerk. "I ordered it Wednesday."

The clerk checked all around and couldn't find it. "Try again on Monday," he suggested.

Pollard was furious. "What am I going to tell Yossi?" he said to himself. He was supposed to drop off the documents at Irit's apartment on his way home from work that Friday evening.

But again, no alarm bells rang in his head. He simply assumed that this was the government's sloppy bureaucracy at work. Thank God he would be leaving that job shortly; he had bigger and better things planned.

And Pollard, in any case, was very excited, knowing that Avi Sella would be in Washington that weekend. They had dinner scheduled for Saturday night. He had not seen Avi since the trip to Israel at the end of July and early August. There was so much to talk about, especially the air strike against the PLO in Tunisia. He assumed that Sella had played some sort of role in the operation, and was very anxious to get all the technical details.

That Friday evening, Pollard, Anne, and a friend ate dinner at the Marrakesh Restaurant in Washington, which specializes in Middle Eastern food. The friend, Pollard later said, was his Saudi contact. The bill for dinner, according to a subsequent government audit, came to $248.40, which Anne paid for by personal check. Included were two drinks before dinner, five drinks after dinner, and a $95 bottle of Dom Pérignon champagne.

CHAPTER EIGHT

Captured

Saturday, November 16, 1985

Aviem Sella was coming to Washington with his wife, Yehudit, to see how his "recruit" was doing. Sella had been in Toronto, where he had met with a very wealthy Canadian Jew who was prepared to donate a sizable sum of money for the construction of a synagogue at the Ramon Air Base in the Negev. It was Sella's pet project.

Although no longer Pollard's "handler," Sella was clearly still very interested in the espionage operation. Through him, Pollard had provided incredibly valuable information to Israel. Sella took personal pride in having played a significant role in establishing the entire connection. He assumed this would help his career, although it was skyrocketing long before he ever met Pollard.

Sella had planned much of the electronic warfare that knocked out Syria's surface-to-air missile batteries in Lebanon. During the Israeli-Egyptian War of Attrition along the Suez Canal in the early 1970s, Sella had become the first Western pilot to actually photograph a Soviet-made SA-6 missile battery; those valuable pictures were immediately provided to U.S. military intelligence. During one encounter on July 30, 1970, he personally downed an Egyptian

MiG-21 fighter flown by a Soviet pilot. Information on that dogfight was also passed on to the U.S. Air Force and Navy. It was no wonder that Sella was a rather popular and well-known figure among American military officers visiting Israel. They often sought him out for briefings.

Now, he was already the commander of the U.S.-built and -financed Ramon Air Base in the Negev and on the fast track to becoming commander of the air force.

But what Sella saw in Washington that cool Saturday evening made him nervous. Both Pollard and his wife had gained a considerable amount of weight. They dined at La Marée, a very expensive restaurant where Sella was struck by the maître d's apparently knowing Pollard by name. Pollard was evidently enjoying the good life which his extra $2,500 a month retainer from Israel enabled him to afford. As the four of them chatted, Sella became even more nervous as he heard of Pollard's grandiose intelligence-gathering schemes down the road. He told him about his Saudi connection.

Sella was beginning to wonder if Israel should terminate the entire operation despite the very valuable information that had been obtained; Pollard might prove too reckless and unstable. Maybe he was not the right man for the espionage assignment after all.

But before reaching that conclusion, Sella wanted to see more, in particular how the Pollards were living. Yossi Yagur, who had succeeded Sella as Pollard's handler, had been badgered by the young Naval Intelligence analyst in recent weeks about his need for a larger, more secure Washington apartment. The current one, Pollard maintained, was simply too small for the kind of entertaining necessary to establish the best contacts. Pollard told Yagur that he was also deeply worried about his ability to escape from that apartment in the event that the operation were ever compromised. He needed a house or an apartment with "special modifications" that would allow them to leave without being observed. There had to be a trapdoor for escape purposes, for example. The Israelis, he said, would have to provide a "secure contractor" to do the job. In re-

cent days, in fact, Pollard had described the existing apartment to Yagur as "a death trap." The apartment itself had
only one way out—and the building was not much better.
There were two exits, one from the front that led to the
street and one in the back that led to an alley. Surveillance
on the building, Pollard told Yagur, was "a piece of cake."

The pilot had been asked to check out Pollard's complaints. It was important, therefore, for the pilot actually to
see the apartment. At the restaurant that night, Sella
thought that Pollard was perhaps exaggerating about the
dangers. He was worried about the Israeli spy. But if he was
going to make a report to his colleagues, he wanted more
hard evidence.

"Perhaps we could come over Monday evening?" Sella
proposed as they were winding up their dinner with coffee
and dessert. He thought that Anne would offer to make
dinner for him and his wife.

"Why don't we go out for dinner Monday night and you
can come over for dessert," Pollard suggested.

That was fine with Sella.

Pollard picked up the tab for dinner, wine, drinks, and tip
that night—$202.02, which he put on his American Express
card.

Sunday, November 17, 1985

It was supposed to be a typical Sunday evening exchange,
one of many Pollard had carried out over the last ten
months.

Pollard drove from his apartment up Connecticut Avenue
to the Van Ness apartment complex to retrieve the suitcase
full of documents he had dropped off the Friday before. Irit
Erb, the young, attractive secretary at the Israeli Embassy
in Washington who lived in the same building, would receive the documents from Pollard on a Friday evening, as
Pollard drove home from work. She would later make copies
in the second flat, purchased by Harold Katz. Because of all
the sophisticated photocopying equipment the Israelis had

installed in the apartment, special security precautions had to be taken. The apartment was provided with a TEMPEST electronic protection system to guarantee that the equipment inside did not radiate signals that could be detected outside. The last thing the Israelis needed was for a neighbor to complain about some interference on his television set.

Three times each week, Pollard would remove documents from his office. As instructed by the Israelis, he would take them to his car and drive to a location where he could not be observed, such as a car wash on upper Connecticut Avenue. While going through the car wash, he would transfer the documents to an Israeli-supplied briefcase which he kept in the car for this purpose. Pollard's neighbors on 17th Street were amazed at how clean he kept his old car.

After receiving the documents on a Friday evening, Irit made copies over the weekend. The machines worked for hours at a time. On Sunday evenings, Pollard would pick up the originals and return them to the national security files, usually first thing Monday morning.

It was extremely difficult—if not impossible—for Pollard to make copies at his office. Some of the documents, for one thing, were huge satellite reconnaissance photographs requiring very sophisticated photocopying equipment— equipment that was installed in Katz's apartment. The pictures could be copied only in sections that would have to be pieced together later. He did not have access to that kind of equipment. And in any case, the Israelis preferred to work from originals; there was less chance for falsifications.

This was basically a very simple operation. Pollard collected documents at his office and brought them to the Israelis. They made copies, and he returned the originals. There were no microdots, fancy skills, or exotic transfers required. That, in fact, was its beauty. But there was also a downside. Precisely because it was so easy to obtain the TOP SECRET documents, there was a built-in temptation to get more and more of them. It was natural to become greedy. And Pollard and his Israeli handlers did.

Pollard said that the information he provided offered Israel "a glimpse into the future. . . . If one is aware of future threats, one can invest scarce money in research and development so that one would be prepared to meet those threats."

For months, this arrangement at the Van Ness had worked very smoothly. But tonight, no one answered the doorbell or his knocking. Irit had always been extremely reliable and prompt. Perhaps some emergency had called her away.

Pollard turned the handle to the door. He was surprised to find that it was not locked. He decided to let himself in. But he immediately discovered that the chain bolt was engaged; the solid metal door would open only a few inches before the chain stopped it. Pollard did not know what was going on. If no one was inside, how could the chain have been engaged? There was no other way to leave the small apartment. Someone had to be there.

"Irit," he called out. "Irit, Irit!"

His voice grew increasingly louder, but no one answered. He could feel his pulse rush, and he backed away from the door. As he left the Van Ness to drive back home, he began to shake as if he had the chills, then to sweat. He lit up a cigarette. It was so unlike Irit to miss an appointment. And what about the chain? It was the first time there had been any serious snag in the operation.

That night, Pollard sat down with Anne in their small living room and told her what had happened. As he stared at a new cactus plant they had just purchased, he said to Anne:

"Look, if I ever call you and use the word 'cactus' in any way whatsoever, that will mean that I'm in trouble. You should immediately take whatever documents we have in the house and get rid of them."

Anne had been aware of Pollard's spying for Israel from the very beginning, even though his Israeli handlers had firmly instructed him against informing her. "Jay had stressed to me over the years the importance of Israel, the survival of the state, and the fact that the U.S. was not being forthcoming with information to Israel, as they had promised," she would later say. "And this was being delayed or kept out by mid-level bureaucrats, not necessarily high-level officials."

Neither husband nor wife could sleep. Irit Erb called later to apologize. She couldn't come to the door, she explained, because she was entertaining a friend. It proved to be a mere trick of fate. It was not, Pollard later discovered, a signal of trouble. Yet at least in the short term, it was a lucky break for him. He was right to have panicked. He did not know that Naval Investigative Service and FBI agents were already closing in on him.

Monday, November 18, 1985

Anne walked from her apartment, down Connecticut Avenue, to the downtown American Express office in Washington to pay the outstanding balance on their account. She gave the cashier a personal check for $86.06 and $2,000 in cash which Yagur had given Pollard in an envelope a few days earlier.

McCullah, Agee, and the FBI agents were ready to pick up Pollard that day, although they were by no means certain that he would first collect the documents waiting for him at the Communications Center; the pattern for pickups, of course, had been on Fridays. As he had not been able to fetch it on Friday, would he come for it today?

The package was taken out of the safe and returned to the computer center. A clerk, acting on Agee's instructions, called Pollard to inform him that it was ready for pickup. In fact, he and two other clerks called Pollard three times— once in the early morning, then in the early afternoon, and finally later in the afternoon.

Pollard, while shaken by Irit's absence, still bit the bait. He was planning to have dinner that evening with Sella, who would deeply appreciate the information contained in the latest package.

He went down to get the package at 4:00 P.M., and

brought it back to his office. Agee, McCullah, and other FBI agents anxiously watched through the concealed video cameras in the ceiling. They saw Pollard—outwardly cool and calm—open the package, throw away the wrapper, and go through the documents. He kept those pages that he wanted, throwing others in the burn bag. He folded the papers and stuck them in one of his desk drawers. It appeared as if he had gone through the routine many times.

Then, they saw Pollard open another desk drawer. He pulled it all the way out. "What the hell is he doing now?" Agee asked.

Pollard reached down way into the back and took out a tiny piece of paper that was folded. He opened it and looked carefully at it before folding it up and returning it back to the drawer.

"That's his shopping list," Agee told the others in the room. "He's trying to memorize something."

Later on, the FBI and NIS discovered several tiny pieces of paper hidden in his desk containing lists of documents that he had been ordered to obtain. The notes had precise numbers and names of classified documents—with unique characters on them, including the proper sequence of codewords. There was no question that Pollard had been told to get those specific documents. The handwriting on the paper was his.

It was this kind of tasking, in fact, that would later convince some U.S. Justice Department and FBI authorities that the Israelis must have had another spy working inside the U.S. intelligence community—a "Mr. X" who was advising the Israelis what documents to obtain. Perhaps this second spy, they suspected, was too high up to actually collect these kinds of documents himself.

Pollard then put the messages in his briefcase and locked it. He called Anne. "I'm on my way home," he said. "I'm leaving the office now." He was anxious to see Sella again.

After hanging up the phone, he straightened out his desk. He looked around the office and casually walked out. He went downstairs to the main lobby and walked out of the building, past the guards. Smiling, he said good-night to them. He was not stopped. The FBI and NIS agents were hovering near the windows watching him leave. It was approximately 5:00 P.M. when he reached his car. There were four carloads of FBI and NIS agents, wearing business suits, waiting.

Pollard sat down behind the wheel, whereupon a NIS agent whom Pollard knew walked up to the window and asked him to get out.

"Jay, would you please step out of the car," he said, "and come back with us into the building?"

Pollard, of course, immediately knew something was very wrong. He had that nauseous sinking feeling in his stomach. "Oh, my God," he said to himself. "I'm in deep trouble."

At that point, he still had no idea what was in store. He knew he had to maintain his composure. A good actor, he feigned total surprise. He did not want to appear ruffled in any way.

"What's all this about?" he asked.

"There are some questions we want to ask you and it will be much easier if we go inside to do it."

Pollard, who again felt his heart drop to the floor upon hearing those words, agreed. He already sensed that this was the beginning of the end.

"Am I under some sort of arrest?" he asked.

He was told that he was not. He was simply asked to answer some questions, which he did.

"Pollard complied willingly," the government would later state in documents filed with the court, "but it soon became clear that his intent was to divert and to stall the agents rather than to assist them in their efforts to recover and secure the classified documents which he had compromised."

At that moment, Pollard remained convinced that he could still stall the authorities long enough to make his escape. He shrewdly anticipated that the agents would suspect the involvement of a foreign nation, and would continue to allow him to remain at liberty in the hope that surveillance might lead the agents to the true recipients of the classified documents.

In the selected office were two FBI agents and two NIS agents. Politely but firmly, they asked him about the package he was carrying since, according to the government, it was "the type typically used by NIS to wrap classified materials."

Throughout the early part of that first interview, Pollard insisted that he was merely transporting the package to a meeting at another secure Navy office within the same Suitland, Maryland, complex. He said that he had to give it to another analyst. The package, according to the government, contained sixty documents, twenty of which were classified TOP SECRET or above.

"I know I shouldn't be taking it out of the office this late in the day," Pollard said. "But I do it all the time. What's the problem?" He professed his complete innocence of any serious wrongdoing.

Jerry Agee, meanwhile, was upstairs, going through everything in and around Pollard's office. "We were inventorying everything," Agee would later disclose. He was especially interested in obtaining names and telephone numbers.

Whenever one of the agents questioning Pollard came upstairs to report on what he was saying, Agee would—in his words—"throw the bullshit flag." Agee kept insisting that Pollard was simply lying.

That evening, the Pollards had been scheduled to have dinner at Mr. K's, a very expensive and elegant Chinese restaurant on K Street in Washington, with the Sellas. Pollard, of course, had called his wife just before five to say that he was leaving the office. He would be home, he said, by around five-thirty.

By 7:00 P.M., Anne became very nervous. It was so unlike her husband not even to call to say he would be late.

"Jay and I have never had a problem with that," she later said. "Some guys would ask Jay to go out and he would always say, 'Fine, I'll bring Anne.' Some girls would ask me to go out, and I said, 'Fine. I'll bring Jay.' That's the only way we would go out. There was never any 'Guys Night Out,' or 'Girls Night Out,' or anything like that. If Jay said he would be home in half an hour, he would be home in half an hour."

Anne also knew that her husband was rather excited about the dinner with the Sellas. She knew how much he looked forward to seeing Sella. By then, Jay had come to love Avi like an older brother. "He thought he was brilliant and generous and extremely kind, a loving individual," Anne would later reveal. "You know when you can instantaneously like someone. He had that feeling about him." In Avi, Jay finally had someone who could value and discuss the things he cared about, from Israel's strategic planning to the Holocaust. They were kindred spirits.

She repeatedly called her husband's office and was informed that he had left at 5:00 P.M.

"It's six o'clock and I'm a nervous wreck," she recalled. "They said he left at five. I thought he may have been in a car accident. I didn't know what was going on."

At approximately 7:30 P.M., Pollard finally called. By then, he had provided the agents with the name of another Navy analyst to whom, he claimed, he was taking the documents. While FBI and NIS agents attempted to locate this other analyst and to confirm Pollard's story, Pollard asked if he could call his wife to explain that he would be working late. Since at that time he was not under arrest, the agents could not say no.

His voice, Anne later recalled, was edgy. "He didn't sound like himself," she said.

"Go see our friends, take the wedding album, give them our cactus, and send them my love," he said, explaining that he was working late.

"What are you talking about?" she asked reflexively. "You said you were on the way home."

"You heard what I said."

He repeated the reference to the cactus and the wedding album.

By then, Anne knew things were falling apart. Of course,

she was stunned to hear the reference to the cactus only a day after their conversation about the codeword.

"Are you sure you want me to give it away?" she asked, quickly attempting to regain her cool. She did not want to sound panicky and suspected that the call was being monitored. "You spent so much time picking it out."

Pollard, also attempting to sound as natural as possible, emphasized that it was very important that she bring the cactus to their friends. "I'll be home soon," he said, ending the conversation.

Ten minutes later, he made a second call to Anne. He repeated the reference to the cactus and added that she should also take their wedding album to their neighbors. Anne knew that some classified documents had been stashed in the album, including those involving the Chinese Embassy. Pollard was confident that Anne would get rid of the classified documents scattered around the apartment and then warn Sella.

After the calls, which were in fact monitored by the FBI, Pollard agreed to further questioning. The agents told him that they had finally located the other Navy employee. He denied any plans to meet with Pollard, or to receive documents from him. But Pollard persisted in his own denial that he had removed the documents for an unauthorized purpose. According to government investigators, he claimed that he had never taken classified documents to any unauthorized locations. But they already sensed that Pollard's story was crumbling.

After the story about the other employee fell apart, Pollard said that he had given some classified documents to Kurt Lohbeck, his friend the freelance journalist who had traveled to Afghanistan to write about the freedom fighters resisting the Soviet military occupation. Pollard would later describe Lohbeck as "a recognized liaison" to the Mujaheddin, or Afghan freedom fighters. By raising the Afghan flag, Pollard hoped to keep his interrogators off of Israel's trail.

"Jay did the classic intelligence agent's dissembling," Agee would later say. "If you're caught, you never tell anything right away. You try to get out of it. Then you give them a little bit of it, and fill up a lot of smoke. And if they finally work their way through that, and find out the truth, you give them a lot more smoke and a little bit of truth. And that's what he was doing. He knew what he was doing. We were spinning a lot of wheels at the time."

Around 10:00 P.M., the FBI and NIS agents were running out of things to talk to Pollard about. Everyone was exhausted. Unless they were going to arrest him, they knew that they had to let him go home. At that point, they did not have enough evidence to arrest him—only to know that something was terribly wrong. They had to stall in order to figure out their next step. They called Agee upstairs and asked him to come to the office to talk to Pollard.

A furious and frustrated Agee took the place of one of the agents and confronted Pollard directly. He was not coy. "What's going on?" he asked angrily.

"I don't know," Pollard replied, professing innocence. "I don't know what they think. All I was doing was taking the stuff down the street."

"Jay," Agee said, "that's a straight lie. You weren't taking that stuff down there. You're doing something else with it. What are you doing with it, Jay?"

"I don't know what you're talking about. I don't know why you keep accusing me of something."

Agee flatly accused Pollard of espionage—which Pollard denied.

Agee had earlier collected all of Pollard's ID cards and badges. He gave him a letter which had earlier been prepared suspending him from his job until the investigation was complete. All security clearances for Pollard were also temporarily withdrawn. "We didn't intend to arrest him at that point, but we didn't want him to have access to anything," Agee explained.

The FBI and NIS agents had been rather soft in their questioning. They did not want to make Pollard overly mad because they feared that he would simply get up and leave—as he could have done. But Agee was different. He quickly became very hostile in his questioning, to the point that he was eventually thrown out of the room by the other FBI and NIS interrogators because of his anger.

"I was rocking the boat," Agee later remembered.

But Agee's tough style actually appeared to get Pollard more nervous and made him talk more, according to Agee and other agents involved in the investigation.

"Every time I accused him of something, he would want to explain why it wasn't true," Agee said.

The agents sought Pollard's consent to search his apartment, but he initially declined, explaining that he was concerned that they might locate small amounts of marijuana. "We don't care if you smoke marijuana," one agent told him.

Pollard then explained that his wife was not feeling well.

"I haven't done anything wrong," he said. "I see no reason to have my apartment searched."

Frustrated, they continued their interview, receiving what they regarded as implausible explanations for the removal of classified documents. They knew Pollard was lying. But they were uncertain about the full nature and scope of his activities.

As the interview continued, the agents became increasingly suspicious. After some six hours of questioning, they finally informed Pollard that they had begun the process of obtaining a search warrant for the apartment. "That was their whole goal," Agee later said. "They felt that whatever he had was probably in his apartment. They didn't know how much."

By sending in different agents to question him, they were trying to wear Pollard down. They wanted to keep him talking while they appeared fresh. "He was stupid," Agee said. "He was so arrogant that he thought he could talk his way out of everything. But all he was doing was digging himself in deeper and deeper. The intent was to let him talk."

Their tactic succeeded. At approximately 11:30 P.M., Pollard finally gave his consent to the permissive search. He assumed that Anne had already "cleaned up" the place by then.

Everyone drove to his apartment. Pollard was relieved to

discover that Anne was not home when he and the agents arrived. He was confident that she had removed the classified documents. It was almost midnight.

"I had heard the word 'cactus' and I knew that something was very wrong," Anne later said. "I gathered up the documents in the house—all the documents. I got nervous."

An FBI agent, Eugene Noltkamper, would later testify that the documents could be stacked fifteen to eighteen inches in height. Many of them were classified TOP SECRET. "That was shown on the front sheet, and then on every page," according to Noltkamper. The documents were related to U.S. weapons and military capabilities.

Anne wasn't sure what to do with the documents. She was afraid to burn them or to flush them down the toilet. Israel or Jay might still need them. Instead, she put them in a suitcase which also contained a pair of women's shoes, an envelope containing wedding photos, and a little plastic bag containing typewriter ribbon, parts of which had been cut into small pieces. She began to walk outside the apartment building at 1733 20th Street, N.W., when she spotted several unmarked FBI and NIS cars outside with their engines running. The cars were double-parked. They were large dark blue, brown, or black Fords and Dodges with extra thick blackwall tires. Inside each car were two men. There were two extra antennas in the rear of the cars. "I knew what they looked like," she said. "Jay had pointed them out to me in the past.

"I could hear radios going off right and left," she continued. "I sat there frozen stiff, scared to death. I didn't know what to do."

After calming herself down somewhat, she hid the suitcase in a basement stairwell and went to the apartment of her next-door neighbors, Christine and Babak Esfandiari, a married couple who were also close friends. "Out of desperation I went there," Anne said. "I begged them to help. I knew the necessity of getting that suitcase out."

She told them that she needed help in removing a heavy

item, a suitcase, from the building. They initially did not take the matter all that seriously, proposing that Anne sit down and have a drink with them. "Why do you want this suitcase?" Christine kept asking. "Why don't you sit down and have a drink?"

"I don't want a drink," Anne replied, losing her cool. "I just want you to bring the suitcase to me. Please."

She pleaded with them for some fifteen minutes.

Finally, when she told them of her concern that something had happened to Jay, they agreed to help. She told them that she had asked Jay to help her out with information on the Chinese Embassy. With two other business associates, Anne was working on a proposal to do some public relations work for the embassy. They were bidding on a contract to do "media training" for Chinese diplomats. The suitcase, she said, contained classified documents; she said she intended to destroy the documents once she was able to get the suitcase outside the building.

Babak, the husband, agreed to help. She asked him to bring the suitcase to the posh Four Seasons Hotel in Georgetown, about a mile or two away. They would meet in the lobby. She urged him to take a circuitous route to get there.

Although never trained to avoid surveillance, she slid outside the back of the building through the alley to R Street. "I walked around the block," she recalled. She thought she was being followed.

"Let me make one thing perfectly clear," she later said. "I am not a spy. I have never been a spy. I am not trained in spying techniques or anything."

But if she was being followed, Anne cleverly managed to escape. At one point, she walked into the front door of a store and exited from the rear. Then she walked through several alleys before reaching Pennsylvania Avenue, where she hailed a taxi. "I told him to take me one place and then we went to more places," she said. Finally, he dropped her off at a street corner and she walked several blocks to the Four Seasons Hotel. She kept checking to make certain she was not being followed.

"I went into the parking garage," she said. "I didn't know

what to do. I was scared. All I knew was that my husband was in trouble, and he had asked me to do this. I had to help him. If he had asked me to jump off the Brooklyn Bridge, I would have. I knew Jay was in horrible, horrible trouble."

But Babak was not there. She called Christine and was told that he should already be there. But she could not find him. Because it had taken her so long to reach the hotel, he had apparently already come and gone—with the suitcase. She became frightened. "I looked everywhere. I couldn't find him. I never found him."

Finally, she went to a pay telephone in the downstairs lobby of the hotel and called Avi Sella at the Holiday Inn in suburban Bethesda, Maryland, where he and his wife were staying. They had been sitting watching television, patiently waiting to hear from the Pollards. Avi had called the Pollards' apartment but there had been no answer. He was getting increasingly more nervous about Pollard's reliability. It was now nine-thirty, two hours after their dinner engagement at Mr. K's was supposed to start.

Anne, holding back the sense of fear and panic in her voice, said that there was a last-minute change of plans. She wanted to meet with Sella alone at O'Donnell's fish restaurant just up the street from their hotel. She said she could not talk on the phone. She would be there in twenty minutes.

Anne took a taxi to the restaurant. It was already 10:15 P.M. Sella was waiting in a corner booth.

"Jay is in serious trouble," she said, carefully selecting her words, chain-smoking. She was not supposed to know about his espionage activities. "I talked around the issue somewhat," she later recalled.

"He asked me to remove certain items from the apartment—items that should not have been in the apartment," she told Sella elliptically. "Avi, you've got to help. Please help Jay. He's in terrible, terrible trouble."

She looked into his eyes. Her hands were shaking, her lips quivering, and she became quite vocal when she sensed that Sella was not responding. She started to cry.

Sella, already very nervous from the Saturday night encounter, began to assume the worst-case scenario was in fact unfolding—Pollard had been compromised. The whole operation was about to crumble. He even began to fear that he was being set up by Anne. He suspected that she might have been "wired" as part of some sort of Justice Department sting operation against him.

"I have to make a call," he said rather coldly, leaving the table.

From a pay telephone at the restaurant, Sella called Yagur, Pollard's chief handler, in New York. He relayed what had happened that night and what Anne had just said. What were the arrangements for escape?

To his horror, Sella was informed that there were no such contingency plans; at least Yagur was unaware of any. Despite Israel's reputation for having the most efficient intelligence service in the world, no one had worked out an escape plan for the Pollards and the other operatives involved. Sella was advised to leave the country immediately. "You better get out of there," Yagur said.

Yagur and Pollard, over the months, had established a very warm relationship of mutual trust. Yagur genuinely liked and admired Pollard. He was deeply grateful for what the American was doing for Israel. Yagur, just before finishing the conversation, strongly assured Sella that Pollard could be trusted. Pollard, he insisted, was a loyal agent. "Don't worry about him," Yagur said firmly. "He's one of us. I trust him completely."

Within five minutes, Sella returned to the table ashenfaced. He knew he was now on his own and would have to escape as quickly as possible. He did not have diplomatic immunity; nor did his wife, who was still watching television in the hotel.

Anne felt briefly reassured when he came back from the telephone. "Avi swore that he would do everything in his power to help us," she later recalled.

He spoke with authority and confidence. "Everything is going to be just fine," he said. "Don't worry. We'll take care of everything. Just calm down."

He provided Anne with Yagur's New York phone number

and instructions for Pollard to telephone Yagur later that night. Pollard had never before received that unlisted number. Before leaving the restaurant, Sella asked Anne if she wanted to come with him.

"I'm not leaving my husband," she said, crying hysterically. "I can't."

The pilot instructed Anne not to reveal to anyone that they had ever met. "You don't know me, you've never met me, you've never heard my name," he said, taking her hand and squeezing it.

She nodded in agreement and said: "Okay."

He promised he would call later that evening to see if Pollard had arrived home and whether, in fact, he was in trouble. He asked that she wait at the restaurant until midnight before leaving; this would be the time necessary for Sella to plan his own escape from the United States. "I understand now that that was his time to get out," Anne later said. "That was the last time I heard from Avi."

There wasn't much traffic on Wisconsin Avenue when Sella walked back to his hotel. It was only a block away. He carefully looked at the few cars in the normally busy street, anxious to discover if Anne had been followed to the restaurant. He saw nothing suspicious. There were no people in parked cars—nor was there anyone walking on the sidewalk. The last thing he wanted was to be followed to the hotel. He walked slowly and occasionally stopped to turn around—quickly—just to make certain that he was alone. By the time he reached the lobby, he was confident that he was.

The elevator door was open. The ride seemed to take forever.

Inside the room, finally, he told his wife that they had to leave the United States immediately. He explained what was happening. She was understandably angry and scared. They quickly packed and checked out of the room.

"Is there anything wrong?" the surprised reception clerk asked when they went to settle their account.

"No," Sella replied. "We've just had a change of plans."

They knew that they had to get out of the country as quickly as possible. But by then it was too late to catch a flight out of Washington, and there were no morning flights to Europe out of Washington's Dulles International Airport either. They had no choice but to get to New York. With the help of an Israeli Embassy official, they managed to rent a car late that night. They then drove all night to New York's John F. Kennedy Airport, where they waited to board the first flight out of the country very early the next morning—a flight to London.

Sella had entered the United States from Canada on his regular Israeli passport, using his real name. But he left the country on a different Israeli passport, using an alias. He feared that U.S. agents could already have been alerted to arrest him. He was a nervous wreck. Indeed, after years of not smoking, he resumed the habit that very long night.

Upon reaching London, he took a deep breath. He was free, he said to himself. He later confided to friends that that ordeal in Washington had been the most frightful of his life—quite a statement for someone who had gone eyeball-to-eyeball against Soviet fighter pilots.

It was well after midnight by the time Anne returned to her apartment. By then, Jay was home. But he had company. The place was surrounded by FBI and NIS agents. Inside, they were slowly searching closets, drawers, books, everything. "My house was being torn apart," she said later.

According to government investigators, the search revealed fifty-seven classified documents hidden in a box, and under some women's clothing, in the master bedroom. Anne, in her panic, had failed to pack them in the suitcase. The documents, according to the government, included some with a TOP SECRET classification. They described the U.S. analysis of weapons systems and military capabilities of the Soviet Union and several Arab countries.

Pollard, according to court papers, "feigned surprise when confronted with the documents." His only explanation was that he must have brought them home in order to continue his work, and later forgot to return them to his office.

While the agents were still in the midst of their search, Sella called, as promised. He was at a pay telephone. Anne answered the ring. "Is everything all right?" he asked, without introducing himself. She, of course, recognized his voice.

"Absolutely not," she replied emphatically.

"I understand," he said, quickly ending the conversation. "Goodbye."

Sella called Yagur to inform him of the bad news. Within minutes, Yagur was on the phone with Rafi Eitan in Tel Aviv.

Because Pollard's possession of classified documents in his home was, at the very least, a violation of Navy security regulations, he was requested to report to NIS offices the next day for a full-scale polygraph examination. He agreed and the agents left the apartment with the classified documents.

They did not arrest Pollard that night. They felt that they had already nailed him. They were confident that he was not in any position to elude their round-the-clock surveillance. They hoped that Pollard would lead them to his superiors. "We had no evidence at that point," Agee recalled. "All we knew was that he was taking stuff out. We had absolutely no evidence of what he was doing with it. So the whole time we were interviewing him and watching him to see where he would go, we were hoping he would go someplace and tell us what was going on."

The working assumption remained that Pollard was spying for Israel. But they had not confronted him directly with that allegation. Agee, who had carefully gone through everything around Pollard's desk, was now more certain than ever that Israel was running Pollard.

After the agents left, the Pollards, badly shaken and scared, went to an all-night coffeeshop near Dupont Circle. They knew they were being followed by FBI agents who did not interfere. From a pay phone booth, Pollard called Yagur in New York, as Sella had instructed Anne.

Pollard said that he was in deep trouble.

"Do they know about Israel's involvement?" Yagur asked.

"No," replied Pollard. "I don't think so."

"Then stall for time," Yagur said. "Don't worry. We'll take care of you."

He said that a special Israeli crew was already standing by to rescue them. He also reminded Pollard to use the special telephone number in Washington that earlier had been given him in case of an emergency. The Pollards, still fearful, returned to their apartment under the watchful gaze, they were sure, of the U.S. government. They knew they would have to escape from the United States as quickly as possible. There was no alternative.

Tuesday, November 19, 1985

After a very long night with virtually no sleep, Pollard told Anne to get out of the apartment that morning and to walk around the neighborhood. "He said that somebody would 'accidentally' bump into me and quietly tell me how we should get out of the country or what we should do," Anne recalled. "That had been an earlier-agreed arrangement."

Pollard that morning appeared, as ordered, at the NIS offices for the scheduled polygraph exam. But as NIS agents began preparations for the test, Pollard asked to speak to one of them alone. He would be unable to complete the test successfully, he said, because he had in fact provided five or six classified documents to a friend who was not authorized to receive them. At that point, according to court documents, the NIS agent advised Pollard of his constitutional right to remain silent, but Pollard said that he was willing to waive it.

His most important objective, for the time being, was to delay for as long as possible any polygraph, which would certainly show him lying. The Israelis had always stressed this point during all of their briefings for him. They did not believe that Pollard could trick the machine. They had also told him never to name Israel if he were ever questioned even without the cables attached to his pulse and sweat glands.

Pollard, who had read hundreds of spy novels, was rather sophisticated in setting small traps for the FBI. He knew what they wanted to hear, and he knew how to delay any arrest.

Upon further questioning, Pollard's estimate of the number of classified documents he had compromised quickly grew to fifty or one hundred each month for the past year. When he admitted receiving money for the documents, FBI agents were contacted and a joint NIS/FBI interview began.

Pollard was interviewed for eight straight hours by the agents. During those interviews, he did not disclose his involvement with the Israelis. Instead, in order to buy more time, he claimed that he had delivered classified information only to his friend, Kurt Lohbeck, an American citizen. Throughout the interviews, he fabricated other tales as well to keep the authorities away from Israel. He ultimately provided the agents that day with an eleven-page handwritten statement detailing the sale of classified documents. He specifically denied personally selling classified documents to a foreign government representative, and disclaimed any actual knowledge that his friend was selling information to a foreign government. He claimed that he merely suspected Lohbeck was using the information to assist "freedom fighters in Afghanistan."

"Perhaps," Pollard said, "he's associated with Pakistani military intelligence."

In the handwritten statement, Pollard described in detail the documents he had provided. Because of the breadth and scope of these documents, as well as the classified documents recovered the night before, the agents suspected that Pollard was himself delivering them to an agent of a foreign country. Moreover, even though Pollard had already provided a lengthy written statement, he insisted that he had more details to provide concerning the specific classified documents he had compromised.

Pollard astutely understood how the FBI and NIS agents

thought and operated. By holding out the promise of further cooperation, he suspected they would let him go home. He needed to delay for as long as possible any decision on their part to arrest him. As long as Pollard was cooperating with the investigation, the agents almost certainly would not arrest him.

"In order to keep my dissembling as 'interrogation-proof' as possible," Pollard later recalled, "I stuck to the truth except for individuals and allegiances. When facing the prospect of round-the-clock badgering, it's simply prudent to build most of your lie around a kernel of truth which can be remembered rather than trust one's powers of creativity and consistency. Although I realized that all the authorities had on me up to that point was the possession of classified documents, which I had not had time to return to their various libraries, such was my trust in Rafi's assurances of rescue that the story I began to weave was more than convincing—it was airtight and fit like a malleable body bag. It should have been since I was well aware of what my interrogators wanted to hear and only had to keep them interested long enough to postpone the inevitable polygraphing. I was hoping by that time I would be out of the country, after having successfully misdirected the security services onto a more appropriate villain."

Later that evening, just as Pollard had hoped, the agents decided to continue their questioning the following day, but to maintain round-the-clock surveillance of Pollard in the meantime. They accompanied him back to his apartment. "Surveillance was initiated in the event that he attempted to contact any foreign representative, or to flee Washington," U.S. court papers said.

Two agents came inside the apartment with Pollard. There, they asked Anne to sign a statement agreeing to waive her Miranda rights and to answer their questions.

"I'm not answering any questions," she said.

They gave her a piece of paper, asking her to sign it. At the bottom of the paper she wrote: "I have refused to answer any questions without the presence of my attorney."

The agents left the apartment.

In anticipation of their escape, the Pollards then began to hand-shred and throw out a large quantity of personal records, documents, and files which they had in their apartment.

Pollard assumed that Yagur, his trusted handler, had already planned their escape to Israel. He was anxious to receive his instructions, and was very disheartened to discover that no one had "bumped" into Anne earlier in the day.

Late that night, the Pollards again went to the all-night coffeeshop to call Yagur. Nervous as they were, they remained confident that the Israelis would still save them. Only a few months earlier, they had spent two wonderful weeks in Israel where they had been so warmly received. The Israelis were "family," Pollard told Anne. And in any case, they were great spies. "They'll take care of us."

But Pollard was stunned when there was no answer at Yagur's apartment. He kept calling. The phone simply continued to ring.

He then called the Washington number which had earlier been given to him to use in an emergency.

"The number you have reached is not in service," the computerized voice of an operator said. "Please check the number and dial again."

He dialed the number again, but the same message was played.

The Pollards returned home thunderstruck. They did not know what was going on. "They'll take care of us," Pollard again told Anne. "Don't worry."

But Yagur, Irit Erb, and Ilan Ravid, the science counselor at the Israeli Embassy in Washington to whose house Pollard early in the operation had delivered documents, already had received instructions from Eitan to get ready to leave the country.

Yagur had strongly protested. "What about the Pollards?" he asked. "We've got to save them."

He received a wishy-washy reply.

Yagur, in arguing against his forced escape from the United States, insisted that Pollard could be counted on to dissemble and not to betray Israel during the course of his interrogation. "We don't have to worry about him," he told his supervisors.

But Eitan, the cold-blooded masterspy, disagreed. The man who had captured Adolf Eichmann in 1960 after hundreds of others had failed, Eitan knew more about espionage and political counterattack than anyone else in the ring. He knew the Americans would have ways of getting the Pollards to talk. Israel, he assumed, would then deny any knowledge of what they were talking about. Who would believe the Pollards and their crazy story of spying for Israel?

He told Yagur, Ravid, and Erb to leave the United States immediately. This was not, he said, a subject for debate.

Pollard, that evening, did not know that he was effectively alone.

He also did not know that earlier in the afternoon, the Esfandiaris, his neighbors and supposed good friends, had contacted NIS agents about the suitcase. The agents, in turn, contacted the FBI, and, together, they went to the neighbors' apartment to retrieve the case.

"Upon obtaining custody of the suitcase from the witness," the government later stated in a memorandum, "the agents saw attached to it a tag bearing the name and address of Jonathan Pollard. The agents did not open the suitcase at that time, deciding instead to seek a warrant to search its contents."

Wednesday, November 20, 1985

On Wednesday morning, Pollard again told Anne to "walk around." He was still certain that she would somehow receive instructions for escape. Israel would not—could not—abandon one of its own agents.

In the meantime, FBI and NIS agents picked him up for more questioning. Pollard provided a second written statement describing further details of what the government called his "unauthorized disclosure of classified documents to the same friend." In the statement, according to court papers, he again recounted information which suggested to the agents that he was in fact delivering documents to a person acting on behalf of a foreign government. Pollard steadfastly continued to deny any knowledge of the involvement of a foreign government. But as part of his ploy to keep the agents intrigued and guessing, he admitted that he and his wife had traveled to Europe in November 1984 and July–August 1985.

With that tidbit, there was growing certainty that Pollard was merely implicating Lohbeck in order to disguise the direct involvement of another foreign country. But the agents did not know which country was involved; they only suspected that it was Israel. Some thought a Warsaw Pact country was perhaps also involved. But there was still no hard evidence.

At the conclusion of the interview, Pollard continued to insist that he had additional details to reveal regarding the specific documents he had been asked to obtain. He agreed to return to NIS offices the following day, after he had accompanied his wife to the doctor for some urgent medical treatment which she had scheduled. The agents complied with his request, but round-the-clock surveillance continued. Court papers later said that this investigative technique "requires the use of as many as twenty agents to cover a single suspect if it is to be done thoroughly and without being detected."

The FBI and NIS also continued extensive interviews of Pollard's co-workers. They already suspected that a significant amount of classified information had been compromised. They later told the court that they were "gravely worried" even though Pollard was still pretending to cooperate with their investigation.

FBI Special Agent Eugene Noltkamper, who had been involved in the earlier questioning of Pollard, was asked to gather and prepare specific information necessary to obtain a search warrant for the suitcase. Late in the day, he alerted the U.S. Attorney's Office to his need for a warrant, and began preparation of what eventually turned out to be a seven-page affidavit. Noltkamper interviewed other FBI and NIS agents to gather additional facts for the affidavit.

Again, a mentally battered and drained Pollard was allowed to return home late in the day. He went to a pay telephone and tried one more time to call Yagur. Again, no answer. He stood in the phone booth crying and shaking. What the hell had he done?

He composed himself before returning home. He did not want Anne to see that he was falling apart.

Pollard once more discussed with Anne what they considered their only remaining option—obtaining political asylum at the Israeli Embassy in Washington. Once inside that building, which U.S. law enforcement authorities cannot enter, they would be safe. The Israelis would then find a way to get them out of the country.

By then, Pollard knew that time was running out. He had managed to delay a polygraph examination by explaining that his wife was sick and he would have to take her to the hospital the next day. The FBI agents agreed to wait one more day. But he would not be able to stall any longer.

Agee later confirmed that Pollard was very worried about the polygraph. "I think he had some real fear of the polygraph," he said. "If he got on the polygraph and they began asking some hard questions, all his successful attempts to dissemble would just kind of evaporate. So I think he wanted to avoid the polygraph and he felt like he had managed to delay this whole thing for four days and it couldn't last forever. Soon, he was going to be arrested, and then he would have no options. If he was going to do anything, he was going to have to do it soon."

From a phone booth that night, Pollard called the Israeli Embassy, asking to speak to the security officer. Pollard later recalled that he had recited the names of his "handlers" and asked that asylum be arranged. "They understood exactly who he was," insisted Anne.

But a truly dumbfounded security officer on duty, who said he would have to look into the matter, asked Pollard to call back the next morning. "We will help you," he said, trying to put the caller's mind at ease.

Thursday, November 21, 1985

Early on Thursday morning, Pollard went to a pay telephone booth to call the embassy security officer again. Pollard would later insist that the instructions he received were firm. He was told that if he could shake his surveillance, he should come to the embassy later that morning. The embassy's driveway gate would be open at 10:00 A.M.

"He asked me what kind of car I would be driving," Pollard said later.

But the embassy's chief security officer testified that he had not instructed Pollard to come to the embassy. The officer insisted that he had no knowledge of the espionage operation or any rescue attempt. However, he conceded that one of his junior officers on duty, whose English was perhaps not very good, may have misunderstood what Pollard was talking about and casually—out of politeness—told him to come to the embassy to straighten out any problem. "It may have been one big misunderstanding," an Israeli official said.

The Pollards packed a bag. Anne grabbed her red-bound wedding album and their cat, Dusty. She also took their birth certificates, marriage license, and Dusty's vaccination papers. She realized that they were leaving the United States, probably forever.

But first, they had to drive across town to the Washington Hospital Center, near Catholic University, where Anne was scheduled to undergo a treatment for biliary dyskinesia, a very uncommon stomach disorder. It was the old problem, no doubt aggravated by the week's terrible stress.

Her internist, Dr. Herbert Moscovitz, would later describe how he had performed an endoscopy on her on November 13. It "revealed that she had a large conglomerate mass of undigested food and secretions in her stomach," he said. "She has a problem with this sort of recurrent situation and we irrigated her stomach."

He asked that she come to the gastro-urology suite on the third floor of the Washington Hospital Center on November 21 for another procedure to try to relieve the pain. "The throat and pharynx are made anesthetic by a spray, a topical anesthetic spray, similar to what's in cough drops," he explained. "And then the patient is sedated with intravenous use of sedative drugs so that a soft, flexible, fiber-optic instrument can be introduced through the pharynx, through the esophagus, into the stomach."

The Pollards were followed to the hospital by the agents. "They followed me into the operating room," Anne later said.

The treatment did not take long but she was heavily sedated. "The sedative makes people very sleepy, somnolent," Dr. Moscovitz said, adding that it "interferes with thinking, and also reduces the gag reflex and decreases their sensitivity to pain and discomfort." He gave her 100 milligrams of Demerol and 10 milligrams of Valium IV prior to the introduction of the endoscope.

From there, they were supposed to return to their apartment. Pollard had been scheduled to undergo more questioning.

But they decided to try to escape even though they knew they were being followed. They drove around Washington in a circuitous route of switchbacks and detours until they reached the Israeli Embassy. Pollard was determined to shake any surveillance—as instructed. He was confident that he had done so. But even if he could not lose the agents, he was certain that he would be safe once he reached the embassy. They could not follow him inside.

Ironically, Pollard had never been inside the embassy before. He had never attended any diplomatic receptions there. It was simply too dangerous for the operation. He would often see the light beige brick building with its semicircular windows as he drove away from the nearby Van Ness apartment complex after dropping off some documents. From Connecticut Avenue, he could see Israel's blue and white Star of David flag flying high on a pole outside the embassy building. Like many others, he thought the building and its distinctive architecture looked as though it belonged in Jerusalem rather than in Washington.

For an hour that morning, according to an FBI field agent involved in the case, several unmarked FBI cars followed him. One car would drop off his tail before another picked it up. Pollard would rarely see the same car in his rear-view mirror. The cars were in close and constant radio contact. And just to be safe, the FBI had planted an electronic signaling device inside the bumper of his green 1980 Mustang that emitted a silent beep, allowing the FBI to pick up the location of the car even if Pollard could shake his surveillance. There was no way the Pollards were going to escape.

They deliberately did not stop Pollard when they discovered that he was driving in circles, hoping that he would lead them to the foreign government involved in the espionage ring—which is exactly what Pollard did.

At 10:20 A.M., Pollard's Mustang entered the 3500 block of International Drive, N.W. It fell in behind an Israeli Embassy automobile—a car belonging to the embassy's number two diplomat, Elyakim Rubinstein. He was not inside, only his driver. The slow-moving, electronically controlled gate did not close after the embassy car passed it. Pollard, as a result, followed the car into the embassy compound. He drove down the long, steeply angled driveway. Anne, still heavily sedated, sat in the front seat next to him, clinging to her cat and her wedding album. The embassy gate closed shut behind Pollard's car.

Two Israeli guards immediately approached. Pollard identified himself as an Israeli agent, working for Rafi Eitan and Yossi Yagur. He was seeking refuge.

"Welcome home," Pollard later recalled one of the guards as saying. The guards saw Pollard literally shaking. His wife was crying. "You're safe now. Everything is fine." The Israeli guards later insisted, however, that they were totally startled by Pollard's arrival.

Anne was seen by the FBI getting out of the car. She

walked out of sight to an area under the embassy, inside the open garage, carrying two bags (one with Dusty inside) and a purse.

But within a few minutes, the embassy was surrounded by the FBI. There were a dozen cars, vans and trucks, and agents spilling out of each of them. They used binoculars to see what was going on.

Realizing what was happening, the embassy's security officer went back inside the building through the underground garage door, while the Mustang remained at the bottom of the driveway. Pollard waited in the driveway.

The agent emerged after about ten minutes.

"You must leave," he told a startled Pollard.

"What?"

"You heard me. You must leave."

"Do you know who I am?"

"You must get out," the officer said in a louder voice.

"Do you know what I have done for Israel? I am an Israeli agent," Pollard said, recalling his Israeli contacts' names.

"Get out," the officer simply said.

Anne, by then, was crying hysterically as she saw her husband arguing with the officer.

"I want to invoke my right under the Law of Return to Israeli citizenship," he said. "We're Jews. We're on Israeli territory. You can't throw us out."

His protestations did not succeed. The officer said: "Get out."

"But you see what's going on out there. We'll be arrested right away. You can't do this." Pollard was himself starting to cry.

The officer pushed him in the car and told him to drive away.

The FBI agents, fearful that they could have lost Pollard, were clearly confused and nervous as they continued to watch from the street. Pollard and his wife were now both standing outside the car engaged in angry and protracted conversation with the embassy officials.

"Please," Pollard pleaded for a final time. "You can't do this."

He again urged the officer to get in touch with Yagur or Ravid or Sella or Eitan or Erb. "They'll tell you that this is all a terrible mistake. They'll tell you what I have done for Israel. I am an Israeli spy. Please. You can't betray an Israeli spy like this. Please, just call them!"

"Drive away now!" the officer screamed. According to the Pollards, he made some wild gestures to back up his message, as if he were anxious for the FBI to understand that the Israelis were throwing them out of the embassy. *"Get out!"*

As soon as Pollard drove off Israeli Embassy property, he was arrested and read his rights. "I can't believe he actually made a run for it," one of the FBI agents later confided. "He must have really panicked."

Pollard was moved to the District of Columbia jail. The car and everything inside was confiscated as potential evidence—with the exception of Dusty. After some initial questioning, Anne was allowed to go home that evening.

"I will never forget the feeling I had leaving the embassy grounds," Pollard later said. "As I looked at the flag on our way out, all I could think of was the song played by the British as they marched out of Yorktown to surrender: 'The world turned upside down.' I was fully prepared—and still am—to give my life for that country, but not this way. What has been accomplished? Oh, I know the information got through and it must gall Caspar Weinberger to no end, but what of the human costs? I hate to say it, but the carnage was all avoidable if Eitan had simply taken the minimum precautions with my personal security."

CHAPTER NINE

Friendly Espionage

On the surface, the Pollard case never really appeared to make much sense. The United States and Israel, close friends, officially share a great deal of intelligence. Why risk that high degree of cooperation for the supposedly smaller amount of intelligence left unshared? Later, the claim would be made that Pollard's espionage activities on behalf of Israel had caused some of the most serious damage ever to U.S. national security, but the government, citing national security, publicly refused to provide specific details of that damage.

Former U.S. Under Secretary of State for Political Affairs Joseph Sisco would later insist that covert operations against each other are "absolutely unnecessary because the amount of cooperation" between the two countries is so strong. "Israel can get ninety-eight percent of what it wants, based on that cooperation," he said. "And whatever one might get from a Pollard-type operation is not worth it in terms of the overall relationship."

Yet nervous Israeli officials, living on a very thin margin of security and always worried about a worst-case threat, were not convinced of this logic. Cooperation—while significant—was by no means that complete. There were still many secrets which Washington, for one reason or another, refused to share with Israel. Neither side would share information that it felt could compromise what the intelligence professionals call "sources and methods"—namely, how that information was collected.

Bob Woodward, in his book on the late CIA director William Casey, explained this logic. He pointed out that the United States had penetrated Palestinian terrorist organizations. The CIA had secret PLO sources that "at times provided operational details about PLO attacks in Israel." But the United States did not share this information with Israel. In "some important respects," Woodward wrote, "Israel was more sinned against in intelligence matters." The CIA's Directorate of Operations had convinced Casey that "such information could not be passed to the Israelis, because the sources would dry up. It was a tough game, and Casey admired the way Israel accepted the rules: sources had to be protected at all costs. They were very sophisticated about this; they realized that an ally could not give everything."

But Pollard did not focus on that element of the relationship. "Imagine yourself sitting at a desk reading a report of an impending terrorist attack against an isolated Israeli outpost in the 'security strip' in southern Lebanon," Pollard would later write in a letter to me.

> Everything is known: the time, place, and method to be used. The assessment clearly states that Israeli casualties are expected to be heavy—perhaps a dozen dead and wounded. Your eyes drift to the bottom of the page where a checked box indicates that a warning notice will not be forwarded to the Israelis. When you contact a friend to discover what the basis for this decision is, you're told that "Sec Def" [Secretary of Defense] wants the Israelis out of the security strip and increased casualties will probably increase the pressure upon them to evacuate the area. So that's the "logic" you have to accept and try to live with as you watch the TV coverage of the subsequent burial ceremonies on Mt. Herzl [in Jerusalem]. Well, I simply got sick and tired

of standing idly by and observing Jews die just so Mr. Weinberger could tell his Saudi friends that he was doing everything he could to promote "stability in southern Lebanon."

For the most part, Israeli officials later said, the kind of information Pollard provided was collected through very sophisticated electronic means. Israel traditionally has been stronger in the "human" areas of intelligence collection—planting agents in foreign countries.

So, while the United States offered Israel a great deal of help, there was also a considerable body of information available that was held back—information which Pollard provided. And according to Israeli officials who justified the creation of the espionage ring in Washington, the information he made available to Israel was seen as absolutely crucial to the security of the state, especially in the event of another full-scale war with Syria.

Pollard carried documents detailing what he later described as "horrifying" threats facing Israel—for example, the existence of Syria's chemical and gas warfare factories. Pollard envisaged tens of thousands of Israelis—men, women, and children—wasted by a surprise Syrian assault. Weren't the Iraqis using poison gas against the Iranians, fellow Moslems? Could he simply shut his eyes to that kind of scenario?

"There's the reality of the intelligence analyst and there's the reality of Joe Citizen on the street," he said. "And if I were scared for Israel's survival when I was Joe Citizen on the street, not being fully aware of the true nature of the threat to Israel's survival, then being immersed in that kind of environment in the intelligence community exacerbated my concern. When you look at an airplane, the first thing you think is, 'My God, how the hell does that thing stay up?' And it was the same kind of experience of wonderment that I felt after looking at all the threats that Israel was facing: My God, how do they cope with it?"

In the real world, all countries spy, not only against their enemies but against their friends as well. The United States tries to intercept Israeli communications; it also takes satellite reconnaissance photographs of Israeli military installations.* American military attachés take pictures of restricted areas. American diplomats will try to learn other Israeli secrets. Israeli officials, in their own way, snoop around the United States as well.

A March 1979 Central Intelligence Agency report on Israel's intelligence services—discovered and circulated by Iranian revolutionaries at the ransacked U.S. Embassy in Teheran—suggested that Israel has long sought to use its contacts among various Jewish communities around the world to serve its interests. "The Israeli intelligence service depends heavily on the various Jewish communities and organizations abroad for recruiting agents and eliciting general information," the report stated.

> The aggressively ideological nature of Zionism, which emphasizes that all Jews belong to Israel and must return to Israel, has had its drawbacks in enlisting support for intelligence operations, however, since there is considerable opposition to Zionism among Jews throughout the world. Aware of this fact, Israeli intelligence representatives usually operate discreetly within Jewish communities and are under instructions to handle their missions with utmost tact to avoid embarrassment to Israel. They also attempt to penetrate anti-Zionist elements in order to neutralize the opposition. Despite such precautions, the Israelis frequently experience setbacks and there have been several cases where attempted recruitments of Americans of the Jewish faith have been rejected and reported to U.S. authorities.

---

*Pollard provided Israel with these pictures, which helped Israel develop more efficient "masking" or camouflaging techniques, including canvases to cover tanks and planes. He justified giving Israel these pictures by noting that the Soviet Union had similar reconnaissance capabilities. Israel could take countermeasures to confuse the Soviets.

John Davitt, former head of the Justice Department's Internal Security Section, would later tell *The Washington Post* that there had been a handful of cases during his thirty years in government service in which Israeli diplomats suspected of espionage were quietly asked to leave the country. But those occurred in the 1950s and 1960s, when the U.S.-Israeli relationship was by no means as strong as it later became.

Still, U.S. law enforcement officials have long suspected that Israel was playing fast and loose with the long-standing U.S.-Israeli understanding barring covert operations against each other. Yes, there is always some spying going on, even among very close friends and allies. But that is a far cry from actually planting a "mole" in a friendly country's intelligence community.

Thus, there is a huge difference between "unobtrusive" intelligence-gathering operations, on the one hand, and the actual running of paid spies in each other's country, on the other. There was supposed to be an unwritten rule that the United States would not use Israeli citizens to spy against Israel and Israel would not use American citizens to spy against the United States. But "walk-ins," U.S. and Israeli intelligence experts have confirmed, were not necessarily part of that rule. It was unrealistic to assume that these kinds of volunteers would be turned away, by either country—as Republican Senator David Durenberger of Minnesota, former chairman of the Senate Intelligence Committee, would later reveal. He said that CIA Director Casey had accepted an Israeli military walk-in during the war in Lebanon in 1982. It was the United States, Durenberger charged, that actually broke the rules of the game first, making it easier for Israel later to accept Pollard.

Still, there are limits within which friendly countries are supposed to operate. Durenberger was referring to a very modest, one-time incident, with no money changing hands. With Pollard, Israel would go way beyond those limits.

By all accounts, Pollard provided Israel with an enormous quantity of documents. The U.S. government maintained that the classified material compromised by Pollard was "immense in volume and far-reaching in scope, including thousands of pages of documents classified TOP SECRET and/or SCI." Many of these documents came from the Defense Intelligence Agency.

Israeli intelligence experts who are aware of Pollard's contribution would describe him as one of the most important spies in Israel's history. An Israeli intelligence official said that some of the information was "so breathtaking" that it did in fact seem to justify the extremely great risk Israel was taking in running an agent in Washington.

Yagur, according to Pollard, would often tell him, without exaggeration, that he was "a one-man intelligence agency" for Israel. In effect, what Pollard did was to make virtually the entire U.S. intelligence-gathering apparatus available to Israel, completing the picture in those areas where Israel's own knowledge was limited. The focus of Israel's interest, of course, was on its Arab adversaries and the Soviet Union, especially their military capabilities.

At a minimum, in terms of the voluminous information provided, Pollard was certainly the most productive. He dazzled his Israeli handlers with both the quantity and quality of intelligence he obtained. Leon H. Charney, a New York lawyer briefly involved in representing Pollard, and someone very close to several top Israeli leaders, would say that what Pollard did "for Israel's security is at the strongest level of anybody who has ever sacrificed his position for the Israeli cause. His help was clearly invaluable to the security of the State of Israel."

Pollard's other lawyers later stated that the information he provided fell into the following general categories: (1) the weapon systems of Arab countries; (2) the intelligence structures and capabilities of Arab countries; (3) daily message traffic concerning events in the Middle East; (4) analysis of Soviet weapon systems that would probably be delivered to Soviet client states in the Middle East; and (5) analysis of Arab leaders, political intentions, and governmental stability.

They insisted that he had imposed restrictions on the information provided to Israel. "He did not adopt the blind attitude that what was good for Israel was good for the United States. Rather, he realized that the interests of Israel and the United States occasionally diverged."

And, they added, "Pollard accordingly insisted, with the concurrence of the Israelis, that he would not divulge information concerning U.S. military or intelligence capabilities, or take any other action deemed to damage the U.S. national security."

Pollard had specifically refused Eitan's request for information regarding U.S. intelligence sources in Israel. "Eitan also demanded documents concerning U.S. knowledge of Israeli arms dealings with other countries, particularly China, and U.S. knowledge of Israeli intelligence efforts in the United States," the lawyers said. "Each time Mr. Pollard would not provide such documentation or information, despite Eitan's threats of recriminations."

Government papers confirmed that most of the documents obtained by Pollard were "detailed analytical studies containing technical calculations, graphs and satellite photographs." Other information included "highly classified message traffic and intelligence summaries," as well as data on "specific weapon systems." Specific documents dealt with the naval forces of certain Middle Eastern and North African countries; the port facilities of a Middle Eastern country; a study on naval mines and mine counterintelligence measures; a study on the lines of communication of a Middle Eastern country; a U.S. Army Intelligence survey of a Middle Eastern country; and a study of the Soviet/Warsaw Pact Heliborne jamming threat to NATO. At the request of the State Department, the government papers did not cite by name the specific Arab countries compromised. The papers referred only to Middle Eastern and North African countries.

Appreciating the value of the information Pollard provided Israel is the only way to truly understand why Israel found itself spying in Washington in the first place and taking such a chance. No sensible Israeli operative would have accepted such a risk if the prize were minor. The rewards had to outweigh the dangers. And Rafi Eitan, the masterspy running Pollard, was no lightweight.

Thus, any understanding of the Pollard affair can only come if details of the information he provided are known. In addition to the information that helped Israel to bomb the PLO headquarters in Tunis, Pollard gave Israel all sorts of other incredibly vital intelligence.

For example, he obtained the most exact U.S.-gathered information about Iraqi and Syrian chemical warfare production capabilities, including detailed satellite pictures and maps showing the location of factories and storage facilities. The United States did not want to make such specific information available to Israel, fearing a preemptive strike. It also feared that American "sources and methods" used to obtain such information could be compromised if it became available to Israel. The first documents Pollard gave Israel, and which so impressed his handlers, involved the details of Iraq's chemical warfare factories.

"With the Iraqis employing nerve agents with impunity in the Persian Gulf War," Pollard later said, "the Israelis were justifiably concerned about the Syrians' intentions to use such weapons on the Golan Heights—as it now seems likely they will. Needless to say, it takes years to prepare troops and civilian population centers to exist in this type of battlefield environment and the Israelis usually operate on a much shorter time frame than that."

Pollard also gave the Israelis the exact details on all Soviet arms shipments to Syria and other Arab states, including the specifics on the SS-21 ground-to-ground missiles and the SA-5 anti-aircraft missiles. Whenever the United States discovered that a Soviet ship was moving through the Bosphorus into the Mediterranean, Pollard passed that information to Israel. He also provided Israel with the U.S. intelligence community's most detailed assessment of the new Soviet MiG-29 fighter.

"It was my plan," he said, "to provide such information on the Arab powers and the Soviets that would permit the Israelis to avoid a repetition of the Yom Kippur War in which they were confronted with nothing less than a technological Pearl Harbor. Given the nature of Israeli defense planning, a situation comparable to 1973 will not be tolerated and, in the absence of reliable intelligence identifying the actual capabilities of newly introduced Eastern bloc equipment, could result in a very destructive preventive war."

For a country like Israel, "which is acutely sensitive to casualties, constrained by limited resources and saddled with highly vulnerable borders," Pollard continued, "the appearance of a new enemy weapon system on the frontier could mean the difference between a quick surgical campaign and a Pyrrhic victory. Therefore, the earlier Israeli military planners know the technical parameters of a given system, the faster they can apportion scarce funds to determine suitable countermeasures, many of which are subsequently turned over to the United States for its own use."

Pollard said that the key for Israel's defense was "to have a sufficiently long lead time for the various research establishments, production plants, intelligence agencies, and operations bureaus to create the requisite hardware and applicable tactics needed to defeat, say, a new Soviet surface-to-air [SAM] system."

He acknowledged that the United States routinely shares a great deal of highly classified information with Israel, particularly on these kinds of weapons. But, according to Pollard, "the information is not detailed enough to allow the Israelis to truly understand the nature of the future threat facing them. Without this type of information, there could be a possibility that the Israeli Air Force might not have indisputable command of the air in the opening days of a war on the Golan Heights, and with distances so short to Israeli population centers, ground forces would have to be left alone to fight costly blocking actions until that time when the air force could decisively intervene.

"For this reason," Pollard added, "much of the material I passed to the Israelis concerned both current and projected Soviet SAM technology, its associated electronic warfare devices and command/control/communications systems."

He noted, for example, that he was congratulated by

Yagur after an Israeli drone, or unmanned reconnaissance aircraft, had been able to "successfully negotiate its way through the entire Syrian air defense system in 1985." Yagur said that this remarkable achievement was possible only because of the information Pollard had provided.

It was the Soviet-Syrian alignment that was uppermost on Pollard's mind throughout the operation. "Of all the threats which Israel is currently facing," he said, "those represented by the Soviets and their Syrian allies are by far the greatest due to the unpredictable nature of the Assad regime and the publicly acknowledged promise made by Moscow to guarantee Syria's strategic parity with Israel. The undisclosed objective of that parity, though, is to allow the Syrian armed forces to mount an unannounced 'standing start' offensive, designed to wrest control of the Golan Heights and Galilee before the Israelis can mobilize. At the very least, the information I provided the Israelis should permit them to cope with most of the all-important Soviet air defense weaponry that the Syrians are relying upon to provide their invasion forces with a mobile umbrella against Israeli air attack."

Assuming that Israel could quickly neutralize those Syrian air defenses, Pollard said, the Syrian attack could be contained as close to the border as possible.

He recalled that those same Syrian anti-aircraft missiles had shot two U.S. Navy jets "out of the sky" during the U.S. involvement in Lebanon. Those missiles, he added, "are the main reason why the current administration would avoid retaliating against Damascus even if the 'smoking gun' of a terrorist incident could be traced back to Mr. Assad's office."

In the event the U.S. Sixth Fleet in the Mediterranean required Israeli assistance for additional air support against the Soviets or the Syrians, Pollard said, "it's going to be very thankful that the Israeli Air Force will be able to handle the threat environment—without the waste of time associated with 'losing a few planes' first."

Pollard did not limit the information he collected to the Soviet Union, Syria, and the PLO. He collected documents on other potential threats facing Israel, including from Pakistan. Specifically, he gave the Israelis information about

Pakistan's program to build an atomic bomb, including huge satellite photographs of its nuclear reactor facility outside Islamabad. An accompanying U.S. intelligence study described in some length a scenario involving an Israeli air strike—along the lines of the Israeli raid against the Iraqi reactor. United States reconnaissance photography has taken incredibly detailed pictures of the Pakistani plant— pictures that are now in Israel's possession.

"Apart from Syria," Pollard said, "I also provided the Israelis with critical strategic information pertaining to their outer ring of enemies: namely, Libya, Algeria, Iraq, and Pakistan. The threats represented by these 'rejectionist front' states are no less real than those from Syria."

He was genuinely surprised by the extent of Israel's needs: "It taught me a very good lesson about how the popularly held perceptions of Israel's intelligence collection capabilities can be totally misleading. They are by no means an all-knowing giant straddling the Middle East, and have been forced to concentrate their best human and technical assets against Syria, which represents the most immediate threat to their survival." Pollard added that as he slowly began to "appreciate the fact that I was providing the bulk of the information reaching Israel on its distant opponents, the magnitude of their precarious position dawned on me."

Pollard also was asked by his Israeli handlers to provide information that could benefit several of Israel's own defense projects, including the feasibility of developing a small trans-atmospheric reconnaissance platform. In addition, he was asked to suggest which arms might prove effective in protecting Iran's Kharg Island oil loading installation from Iraqi air attack.

He had also prepared a lengthy letter to Yagur describing various missile systems designed or manufactured by various non-Communist countries that might be available for sale to Iran, including the French system sold to South Africa known as CACTUS. This letter would later come back to play a very special role in haunting Pollard.

Pollard defended his decision to help the Israelis in learning about potential arms sales to Iran. He acknowledged that

Iran's "clerical leadership is adamantly opposed to Israel's existence." But he still maintained that "the defeat of the Iranian armed forces in the current Persian Gulf War would leave Iraq free to redeploy a large number of units either to the Golan Heights or Jordan River Valley, thereby compounding the threat to Israel's eastern border.

"Put in more biblical terms," Pollard continued, "Israel's interest in Iran's continued viability is a modern-day version of 'the enemy of my enemy is my friend.' Although this line of reasoning may not, on first sight, seem acceptable to many Americans, who are accustomed to a more idealistic foreign policy, it is a little-known tenet of U.S. strategic policy that the territorial integrity of Iran must be maintained so as to prevent a vacuum from arising, which could facilitate a Soviet advance to the Indian Ocean.

"I'm sure Churchill no more enjoyed dealing with Stalin during the Second World War than I did recommending appropriate defense armaments for Iran, but the logic of realpolitik often requires a person to choose between the lesser of two evils. For me, the need to keep the Iraqi regime preoccupied fighting a militarily strong Iran on a battlefield far removed from the Israeli frontier was paramount if the delicate strategic balance between Damascus and Jerusalem were to be maintained."

Thus, he sought to place the letter to Yagur into some sort of context. "Israel is committed to maintaining Iran's conventional military capabilities in order to assure a stalemate in the Persian Gulf War," he maintained. "Since the U.S. has repeatedly warned Israel in the past against openly shipping arms to Iran, the Israelis have very conveniently delegated this activity to trusted private brokers, who can also be repudiated if exposed."

"Uzi" had been assigned to that project, according to Pollard. Specifically, by the fall of 1985, the Iranians needed to defend their Kharg Island facility from Iraq's numerous air strikes. "My suggestions were solicited as to how that objective could be realized, given the fact that I was in the best position to know exactly what weapons the Iraqi Air Force was using to interdict the oil-loading complex."

Pollard also gave the Israelis a considerable amount of U.S.-collected intelligence on what are considered the more moderate Arab states—Egypt, Jordan, Saudi Arabia, and others. He described those states as "latent threats to Israel which no amount of propaganda to the contrary can alter."

Thus, he charged that despite Egypt's peace treaty with Israel, "the Egyptian General Staff is still calculating how best to fight a war in the desert wasteland of the Sinai Peninsula." And the Saudis, he added, have been involved in an "incredible expansion" of their Tabuk military-industrial complex, not far from Israel's southern port of Eilat. Moreover, the Saudis have been providing the Syrians "with over ninety percent of the hard currency" needed to purchase arms from the Soviet Union.

"However," Pollard continued, "no information was provided that either dealt with joint U.S.-Egyptian or U.S.-Saudi military exercises, diplomatic agreements, or secret military contingency plans."

Perhaps the most important single document Pollard provided to Israel consisted of a lengthy, extremely sensitive U.S. handbook on communications intelligence that had been his handlers' number one priority in obtaining. It was this handbook, the Israelis believed, that would help them win the next war. The United States had no intention of ever sharing it with Israel or any other country because that could endanger the future collection of that kind of intelligence. If Israel knew what was in the handbook, U.S. officials said, it would undertake certain actions that would almost certainly signal to hostile powers that the United States had penetrated their most sensitive communications. In effect, the handbook virtually allowed Israel to spy almost anywhere it wanted.

"In the final analysis," Pollard maintained, "the value of the material I provided the Israelis actually goes far beyond the immediate tactical advantage it will confer upon their field commanders: by giving high-level Israeli defense planners a detailed look at the nature of their future threat environment, it permits the country's political leadership to articulate an external policy based on certainties rather than debatable risks."

He further rationalized his activity by convincing himself that he was actually promoting peace. Israel's military advantage, he said, "would tend to work as a stimulant for the peace process since no responsible Israeli government could ever consider yielding valuable territory unless it had an accurate assessment of what the potential loss to the nation's military security would be from such a decision. . . . I am satisfied that what I did will hasten the day that peace can be reached in the region because without much of the information I provided, the Israeli military establishment would be less inclined to trust the assurances of its own political leadership, let alone those of a traditional enemy."

PART TWO

The Prisoner

CHAPTER TEN

Embittered, Disappointed, and Befuddled

Sitting in jail, Pollard was still dumbfounded about the scene at the Israeli Embassy. Why had they kicked him out? Rafi Eitan had repeatedly assured him that Israel would rescue him if the operation were ever compromised. "Why Rafi lied to me in this regard is beyond my powers of comprehension," Pollard would later say. "Instead of running when I had a chance, I purposely dissembled in order to assure the escape of Avi and redirect the focus of FBI suspicion onto other diplomatic establishments, thereby guaranteeing the departure of Yagur and Ravid. I did everything I was supposed to do. It just never dawned on me that I was to act as an expendable rear guard since the fundamental rule of such affairs is to pull the agent out of harm's way as quickly as possible."

During that first post-arrest interrogation, Pollard acknowledged that his written statements of November 19 and 20—the previous Tuesday and Wednesday—were correct insofar as the operational details were concerned. He thus confirmed the nature of the documents he had compromised, the timing and frequency of the unauthorized deliveries, and the amount of monthly compensation he had received. But he admitted that the person to whom he had been selling the documents for more than a year was not Kurt Lohbeck, the American friend he had earlier named. He acknowledged that he had falsely identified Lohbeck so as to throw the agents off the real trail.

At that first post-arrest session, Pollard also admitted that he sought to evade further questioning and ultimate arrest by obtaining asylum at the embassy. He explained that as a Jew, he expected to be routinely granted asylum under Israel's Law of Return, and was astonished when the embassy security personnel refused to admit him and his wife. Despite persistent questioning, however, he steadfastly refused to provide the nationality, let alone the names, of the persons to whom he had been providing the information.

Pollard would also not disclose the whereabouts of classified documents he had removed from his office, or reveal the location to which he had delivered them, except to state that the documents kept in the suitcase in his apartment had been delivered to his "contact," and then copied and returned to him. He would only provide a one-word response when asked by the agents if he had ever provided classified information to a representative of the Israeli government. "Yes," he said.

But according to government documents, this affirmative response "did not materially advance the agents' investigation since Pollard had on two occasions served as a member of U.S. teams who met with their Israeli counterparts for the authorized exchange of information and documents." Even after being kicked out of the embassy, Pollard, embittered, disappointed, and befuddled, was still trying to protect Israel.

"Assumptions acquired over the course of a lifetime do not simply vanish overnight and I kept believing, in spite of all the evidence to the contrary, that we would not be abandoned," Pollard later said.

Still, he was beginning to lose faith. In the back of his mind were the other Israeli spies who had been arrested elsewhere and sent to jail for many years. He knew of the ill-fated Lavon affair in 1954, when Israeli agents in Cairo were captured following their efforts to plant bombs in U.S. and British installations there. Defense Minister Pinchas Lavon was blamed by some in Israel for the mishap. The Israelis, using Egyptian Jews in the operation, had sought to undermine Egyptian President Gamal Abdel Nasser's relationship with Washington and London by giving the impression that the Egyptian regime could not protect their interests.

Pollard later said that he was also aware of the Israeli espionage operation in Switzerland in 1968 to obtain the plans for the French-made Mirage jet fighter. Israel subsequently used those plans to help in the development of its own Kfir jet fighter. But a Swiss engineer, Alfred Frauenknecht, who was working with the Israelis in the smuggling operation, was eventually captured by Swiss authorities and sent to prison for several years.

"I knew about the Lavon scandal and what happened to Alfred Frauenknecht, but I convinced myself that these were nothing more than aberrations which would certainly never be repeated," Pollard said. "When I walked into that first interrogation on November 19 and began my 'confession' as an agent for Pakistani military intelligence, I began to appreciate how the kamikaze pilots felt just before they crashed into their targets. It's an unearthly feeling that sweeps over someone who voluntarily puts his own head on the block for a cause greater than himself. In a sense, I'd spent the past eighteen months creating elaborate cover stories as a prelude to the grandest one of all."*

---

*Pollard would later clarify this in a letter to me. "I want to be very clear. I do *not* believe the operation was a mistake" (the word "not" was underlined). "Given the dangers it set out to neutralize, the affair was an essential undertaking. Assuming a proper escape plan had been developed the risks of exposure would have been reduced to truly acceptable levels." Clearly bitter, Pollard wrote of "the criminally inadequate measures taken with regard to guaranteeing my security in the event of exposure."

When I was subsequently told to come to the embassy, I couldn't believe my ears since that was sure to undo everything I'd been able to establish over the preceding two days of rather "unfriendly" interrogation. It was at that point that I realized the whole affair was coming apart at the seams since one hand obviously did not know what the other was doing. Making matters worse, there was no alternative for me at that moment since I had already sealed my fate as a spy.

Despite the fact you may doubt this, believe me when I say my skin literally began to crawl when the full understanding of what was occurring dawned on me.

During that incredibly tense day, Pollard was especially worried about Anne. "The only person I was concerned about then was Anne because she was supposed to accompany me to the embassy and if that gambit failed, she would be inexorably sucked into a vortex not of her own making. She could have left the country with Avi but decided to stay behind because she felt her place was by my side, despite the risks this posed to herself. Leaving aside the fact that she was the one responsible for saving Avi's neck, the Israelis knew how precarious her state of health was and still those bastards let her rot in prison for three months without any medical treatment. They could have at least told the Americans that she had never been part of the operation and that her release was therefore appropriate on humanitarian grounds. I have no doubt that any such appeal would have fallen on deaf ears but at least an attempt could have been made on her behalf.

"I'm confident that if the Israelis had told me that it was impossible to rescue me because no plan had, in fact, been organized by Rafi for such a contingency but that they were predisposed to take Anne [forcefully] out of the country, I would have gone ahead and pulled the temple down about my head. It's not that I'm a martyr, just that I understand there are some moments when an individual has to place the interests of his state ahead of himself. But this type of choice need not have faced me had Rafi shown even a minimal degree of concern for my security. What could he have been thinking?"

From the very start, Pollard recalled, he had repeatedly warned of flaws in the operation. But Eitan did nothing to correct them. "I pointed this out to him constantly during the course of the operation with regard to the money I couldn't recycle, the trips I couldn't explain, the hotels we were told to stay in which were clearly beyond our means, the credit cards he insisted we use despite their obvious disadvantage, and the volume of material he wanted that had me running around the city like a chicken with its head cut off. And, lest we forget it, a Swiss bank account which I never asked for and never expected to use. What the hell did he think he was doing? This was not supposed to be a suicide mission, but even if it had been, I have this gut feeling my 'L' pill would have turned out to be a placebo!"

Within hours after Pollard's arrest, FBI agents obtained a search warrant to open the suitcase Anne had asked her neighbors to retrieve. Special Agent Noltkamper and an Assistant U.S. Attorney had brought their affidavit to the court, and the warrant was routinely approved.

The suitcase was found to contain twenty-five classified documents relating to national defense, including one stamped TOP SECRET. It also contained drafts and copies of a letter from Pollard to "Yossi" that recited certain classified information which Pollard had obtained—namely, the missile systems designed or manufactured by various non-Communist countries, which might be available for sale to Iran, including one known as CACTUS. This letter was actually drafted shortly after the United States and Israel began their own covert arms-for-hostages negotiations with Iran. Israel had already received President Ronald Reagan's permission to sell U.S.-made TOW anti-tank and HAWK anti-aircraft missiles to Iran. Israel did not need to receive American authority to sell Iran non-U.S.-made weapons.

The search of the suitcase began Thursday afternoon and continued late into the night. "It is notable," the government later stated,

> that the search of a container in a foreign counterintelligence case, particularly one containing 15 to 18 inches of classified documents, cannot be hastily performed. A searching agent cannot merely leaf through the documents looking for clues; the documents must be carefully handled with gloves and separately packaged so as not to disturb other physical evidence which may be present, such as fingerprints or microdots. Moreover, if the agents searching the suitcase on Thursday night had simply paged through the documents, the significance of code words like "cactus" would not have been apparent.

The agents involved in the search, while clearly experienced in these matters, were not the same ones who had earlier questioned Pollard. The searching agents therefore did not—in the words of court documents—"have the collective knowledge of all other agents who had been involved in the investigation, nor could this be expected in an investigation which involved literally scores of agents."

Jerry Agee, who had not slept in days, was ordered to try to recreate exactly what information Pollard may have had access to and what he may have passed. This was part of the so-called damage assessment operation. Other officers were assigned to an exhausted and drained Agee to help with the collection of information. "I was working very long hours," Agee later said.

As ostensibly bizarre as his original suspicion was—that Israel was the country involved in the espionage operation—Agee had been proven right.

On that same Thursday afternoon, Pollard was brought before a U.S. Magistrate for the District of Columbia, Patrick J. Attridge. An Assistant U.S. Attorney, Harry R. Benner, represented the government. Gordon Coffee, who worked with Richard Hibey, represented Pollard. A stunned Dr. Morris Pollard, upon learning that his son had been arrested earlier that day, had frantically asked a friend at the Notre Dame Law School to recommend a good criminal lawyer in Washington. Hibey's name came up. He, in turn, sent Coffee to that first hearing because he was in California on other business.

"I received a call from Anne saying that they needed an attorney right away," Dr. Pollard recalled. She told him that his son had been arrested for espionage—"It hit me like a bolt of lightning." He immediately flew to Washington to see what was going on.

Attridge, who convened the hearing in a small, crowded courtroom, asked the clerk to swear in Pollard. He stood in front of the judge, clearly nervous, his voice barely audible and cracking.

"Will you tell us your full name for the record, please?" the judge asked.

"Jonathan Jay Pollard."

The judge then asked a series of routine questions about any disabilities Pollard might have that would prevent him from understanding the hearings. Pollard said he had none. The judge asked whether Pollard was under the influence of any drugs. "No," Pollard replied.

Attridge then informed Pollard that the purpose of the hearing was simply to advise him of his rights. A preliminary hearing would be arranged, "at which time the government will have to produce evidence to show that there's probable cause that this crime you have been charged with was committed and probable cause it was committed by you."

Pollard listened, shaking his head. His hands were folded. He could not believe what was happening in his life.

"Now," the judge continued, "you have been advised that you've been charged with a violation of Title XVIII, Section 794 (a) of the United States Code in that during November of 1985 within the District of Columbia you, with intent and reason to believe that it was used to the advantage of a foreign nation, did communicate and deliver to a foreign government directly or indirectly documents, writings, and information relating to the national defense.

"If convicted of a violation of that section, the penalties are death, imprisonment for any term of years or for life."

Pollard grimaced when he heard that last sentence.

"You also have been charged with a violation of Title XVIII, Section 793 (e) of the United States Code, which makes it unlawful to possess any documents and writings relating to the national defense and wilfully retain the same and fail to deliver them to the officer or employee of the United States entitled to receive them.

"If convicted of a violation of this section, the penalties are a maximum fine of up to $10,000, imprisonment for up to ten years, or both."

Attridge then asked Pollard a series of additional questions to determine whether he should be released on bail. "I want to remind you and caution you that you are under oath," he said.

Pollard was asked to state his address, his marital status,

his employment, his place of birth, his education. He was also asked whether he had ever been arrested. He said he had not. He replied in a soft but steady voice.

At that point, the judge asked Benner, the Assistant U.S. Attorney, to spell out the government's case against Pollard. Benner recommended that Pollard be denied bail.

"Your honor," he said, "with respect to the question of bond, the government is going to ask that Mr. Pollard be detained, both because he is a danger to the community and because there's a serious risk of flight in this case. In addition to the fact that he is charged with an offense for which he could receive up to life imprisonment, your honor, our information is that Mr. Pollard has traveled twice this year outside of the United States.

"By his own admissions, he is in possession of a large amount of money that he received as payment for the activities mentioned in the complaint. And there are other facts that we think would justify the court in detaining Mr. Pollard so that we have a detention hearing at the earliest convenience of the court and of the parties."

The judge agreed—Pollard would not be released on bail. He set the preliminary hearing for the following Wednesday.

Pollard was escorted out of the courtroom and returned to D.C. jail, where he wept. His mind continued to dwell on his expulsion from the embassy. Why? he repeatedly asked himself. He had no answer.

Joseph E. diGenova, the U.S. Attorney for the District of Columbia, when asked that same day by reporters about the nature of the documents obtained by Pollard, replied: "He has been charged with espionage. This was not the list of lunchtime attendees at the Press Club. The documents were highly classified."

Elyakim Rubinstein, the number two diplomat at the Israeli Embassy in Washington, was summoned by Under Secretary of State for Political Affairs Michael H. Armacost later that evening to come to the seventh floor of the State Department, where he was questioned about Israel's association with Pollard. The Israeli Ambassador, Meir Rosenne, was in Paris delivering a lecture. Rubinstein said he did not know anything about Pollard or the alleged espionage operation. He said the Israeli government was looking into the matter on an urgent basis.

On Friday, November 22, FBI agents obtained warrants to search the 1980 Mustang, the Pollards' apartment, and the bag and purse which Anne had carried to the embassy. They were delayed somewhat in their investigation when a frantic agent assigned to conduct surveillance on Anne called headquarters from the District of Columbia jail, where she had gone to visit her husband. The agent, according to court documents, reported that a bondsman at the jail was attempting to arrange the release of Pollard on bail—despite the magistrate's ruling the day before. "Considerable time and manpower," the government later said, "was expended in an effort to prevent Jonathan Pollard's release." Agents notified the court chambers and the Department of Corrections. But if they failed to keep him in jail, they planned around-the-clock surveillance on Pollard. "Needless to say," the government later disclosed, "this apparent crisis, which was finally resolved without incident by the Department of Corrections, delayed the analysis of the evidence."

Dr. Pollard would later say that he, too, was initially alarmed when he discovered shortly after his arrival in Washington that arrangements were being made to get his son released on bail. "I felt that this was wrong," the father said, "because who knows who's behind the release? They could release him so that he could get out and get killed." He said that there was "something screwy" going on, and, ironically, he was actually relieved when his son was denied bail.

It was not until the next day, Friday afternoon, November 22, that the agents, together with several assistant U.S. attorneys, could sit down to review the evidence involving the documents found in the suitcase.

Later that night, FBI and NIS agents searched the Pollard apartment again. Four additional classified documents and notations were discovered from hidden locations. They had been overlooked by the Pollards the previous Wednesday evening when they were preparing their escape. The apartment revealed what the government later described as "clear evidence" of the Pollards' intent to abandon it, including three large bags containing hand-shredded personal papers, letters, notes, and U.S. government documents.

Anne and her father-in-law—both deeply confused and pained by what was unfolding in their lives—spent most of that Friday trying to win permission to visit Pollard in jail. But because her purse and its contents had been confiscated, she had no identification papers, such as her driver's license, required to enter the jail. She needed identification with a picture to get into that jail. Eventually, however, she returned to her apartment and found her passport, which she used to see him that day.

Later that evening, she and Dr. Pollard had dinner in the drab cafeteria at D.C. General Hospital, near the jail. They could hardly eat. She recounted in very general terms some of the extraordinary events of recent months. He could not believe what he heard. They whispered, knowing that they were being watched. As they walked out, two FBI agents approached her.

"Anne Pollard?" the taller one asked in a low voice.

"Yes," she said. "Who are you?"

"We're with the FBI. You're under arrest," he said, reading her her rights.

Dr. Pollard, a short man with a sweet and reassuring presence, grimaced. He tried—unsuccessfully—to intervene. She was handcuffed and sent to the District of Columbia jail.

The next day Superior Court Judge Rufus King ruled that Anne could be held without bail until a preliminary hearing could be arranged for Monday, November 25. She would spend the weekend in jail. Her roommates were some of Washington's veteran prostitutes and drug dealers, who taunted her nonstop.

On that same Friday, the State Department's spokesman, Charles Redman, told reporters at the daily news briefing: "We are shocked and saddened at the notion that something like this might occur. We have been in touch with the Israelis to try and get to the bottom of this. We don't have all the facts."

Republican Senator David F. Durenberger, chairman of the Senate Select Committee on Intelligence, released a statement which said: "This treacherous and traitorous act by a trusted employee motivated simply by money is appalling. It once again reinforces the need for immediate action on the numerous proposals for improvement in counterintelligence that are under consideration in the administration and before our committee."

In Jerusalem, the Foreign Ministry's spokesman, Avi Pazner, stated that the Israeli government had no knowledge of Pollard. "We don't have the slightest idea about this matter," he said. "We are checking that story and after we find out what the facts are, then and only then will there be an official reaction."

Late Friday afternoon, Minister Without Portfolio Moshe Arens, a former Israeli Ambassador in Washington, went to the State Department for a previously scheduled meeting with Secretary of State George Shultz. Arens was accompanied by David Matnai, the Israeli Embassy's political counselor, and Yossi Gal, the embassy's press spokesman. Rubinstein, an Orthodox Jew, did not want to drive Friday evening—after the start of the Jewish Sabbath.

Arens and Shultz had developed a close personal friendship during the Israeli's tenure in Washington. Arens had served as Defense Minister in the spring of 1984, when Pollard first established contact with Sella.

Near the end of their meeting, Shultz raised the question of the Pollard affair.

"Misha," Shultz said, calling Arens by his nickname, "I must discuss another issue with you." He expressed his deep dismay in learning about Pollard's association with Israel.

"I am no less amazed than you," replied Arens, proposing that they wait until they obtain all the facts before reacting to the case.

Shultz said President Ronald Reagan had also been puzzled, having painfully asked the Secretary on their return flight aboard Air Force One to Washington from the U.S.-Soviet summit in Geneva: "Why are they doing it?"

Arens would tell reporters when he returned to Israel two days later that he had failed to ease American concerns. "It will take time for the smoke to clear," he said. "We have a problem here and it is important that we solve it. I don't think we have succeeded in calming the situation."

Later that Friday, the Foreign Ministry revised its position when it released this statement:

> Israel's political leadership received with shock and consternation the reports from Washington according to which an employee of the U.S. Navy was accused of espionage for Israel. Actions of this kind in the United States stand in total contradiction to the policy of the Israeli government. It is Israel's policy to refrain from any intelligence activity related to the United States, in view of the close and special relations of friendship prevailing between the two countries. A thorough examination is being undertaken to determine whether there has been a deviation of any kind from this policy. Should such a deviation be found to have occurred, then necessary conclusions will be drawn.

A former chief of the Mossad, Isser Harel, was asked by the Israeli newspaper *Ha'aretz* whether it would be possible for espionage activity to have taken place out of the Washington Embassy without high-level authorization from Jerusalem. "Theoretically this is possible, even though as a rule activity such as this is not carried out without directives from above," he replied.

On Monday, Anne Henderson Pollard, having spent three days in jail, came before Magistrate Patrick Attridge. James Hibey (Richard Hibey's brother) represented her. Charles Leeper, a no-nonsense Assistant U.S. Attorney, represented the government. She was sworn in and asked the same routine questions her husband had been asked the previous

Thursday. When she was asked her full name, she replied: "Anne Henderson Pollard." She noted that she did not have any sight or hearing disabilities, but her lawyer reported that she was taking a certain prescription medication. She said "No" when asked whether it would have any effect on her ability to understand the proceedings.

"Now," the judge said, "you've been charged with a violation of Title XVIII, Section 793 (e) of the United States Code which, in substance, is unauthorized possession and transmission of classified defense documents. If convicted, the penalties are: a maximum fine of $10,000, maximum imprisonment of up to ten years, or both."

The judge asked Leeper whether the government had a position on the matter of pre-trial release.

"Yes, your honor," he replied. "We're requesting that the hearing be scheduled for Wednesday."

"That the same time as the husband, Mr. Pollard?" the judge asked.

"Yes, sir."

"All right, Mr. Hibey?"

"Your honor," Hibey replied, "for the record, my name is James Hibey. I represent Mrs. Pollard. We will enter a plea of not guilty and request preliminary hearing and we'll be prepared for the hearing on Wednesday."

"Anything further at this time?" Attridge asked.

"There has been a bit of a problem at the jail in the sense that, as she indicated, she takes prescription medicine for some health problems that she has, and she's been unable to receive it at the jail thus far," Hibey said, going on to ask that she be allowed to take her medicine. "Without it," he continued, "she can't eat, and she hasn't eaten, so it's imperative that she be given that medicine."

"Mr. Leeper?" the judge asked.

"No objection, subject to the doctor's approval, of course," he replied.

"All right," the judge agreed. He ruled that a physician at D.C. General Hospital interview Anne "for the purposes of corroborating her need for prescription medication. . . . In the meantime, defendant is held without bond."

The small courtroom of the U.S. District Court for the District of Columbia was packed with reporters, network artists, and others on Wednesday afternoon, November 27, when Magistrate Attridge called the preliminary hearing into session. Leeper, this time, was joined by David Geneson, another Assistant U.S. Attorney. Both Hibey brothers were present as well.

Pollard, wearing a brown suit, pink dress shirt, and matching tie, was brought into the courtroom—as was his wife, who wore a simple purple and black dress. The room was silent. They were seated next to their lawyers when Attridge asked the government to call its first witness, FBI Special Agent Eugene Noltkamper, who was sworn in.

"I'm assigned to the Washington field office," he said, as he began to answer Leeper's questions. "I'm assigned to the Foreign Counterintelligence Squad." He said that he had worked for the FBI for fourteen years—the last two on the Squad.

Noltkamper stated that the FBI and the Naval Investigative Service were jointly involved in the investigation of the defendants. He said that Pollard, in the course of his work, had access to "documents relating to national defense."

Under fast-paced grilling, Noltkamper said that Pollard was picked up for initial questioning on November 18. He was carrying an envelope containing national security documents which were so sensitive that they required "a specific safe, and also that there be twenty-four-hour guard service or alarm service."

The FBI man said that the approximately sixty documents in the envelope focused on the weapons capabilities of foreign countries, which he did not name. He had been briefed in advance not to name names of foreign countries, lest some sort of diplomatic crisis erupt.

Noltkamper said that the documents involved "the intelligence-gathering capabilities of foreign countries."

Speaking in short, crisp phrases, he then described Pollard's two phone calls to his wife, using the codeword "cactus" to get her to remove the classified documents from the house. He recounted her efforts to convince the neighbors to help. "She wanted them delivered to her at a hotel where she would then burn them." A search later revealed that those documents involved information on both U.S. and foreign military capabilities, he said.

Noltkamper pointed out that neither Anne nor the neighbors were authorized to see those documents, which had "a cover sheet, which is bright red, saying TOP SECRET."

He then recalled the Pollards' effort to enter the embassy. "A diplomatic vehicle was going into the compound, through the gate, and the Mustang followed it through."

"What happened to the gates at that time, sir?" the Assistant U.S. Attorney asked.

"They closed."

The agent described the scene at the embassy. He noted that Pollard, after his arrest, had told the FBI that he had called the embassy and was told that "if he could shake his surveillance, to come on in." Pollard knew he was under surveillance but still decided to make his break.

During that interview, Noltkamper continued, Pollard also acknowledged that he had previously disclosed national security secrets for about eighteen months. Asked whether Pollard admitted receiving payment, the agent replied: "He was paid $2,500 per month, plus he received two trips to Europe."

Noltkamper went on to quote Pollard as saying that the documents discovered in the suitcase had been delivered to Israel for copying and were going to be returned to his office "because he had signed out for them, and charged out with them."

Leeper, a tough, even mean-looking prosecutor who gives the impression that he simply does not know how to smile, then directed his questions to the FBI agent on Anne. In the process, Noltkamper said that when Anne was finally arrested, she had her passport in her purse. His implication, of course, was that she was planning to flee the country.

But her lawyer, James Hibey, explained why she had her passport; it was the only piece of identification she had left with a photograph of herself on it. She needed it to gain entry into the jail. Hibey also insisted that there was nothing "sinister" in her contacts with the Chinese Embassy. Together with other executives of a New York-based public relations firm, she was simply trying to win a media training contract from the Chinese. There was, Hibey said, "a very innocent explanation" for Anne's "presentation that was made at the Chinese Embassy."

"They've made no sinister insinuations," the judge said. "The testimony is that she had unauthorized classified documents on her person, and furthermore, she had them in a bag under the stairs or something, or a suitcase under the stairs, and asked somebody else to take them. The other area—about the Chinese Embassy—is not that important at this stage, as far as I'm concerned."

James Hibey, who has a high-pitched voice, called Anne's doctor, Herbert Moscovitz, to testify about her health. He described the procedure he performed on her that previous Thursday morning, November 21. Under questioning from the judge, Dr. Moscovitz said that she had been "drowsy" when she left the hospital that morning. "She might be somewhat slow in response, but she would be oriented as to time, place, and circumstances," he added.

Dr. Morris Pollard was called to testify later in the hearing. Magistrate Attridge questioned him about his relationship with his daughter-in-law. "How long have you known your daughter-in-law?" he asked.

"About four years."

"Under what circumstances have you met her in the past?"

"Well, they came up to visit us on one occasion and I would meet her whenever we'd come to Washington."

"And on how many occasions did you come to Washington and visit them, within the last four years?"

"Oh," Dr. Pollard replied, "I would say once every four months, perhaps."

"And what were the circumstances that you met her on those occasions?"

"We had dinner."

"Would that be at their home, or at a restaurant?"

"No. At a restaurant."

"At a restaurant?"

"On one occasion we had dinner in the home."

Later during the questioning, the judge asked Dr. Pollard how he had come to feel about Anne. "I don't know how to explain it, how to answer that," he replied. "I know her. I respect her. I've developed an affection for her."

Under questioning from James Hibey, Dr. Pollard maintained that Anne, if released on bail, would not flee the District of Columbia. "I've very sure that she would not," he said.

But the Assistant U.S. Attorney, in arguing that she should be denied bail, recalled that even after her husband had been arrested she was still planning to travel to New Jersey that following day on previously scheduled business. He pointed out that Dr. Pollard had arrived in Washington on Thursday, shortly after receiving word that his son had been arrested. "And on Friday you went to the D.C. jail with the defendant Anne Henderson Pollard?" he asked Dr. Pollard.

"Correct," Dr. Pollard replied.

"That Friday morning she was still considering a trip that she described as a business trip?"

"That's correct."

Anne's father, Bernard Henderson, was then called to testify. He confirmed that he had advised her to make the trip to New Jersey. "I'd been aware of that trip for some time," he said in response to questioning from James Hibey.

"How are you aware of it?"

"I'm aware of it because one of the principals in the corporation is a friend of mine and we had discussed the trip and discussed the advisability of Anne going on that trip. We did so by telephone, and also in person at a meeting with the principals, recently."

"And you discussed it with Anne as well?"

"Discussed it with Anne as well."

"Did you talk to Anne on Friday, the past Friday, November 22, about the trip?"

"Yes. I telephoned Anne from Los Angeles, and that trip came up during the conversation."

"Did you advise her with respect to whether she should make the trip or not?"

"I advised her to make the trip because I felt the trip was

important to the continuance of her career in public relations."

"If Mrs. Pollard is released, will she leave the District of Columbia?"

"I don't believe she will, because in that same conversation, I suggested to Anne that she might want to come and stay with me in Pennsylvania for a while, and she said, 'No, Dad. My place is here in Washington.'"

Later during the hearing, Richard Hibey stated that he was not asking that his client be released on bail. "Your honor," Hibey said, "I am prepared to state to the court at this time that there will be no argument made on behalf of Mr. Pollard on the question of either probable cause or bond, so I think all counsel need do is address his case against Mrs. Pollard."

James Hibey insisted that his client—Anne—be released. Leeper argued the opposite. He said she might in fact attempt to flee, and recalled her effort to gain entry into the Israeli Embassy with "multiple, numerous family photographs, the heirloom type, beginning with photographs of when she and her husband were small children until the present time." He maintained that "the risk of flight, in the government's opinion, as to the defendant, Anne Pollard, is as great as the risk posed by her husband. It may be that she only stands charged at the present time with a ten-year offense, but undoubtedly after the testimony which was elicted today it is reasonable for her to expect that she, too, will be indicted by the Grand Jury on the charge of espionage because of her aiding and abetting her husband in his activities in disseminating information to the Israeli government or, for that matter, her own activities that concerned the People's Republic of China."

Leeper continued: "I think that it's important to view her position in the context of her husband's admission that he and his wife were going to the Israeli Embassy on Thursday morning to seek asylum, and that admission is corroborated by the contents of Mrs. Pollard's purse. Not documents in the possession of the defendant Jonathan Pollard, but rather, documents that she had in her purse which undoubtedly she put there before she ever underwent this procedure that was described by Dr. Moscovitz.

"And those items of identification are precisely what one would need to start a new life in a new country: marriage license, birth certificate. They even had what they needed for the cat to start a new life in a foreign country.

"She had the family photographs with her, photographs which covered the period from when she was a child through the time that they were adults. And, as I said before, it was she who was carrying these documents, not the defendant Jonathan Pollard."

Leeper also referred to the paper in the purse which described the Pollards' itinerary during their trip to Israel and Europe the previous summer—their honeymoon. This was a trip, the prosecutor said, which was "financed by the parties to whom he was giving this classified information. What assurance do we have that that party, a representative of the Israeli government or, for that matter, another foreign government representative interested in obtaining classified information that the Pollards had access to wouldn't finance another trip?

"In the case of the Israelis, it would of course be for services—past services rendered, but as the court has heard during the course of the testimony here today, the documents to which both those defendants had access are, or constitute, national secrets. I don't think the court would have to engage in speculation to conclude that a foreign government, particularly a hostile foreign government, would have a great interest in obtaining this information and be willing to pay for it."

The judge interrupted Leeper to ask whether the U.S. government suspected that other classified documents may still be outstanding. "Well, your honor," Leeper replied, "I can't say, but I do know this: the defendant, Jonathan Pollard, on Monday was asked if he had any other classified documents aside from the ones he had in his envelope. He said no. Lo and behold, they find some back in the apartment.

"He's asked Thursday night, after his arrest, 'Do you have

any more classified documents?' He says no. Lo and behold, when they do a complete search of the apartment pursuant to the warrant on Friday, they find some more."

Leeper said that Anne had been very familiar with the documents, especially those relating to the intelligence-gathering capabilities of China in the United States. This kind of information, he said, "is still of value to foreign governments, particularly the People's Republic of China. And so she has more to sell than just documents that may be out there; she has knowledge to sell."

The U.S. Attorney then cited Anne's consideration of making the scheduled business trip to New Jersey. He asked how she could consider "for a single moment making a business trip to further her two-month career? I suggest to the court that it was a ruse. I suggest to the court that she does intend to make a trip at the first opportunity she gets."

He recalled that she and her husband had been "turned away by the very government" they had been assisting. But she could try again elsewhere. "The court should be aware that the arrest for espionage is not an extraditable offense," he said. "So this defendant doesn't have to get to Israel. She doesn't have to get to Europe. All she has to do is get to the Canadian border."

Leeper said that the documents read by Anne contained "the highest government secrets—documents relating to our weapons systems and military capabilities, the weapons systems and military capabilities of foreign nations, and the intelligence-gathering capabilities of those nations here in the United States. And having traded this information in the past for money, there is every reason to believe that they would be prepared—that Anne Henderson Pollard would be prepared to do it again.

"I think the situation could just be summed up by saying, 'Desperate circumstances produce desperate actions.' And the government with which they had been primarily cooperating closed the door on them. I suggest to the court there's every reason to believe that that information that she has in her head may be put up for the highest bidder."

Asked by Attridge to spell out that last point, Leeper

replied: "I don't think that we can take comfort in the fact that she may not have a photographic memory, because reasonable people, I think, can conclude that even a small part of that information, if disseminated to what many people consider to be a hostile country, or a country whose interests are antagonistic towards ours, the People's Republic of China, would be injurious to the United States."

James Hibey rejected Leeper's arguments. "Your honor," he said, "with all due respect, I'd suggest that perhaps Mr. Leeper's rhetoric makes good copy, but it's not supported by the evidence." The business trip to New Jersey, he stressed, was not sinister. Nor was the presentation to the Chinese Embassy. "She did so with her business associates from the company. The government has interviewed those witnesses. Now to come to the court and to make a big deal out of that, I think is inappropriate."

But the judge was clearly moved by the fact that Anne had accompanied her husband to the embassy, and that that was not a spur-of-the-moment decision. "Why would it be on the spur of the moment when the testimony and the evidence shows that there were telephone conversations before that with the Israeli Embassy and the defendant Pollard is alleged to have been told that if they can shake their surveillance, they'll take them in?"

At the end of the two-hour hearing, Attridge ruled that Anne—like her husband—should be held without bail. Both were handcuffed and sent back to different wings of the District of Columbia jail.

Pollard, ten years old, playing the cello at the Marshall Elementary School.

Pollard at Riley High School, South Bend, Indiana.

Jonathan Jay Pollard, Riley High School, class of 1972.

Pollard dressed for fencing at Notre Dame.

Pollard at the Virginia Federal Penitentiary at Petersburg, November 20, 1986, while awaiting sentencing. (*Wolf Blitzer*)

Pollard's boss at Naval Intelligence, Commander Jerry Agee, was the first to suspect Pollard. (*Timothy A. Murphy,* U.S. News & World Report)

The driveway of the Israeli Embassy, where Pollard sought and was denied asylum. (*Wolf Blitzer*)

Pollard at the Virginia Federal Penitentiary at Petersburg, November 20, 1986, while awaiting sentencing. (*Wolf Blitzer*)

Pollard's Naval Intelligence identification photograph.

Israeli air force colonel Aviem Sella at Ramon air base in the Negev Desert. (*Eyal Fischer*)

Rafi Eitan, Israel's master spy and Pollard's handler. (*David Rubinger*)

Pollard and his wife honeymooning in Venice, 1985. They were on their way back to the United States from Israel, where he had met his Israeli handlers.

The Pollards in their Washington, D.C., apartment in 1985 before Pollard's arrest.

Pollard, ten years old, playing the cello at the Marshall Elementary School.

Pollard at Riley High School, South Bend, Indiana.

Jonathan Jay Pollard, Riley High School, class of 1972.

Pollard dressed for fencing at Notre Dame.

Mrs. Mollie Pollard, Jonathan's mother; Carol Pollard, his sister; Bernard Henderson, his father-in-law; and Dr. Morris Pollard, his father, at a "Justice for the Pollards" rally in New York City, 1988. (*Robert Kalfus*)

Pollard and his parents in Washington, D.C., pre-arrest.

UNITED STATES DISTRICT COURT
FOR THE DISTRICT OF COLUMBIA

Holding a Criminal Term

Grand Jury Sworn in on November 7, 1984

UNITED STATES of AMERICA	:	Criminal No.
	:	
v.	:	Violations: 18 U.S.C. § 794(c)
	:	(Conspiracy to Commit
JONATHAN JAY POLLARD	:	Espionage)

I N D I C T M E N T

The Grand Jury charges:

COUNT ONE

Introduction

1. At all times material to this Indictment, defendant, JONATHAN JAY POLLARD, was employed by the United States Navy.

2. On September 19, 1979, defendant, JONATHAN JAY POLLARD, was hired as an Intelligence Research Specialist by the Field Operational Intelligence Office of the United States Navy in Suitland, Maryland. Between September of 1979, and June of 1984, defendant, JONATHAN JAY POLLARD, held the position of Intelligence Research Specialist within various divisions of the United States Navy.

3. In June of 1984, defendant, JONATHAN JAY POLLARD, was assigned as a watch officer for the Anti-Terrorist Alert Center,

A page from the U.S. government's indictment of Pollard.

Carol visits her brother Jonathan in jail in 1986.

Pollard, in 1988, serving his life sentence.

CHAPTER ELEVEN

The Cover-Up:
Code Name "Siren"

Just as the bail hearing was winding down, Under-Secretary of State Michael Armacost called Ambassador Rosenne to the State Department. By then it was apparent that a serious rift in U.S.-Israeli relations had erupted. The Americans were angry. They wanted answers quickly.

Armacost, a polished and impressive career diplomat, pressed for assurances of Israeli cooperation in the investigation. The ambassador assured him that the Israeli government wanted those answers just as quickly.

Upon leaving the C Street entrance to the State Department, Rosenne was asked by waiting reporters whether any Israeli diplomats had left the United States. He replied: "Nobody has left."

Both Prime Minister Shimon Peres and Foreign Minister Yitzhak Shamir, who had been bombarded with telephone calls from angry American Jewish leaders demanding that the incident be clarified, sent messages to Shultz stating that Israel's senior political leadership was caught by complete surprise by the affair and shared the Secretary's desire to learn all the facts as soon as possible. The State Department, after receiving those messages, issued a statement noting

that the United States had been "assured of the full cooperation of the Israeli government" in investigating the affair.

Indeed, Peres sent Shultz another message the next day
promising that Israel would return any stolen classified documents.

In Jerusalem, Peres, Shamir, and Rabin were meeting
daily at the Prime Minister's office to plan their joint strategy. Each was clearly nervous; their careers were on the
line. They anxiously wanted to make certain that Rafi Eitan's
operation could not be linked to the highest elements of the
Israeli government.

The heads of the various intelligence agencies in Israel
were asked to participate in the initial post-arrest investigation, which was code-named "Siren." By then, the Israeli
leadership was well aware of Eitan's involvement. He explained what had occurred—he had simply assumed that
LAKAM was fully authorized to run Pollard in Washington.
He documented some of the vital information that Pollard
had passed on to Israel.

Within a few days, the government formally appointed a
three-member panel to take charge of the internal inquiry:
Avraham Shalom, the head of the Shin Beth, the domestic
intelligence organization; Hanan Bar-On, the deputy direc-
tor-general of the Foreign Ministry; and Ram Caspi, a well-
connected Tel Aviv lawyer who was a close political associate of Peres.

This damage control committee completed its report on
Wednesday, November 27. It concluded that Pollard was
part of a "rogue" intelligence-gathering unit. The government, per se, was unaware of what had been going on. This
line had to get out quickly in order to limit the damage to
U.S.-Israeli relations.

Rabin's popular press spokesman, Nachman Shai, that
very same day called Thomas L. Friedman, the Jerusalem
Bureau chief of *The New York Times.* Shai invited him to the
Defense Minister's office to hear the results of the report
that were being relayed to the U.S. Ambassador in Israel,
Thomas Pickering, at the very same time. Friedman's
lengthy report, published the next day, November 28,

quoted an unnamed "highly placed Israeli source." Rabin did not want to be quoted by name.

The findings, according to the Defense Minister, asserted that Pollard had approached Israeli officials. They did not approach him. The report suggested that one motive for using Pollard was to find out if the United States was spying on Israel. Eitan made a major point of this during his debriefing.

Pollard, the report continued, was initially motivated by his zealous pro-Israeli sentiments; the subject of money was raised only later. According to the report, Pollard said he needed money to help support his wife and to pay for her illness. He said the money could also be useful in getting secret documents.

Rabin told Friedman that the senior Israeli intelligence official in charge of the Pollard operation—whom he did not name—had not informed the Prime Minister or anyone else in the Israeli government about it so that he would not be instructed to stop it. Rabin conceded that that sounded incredible but it was indeed the case. "He interpreted our basic policy of not carrying out espionage inside the United States as meaning not carrying out espionage against the national security interests of the United States," Rabin said. "There was no doubt that it was a mistake on his part to interpret the guidelines in this way. And there is no excuse for obtaining information through nonlegal means. But there was no malice on his part. It was a wrong interpretation of guidelines, a sincere mistake."

With the publication of Friedman's story, Rabin and other Israeli officials believed that they had limited the damage. They were becoming increasingly confident that they could ride out the storm. They now assumed that they could quietly patch up the loose ends with Washington—the way friendly countries often resolve diplomatic embarrassments.

But the report in the *Times* and the repeated Israeli assurances of cooperation failed to ease concerns in Washington. Indeed, in the face of what U.S. officials charged was Israeli stonewalling, the State Department on Friday, November 29, expressed "dismay" that Israel had not given its "full and prompt cooperation" to the American investigation. "Our objective now is to obtain all the facts promptly so that our laws can be enforced," it said in a statement. "We've asked the Israeli government specifically for their full cooperation with our law enforcement officials in providing us with all information it has in connection with this case, including the return of any documents and access to Israeli officials involved. The Israeli authorities have assured us of their willingness to cooperate. However, they have not yet provided the full and prompt cooperation we requested a week ago. We regret this delay and are urging the Israeli government to respond promptly."

Asked about press reports that he was somehow involved in the affair, Eitan on that same Friday told the Israeli newspaper *Ma'ariv:* "I may have something to say, but at a later stage. At this point, the wisest thing is not to respond to all of the attacks against me because past experience proves that the best thing an intelligence man can do is stay away from the media. Concerning the mention of my name in the American and local press as the man who recruited and operated Pollard, perhaps this is a mistake. My name is in the news by mistake."

The Americans remained angry. Indeed, it was the middle of the night, 3:30 A.M. in Jerusalem on Sunday, December 1, when Shultz personally telephoned Peres to complain. Because of the time difference, it was only 5:30 Saturday afternoon, November 30, in California—where Shultz then happened to be. "We have to resolve this matter once and for all," an upset Shultz said. Peres, in his pajamas, agreed.

They spoke at length, reviewing the entire incident. Peres firmly stuck by Israel's official contention that the operation was indeed unauthorized. Still, he apologized and again promised Israel's full cooperation. He also assured Shultz that a team of U.S. investigators could come to Israel to question the Israeli officials involved, provided that mutually acceptable ground rules could be reached. Israel wanted to make sure that the Israeli officials would obtain immunity from any criminal prosecution. Peres ended the conversation by promising that he would issue a formal statement outlining their agreement later in the day.*

The six members of a Knesset investigatory committee would later split along party lines in reviewing this decision by Peres, the Labor Party leader, to offer full cooperation with the U.S. inquiry. The three Labor parliamentarians, Abba Eban, Simcha Dinitz, and Micha Harish, supported the decision, while the three Likud members, Ehud Olmert, Eliyahu Ben-Elisar, and David Magen, opposed it. The Labor members pointed out that Peres had the backing of Shamir and Rabin in the decision-making process. "The urgency of the pressure exerted by the U.S. to clarify the matter, together with salient indications that the political echelon in the U.S. sincerely wished to contain and extinguish the blaze, compelled the three ministers to turn their attention urgently to the American front," the Labor members said. Shamir had told the panel that there were consul-

---

*And that is exactly what the Prime Minister did. "The government of Israel is determined to spare no effort in investigating this case thoroughly and completely and in uncovering all the facts to the last detail no matter where the trail may lead," the statement said.

The full inquiry is still incomplete and therefore the government of Israel is not yet in possession of all the facts; but the inquiry is progressing vigorously.

The government of Israel assures the government of the United States that in the wake of the inquiry, if the allegations are confirmed, those responsible will be brought to account, the unit involved in this activity will be completely and permanently dismantled, and necessary organizational steps will be taken to ensure that such activities are not repeated. Our relations with the United States are based on solid foundations of deep friendship, close affinity and mutual trust. Spying on the United States stands in total contradiction to our policy. Such activity to the extent that it did take place was wrong and the government of Israel apologizes. For the time being, we have nothing further to say on this.

Within a few hours, Shultz issued the following statement:

The Government of Israel has issued a statement on the Pollard case which has been made public. It is an excellent statement. We are satisfied with it. We wholeheartedly welcome it. We have full confidence in Israel's determination and ability to pursue this case to the last detail and to bring those responsible to account.

tations in advance of the Peres-Shultz phone call. "It was clear that we were going to full cooperation in order to conclude the episode," Shamir testified.

The Labor parliamentarians also said Peres's actions "prevented a debacle and forged tight cooperation" with Shultz. "The senior political echelon in the United States reacted positively to the conversation with Mr. Peres and to the messages that followed in its wake. Mr. Peres and Mr. Shamir received messages from Mr. Shultz that were steeped in esteem and exuded friendship, evincing a desire on his part to contain the affair. There were grounds for believing that the tension was dissipating and that relations with the United States would again be smooth. It is difficult to describe as a blunder a diplomatic move that was crowned with this degree of success. The alternative to this policy would have generated a serious setback in relations between Israel and the United States, with all that this entails. It would have generated an extreme and furious reaction by all the elements of American society, would have thrust Israel into a confrontation with Secretary of State Shultz and

---

I have been assured by Prime Minister Peres that he and his associates were completely surprised by this development and were not aware of the activities alleged in this case.

The Israelis have assured us that they will work cooperatively with our law enforcement authorities and we will cooperate with them.

We are assured, as well, that Israel will provide us with access to those individuals who are knowledgeable about the case and that Israel will give us a full report on whatever activities their investigation reveals to have taken place.

The test of a good relationship is not so much what happens when things are going smoothly, but when difficulties arise. That is when it is important that the people involved work closely together to deal effectively with the problem.

That is what is happening here. In doing so, this process can even result in a relationship that is deeper, more enriched, and marked by a greater mutuality of trust.

To sum up: We welcome the statement of the Government of Israel and appreciate its willingness and commitment to work cooperatively with us to see this issue fully resolved. For our part, we will work closely with Israeli authorities so that both countries can expeditiously get to the bottom of the case and ensure that justice is done. As the U.S. investigation into this matter is concluded, we will make an appropriate report public. For the moment, the U.S. Government will have nothing further to say on this issue.

thereby with the White House as well. The result would have been reactions against Israel both among public opinion and in the Congress."

But the Likud members of the panel disagreed. While they conceded that some cooperation with Washington was essential, they questioned the extent of Peres's assurances. "Prime Minister Shimon Peres's agreement to return the documents which had been brought by Pollard was fundamentally wrong and caused extremely serious damage," the members said. Peres should have known that the material would be used against Pollard.

They also noted that Peres "did not heed the advice of those who were dealing with the matter on his behalf who believed that it was not possible to return these documents."

The Likud parliamentarians charged that the three-member, Peres-appointed investigatory panel had done a poor job in assembling all of the facts. They concluded by noting that had Peres "directed that a proper investigation be conducted, as he was obliged to do, he undoubtedly would have refrained from proposing that the documents be returned, and perhaps even have refused to permit the questioning of the Israelis involved in the affair. But Mr. Peres refrained from ordering an investigation or examining the requisite details, thereby becoming entangled in an undertaking he should never have given."

Peres, two days after his phone call with Shultz, dispatched a high-level delegation to Washington to work out the exact details involving Israel's cooperation with the U.S. investigation. It included Arens, Avraham Shalom, and Ram Caspi. The Israelis met with Shultz at the State Department on Thursday, December 5. It was a productive session.

The next day, Shultz said that FBI agents would join a delegation of other U.S. officials on an investigative trip to Israel. Israel, he recalled, had pledged "full cooperation" in the investigation, and was now going to live up to its promise. They would make available Eitan, Yagur, Erb, Ravid, and other Israeli officials for questioning. "We have every reason to believe that the issues involved will be resolved satisfactorily," Shultz said.

The delegation was led by the State Department's Legal Affairs Adviser, Abraham Sofaer, and his staff assistant, Pat Schaubel. He was joined by the U.S. Attorney for the District of Columbia Joseph E. diGenova and his wife, Victoria Toensing. Also in the delegation were Deputy Assistant Attorney General Mark Richard; John Martin, the Justice Department's chief of the Internal Security Section; two assistant U.S. attorneys—Charles Leeper and Stephen R. Spivack—and two FBI agents, Joseph Johnson and Eugene Noltkamper. Agee was also included.

The meetings in Israel lasted for several days. In the course of the sessions—held at the Country Club just north of Tel Aviv along the Mediterranean coast—the Israeli officials admitted that Pollard had passed information but insisted that it was not in the quantity suspected by the United States. They, of course, repeatedly maintained that it was not an officially approved operation.

During the questioning, the Israelis mentioned that another Israeli had been involved very briefly in the affair but they did not want to identify him. They insisted—referring to Avi Sella—that he had in any case played only a very marginal role in the operation. They would later insist that the Americans did not press for his identity, clearly relieved that this individual was not another American citizen.

There were several reasons why the Israelis did not want to reveal Sella's identity. The top leadership, at that time, appeared to be genuinely convinced that he had in fact played only a relatively minor role in getting the operation off the ground. They thought that it would be a tragic waste to upend Sella's brilliant career simply for that initial introductory role.

But there were other good reasons for keeping Sella's identity a secret. The Israelis suspected that no one in Washington would believe that the operation was unauthorized if it were revealed that a high-ranking Israeli Air Force officer was actually involved—even if only marginally. The

Americans are simply too knowledgeable about the Israeli military to accept the notion that Sella could have been involved without higher authorization. That, of course, meant the commander of the air force, Gen. Amos Lapidot, and probably the Chief of Staff himself, Gen. Moshe Levi. Revealing to the Americans Sella's identity would have thus opened up a whole series of other questions that the Israelis desperately wanted to avoid.

In fact, they took no chances. They ordered Sella to leave the country just as the Sofaer delegation was arriving in Israel. Sella, as instructed, flew to West Germany with his Israeli passport falsely dated a few days earlier to make it appear that he was out of the country before the delegation arrived. The Israelis wanted to be in the position of saying to the U.S. investigators that this unnamed other Israeli was not available in any case for questioning since he was abroad. West Germany was selected because its customs officials do not routinely stamp entry dates into visiting Israeli passports. The Americans did not press to interview the other Israeli.

At that point, the Israelis believed that Sella's identity could indeed remain secret. They felt confident that Pollard would not reveal it. If he did, that would then mean that Pollard would also have to disclose the involvement of his long-time family friend, Steven Stern. Pollard, the Israelis believed, would keep quiet about both Sella and Stern.

But it was not very difficult for the FBI to independently learn about Stern. A thorough review of Pollard's long-distance telephone calls from his home and office showed a consistent pattern of conversations between the two friends. Who was this man that Pollard was also talking to?

Stern's lawyer would later tell *The New York Times* that Stern had no idea that the initial Pollard-Sella contact would eventually lead to espionage. The lawyer, Jonathan L. Rosner, said that Justice Department officials had told him that Stern was designated a "witness" in the case, a term he said refers to "someone against whom they do not intend to proceed or do not have the evidence to proceed." Rosner added: "Mr. Stern's involvement in this whole affair is of such little consequence that it shouldn't even be the subject of a story."

Stern, for his part, would later confirm that he had testified before the federal Grand Jury investigating the case. He cooperated with the FBI investigation. He professed complete innocence, and was never charged with any crime.

But in Pollard's view, Stern's matchmaking was by no means all that innocent. Believing that Stern had bad-mouthed him during his sessions with the FBI, Pollard bitterly suggested that Stern must have known what Pollard's intentions were.

Pollard would later also flatly deny that he was first to tell the FBI about the pilot or Stern. He suggested that Stern may have revealed Sella's identity. Stern, for his part, has maintained that when the FBI agents first came to question him, they already knew about Sella. Stern, at that point, assumed that they had received the information from Pollard.

U.S. law enforcement authorities, while refusing to say flatly who had disclosed Sella's role, indicated that it was Pollard who began to "sing" after he learned that the Israeli government had betrayed him. They also noted that it was largely Pollard's testimony before a secret U.S. federal Grand Jury that resulted in an indictment against the pilot.

Back in Israel, Peres, Shamir, and Rabin were coming under increasing criticism for their willingness to cooperate with the Americans. This was underscored in a dispatch in *The New York Times:*

> Whatever his public image, Mr. Pollard is seen in the Israeli military apparatus as just another agent doing his job, and Israeli intelligence cannot afford to sacrifice him without undermining its credibility with its other spies around the world. Israeli military officials believe that Mr. Pollard passed on some very valuable information. That he was discovered is generally viewed in the military establishment as an

intelligence failure, a frequent occurrence in the espionage business, but not a mistake in its original conception.

That opinion was also expressed in an Israel Radio interview with Col. Menachem Digly, a retired Israeli intelligence officer. "I don't know anything about how the Pollard affair happened," he said. "But one thing I know is that the people who handled it were not fools. Whoever made the public believe that was so, only shows that he knows nothing about intelligence." Digly said gathering intelligence was similar to looking for oil. "In the case of Pollard, the drill hit the main vein that was full of information. The hunger for that information was great, but the well happened to be in the yard of a good friend—but not good enough to have given us the information voluntarily. . . . Imagine if Pollard had provided information for years without anyone knowing about it. Does anyone doubt that it would have been viewed as vital and worth it—in spite of everything?"

The U.S. delegation stayed in Israel for one week. During that entire time, they were observed carefully by Israeli agents. The Americans, in fact, were certain that their hotel rooms were bugged. One man actually tried to find bugs but could not. He also searched for possible pinhole lens video equipment hidden in the rooms, but could not find that either.

In the early days of their questioning, they felt they were getting the runaround. They were. The Israelis initially refused to return documents obtained by Pollard; they also hedged in answering various questions about the operation. At one point, Sofaer threatened to take his team back home unless the promised "full cooperation" was in fact forthcoming. The Israelis relented. Another order was given from the Prime Minister; Sofaer stayed.

Pollard was understandably shocked when he subsequently learned of Israel's cooperation. Israel's "inexcusable decision to cooperate with the Justice Department probe without first guaranteeing my release," he later confided, "clearly indicates that the Cabinet actually believed that a human sacrifice and a lame 'rogue' alibi would successfully ameliorate the administration. This was a classic manifestation of grotesque miscalculation at work since their 'cooperation' did nothing more than fan the flames of Weinberger's anti-Israel bonfire." Pollard was becoming obsessed with blaming Defense Secretary Weinberger for his problems.

He later said that the unraveling of the operation was the result of Rafi Eitan's "stupidity" and "greed" as well as Israel's "inexplicable failure to appreciate the hostile nature of the present administration towards Israel." According to Pollard, both of these factors led to Eitan's failure to have a workable contingency plan to rescue Pollard and his wife.

"Leaving aside the propriety of Israel operating a Jewish agent within [not against] the U.S. intelligence community," Pollard said, "it has become painfully evident to me that someone back home was living in a dream world when it came to assessing how this particular administration would react if an Israeli agent were discovered deep within its security services. Although part of the reason for this lamentable miscalculation may be ascribed to Peres's belief that the administration would never threaten his chances of reaching a modus vivendi with Jordan by sensationalizing an espionage scandal, I think the fundamental flaw in Israeli 'thinking' on this matter was their underestimation of Weinberger's desire to recast Israel in the image of Russia as far as its threat to American security was concerned. This was, however, simply to be a means to an end for the Defense Department Arabists. Unfortunately, the folks back home evidently couldn't appreciate the propaganda value this type of scandal would represent for people like Weinberger who have been trying for seven years to redirect the focus of American strategic concern and commitment away from Israel and toward Saudi Arabia and the various Persian Gulf sheikdoms."

Pollard said that his handlers' big mistake was to assume that the espionage operation was being run in a friendly environment. If Israel had assumed that the environment was hostile, it would have taken more precautions. It also would have worked out in advance an escape plan for the Pollards.

"So, rather than treat this operation as if it were being conducted behind enemy lines, which it was in many respects, my control decided to believe that the 'special relationship' between the two countries would adequately ensure a limitation of political 'fallout' should I be exposed," Pollard said. "This was a fatal misreading of the actual state of affairs that existed in Washington: it was widely known that Weinberger favored an 'evenhanded' arms sales policy in the Middle East and Meese never hid his desire to have Israel placed on the 'Criteria Country List,' which would have categorized her with such pariah states as Libya, Cuba, and North Korea. Indeed, the position of those pro-Israeli bureaucrats that existed at the time was so precarious that many were purged without even a congressional outcry shortly after my arraignment. By that measure alone, one can gauge the absolute imbalance that existed between the two sides during my operation."*

Pollard said he was always urging the Israelis to take another look at some of their underlying political assumptions about Washington. "I constantly warned Rafi about the type of overtly hostile, anti-Israeli environment which existed in town, particularly within the military intelligence community, but he always felt that I was too low down the political ladder to appreciate what was happening on his Olympian heights. There was a reason why the information was not reaching Israel through the exchange agreement which had less to do with the commonly found antipathy towards Israel of the military intelligence community than it did with the Weinberger political appointees in the Pentagon who operationalized this bias and quietly countenanced the reduction of critical intelligence to Israel. That was something Rafi flatly refused to believe was occurring because he was still

---

*Criteria countries are those designated by the State Department and the Justice Department as especially hostile to the United States. Their representatives in the United States are subjected to close surveillance. High technology transfers are not approved to them. Israel was never seriously considered for this category, though some U.S. counterintelligence officials often wanted tighter surveillance.

an honored guest at the Pentagon." Pollard called this "a case of terminal hubris, I'd say."

Pollard also suggested that Peres may have simply assumed that CIA Director William Casey—a strong supporter of Israel—would contain the damage to the relationship following his arrest because of the CIA's close ties with the Mossad and "the agency's evident recruitment of an Israeli officer during the Lebanon War." This was a reference to an assertion by Republican Senator David Durenberger of Minnesota that the United States "broke the rules of the game first" by running an agent in Israel during the war.

But this, too, was a miscalculation of Weinberger's "ability to outmaneuver" Casey on Middle East policy, "at least by playing his Saudi trump," Pollard said. "Despite the rhetoric about Reagan's love of Israel, he's never once overruled Weinberger's advocacy of balancing the military capabilities of the Arabs and Israel. Quite the contrary. Hell, even the granting of major non-NATO ally status to Israel was a farce since in the interests of 'evenhandedness,' a creature of Weinberger's invention, the U.S. simultaneously conferred this status upon Egypt as well. Now the Israelis will have to be careful about what military equipment they ask for lest the Egyptians pop up demanding 'equal access' to the same material as per their upgraded relationship with Washington.

"Even though we could go on ad nauseam trying to unravel this political equivalent of an R. D. Laing 'Knot,' when all is said and done the Israelis simply failed to appreciate the 'threat environment' and decided that in view of the quality of the information reaching them, the residual risks to the operation were acceptable."

And Pollard was convinced that Eitan did not make this decision on his own. "The notion that Rafi made this kind of decision by himself seems rather remote to me," he said. "Despite the evasive quality of the Eban/Rotenstreich–Tzur reports, they did establish the fact that my material was incorporated in reports which reached the Defense ministers. Those fellows at the very top knew very well where the information was coming from and simply got greedy and short-sighted; they were thinking tactically rather than strategically if you will. Given the nature of the threats I was uncovering, perhaps this perspective was warranted but it was taking an awfully high risk with my operational security."*

Pollard, of course, had been repeatedly assured that if he were exposed and arrested, the Israelis would get him out. "Time and time again I was assured that if I were somehow caught in such a way that rescue was impossible, the Americans would be quietly approached and asked for my expulsion," he recalled. "That was quite an assumption to make although it may have been based on the belief that Mr. Casey would successfully intervene on my behalf—as he evidently tried to do. However, this assumed the Israeli link would be acknowledged, which I was repeatedly told must never under any circumstances be revealed, hence the disinformation effort I was expected to mount if arrested. This inconsistency was never resolved."

According to Pollard, Eitan was also working under other false assumptions. "Rafi was quite confident that since I was in counterintelligence, I would be alerted to any decision made to increase surveillance against Israeli legals in the country like Ravid and Yagur with whom I was working," he said. But there were two reasons why this line of thinking was dangerous. "Firstly," Pollard said, "the counterespionage function is widely distributed against a plethora of very compartmentalized agencies, most of which I would not have access to. To make matters worse, these agencies would be expected to concentrate their activities in the Washington area, given the number of sensitive targets and Communist diplomatic establishments in the capital. There

---

*Two commissions of inquiry were established in Israel to look into the Pollard affair. Abba Eban, a Labor Member of Knesset and Chairman of the Knesset Foreign Affairs and Defense Committee, chaired one panel. A second was composed of the late Yehoshua Rotenstreich, a prominent Tel Aviv attorney, and General Zvi Tzur, a retired IDF officer. This second panel was created by the Israeli government. Both reports were released on the same day—May 27, 1987.

would be no way for me to be sure, then, that the Israeli legals were not being followed." Since Israel was not a Criteria Country (see footnote, page 209), he continued, "perhaps this was a valid risk but it was one I was never happy about because it was avoidable."

The second reason dealt with what Pollard called "a cardinal rule of Israeli operations, even when they involve someone like myself who was considered one hundred percent loyal to the cause." Specifically, he said, the actual handlers "must not be tied to a diplomatic post" and the agent "must not know the names of his team members." But the Israelis did not observe those rules.

"No attempt was made to use aliases by the Israeli diplomats since being in counterintelligence I could discover who they were without any problem and as I was considered to be an Israeli for all intents and purposes the need for such 'bothersome' circumventions was not indicated. All of these operational characteristics can be ascribed to one bedrock belief: we were not working in a hostile environment."

Pollard said the Israelis had other misconceptions as well. They had hoped that if Pollard were captured, the Americans would treat him gingerly since the information he obtained for Israel dealt strictly with Arab and Middle Eastern threats facing Israel. "I was not directed to collect information pertaining to U.S. military capabilities or diplomat secrets." The Israelis felt that "the geographical and functional focus of my activities would tend to blunt any American criticism were I to be exposed. Although under ordinary circumstances this line of reasoning might have been appropriate, with the spy paranoia sweeping Washington at this time as well as the probable attitude Weinberger was sure to adopt once he realized what kind of damage I'd done to his Arab friends, it simply didn't make any sense. No one seemed to realize that my exposure would be seized by the anti-Israeli factions in the administration as a golden opportunity to have the state portrayed as a clear and present danger to American security regardless as to whether my collection activities were confined to third parties."

Was Rafi Eitan, Israel's masterspy, "simply getting too old

and infirm for the job?" Pollard asked. "Even if his field operatives were really unsuited to the task at hand, since neither Ravid nor Yagur were agents in the real sense of the word, but were 'applied scientists' first and foremost, if an escape plan had to be undertaken, they lacked both the training and the temperament for its implementation. The only thing I can think is that people simply didn't assume that I was operating in a high threat environment and believed that if caught, I would either willingly sacrifice myself by misdirecting the authorities toward other parties screaming 'Valhalla' or go to prison for a 'few' years on a possession charge. However, nothing really had been thought through except that I would be rescued 'somehow' and that I absolutely had to make sure my Israeli connection was covered before dropping out of sight.

"But if there were no mechanism to guarantee my escape," Pollard continued, "then the order to implicate a third country was tantamount to having me commit suicide." Believing he was told to go to the Israeli embassy, Pollard could not understand the rationale behind telling him to do this. "Unless," he said, "someone thought that things would quietly blow over once the authorities realized that I wasn't an Eastern bloc agent. What's more likely, though, is that there was a grand foul-up precipitated by the sudden departure of Ravid and Yagur. All I know for sure is that I was specifically told to come in."

Pollard insisted that during those first two days after his initial interrogation, he could have escaped on his own if he had so decided. "While it's true that I could have arranged for my own escape independent of Messrs. Eitan and Yagur," he wrote,

> there were several factors which prevented this from occurring. Firstly, I lacked the innate distrust of my immediate control officer [Yagur] that would have been the foundation for any predisposition on my part to guarantee my own survival. I simply couldn't believe that Jews were capable of abandoning their own since this was something only the goyim did. I

think it must be said, though, in all fairness to Yossi
that if he had been given the means and authority,
he would have done his level best to get us out of
the country.

Secondly, as my collection assignments mounted in
volume, I simply didn't have the time to think about
my own vulnerability. Everything I thought about at
the time was getting the material to Israel as soon as
I could because so much of it was both time sensitive
and threatening. Under the circumstances my
personal concerns seemed to be of secondary
importance. This may seem incredible to you but
such is the nature of true believers, particularly
when they find themselves in a situation that calls for
immediate action rather than reflection. I suspect it
really revolved down to a question of instinctual
priorities: I had to balance my personal fears against
a state I'd been raised to believe represented the
survival of our race.

Pollard pointed out that he simply did not have the money
necessary to organize an escape. "I simply lacked the funds
needed to put together an escape plan which would have
guaranteed our disappearance overseas," he said. "Moreover, as Yossi held our Israeli passports, how were we to
cross borders and get back to Israel on our own? It was
simply an impossible undertaking which neither Anne nor
I were in a position to implement. In retrospect, even if we
might have been able to reach Canada, then what? Were we
then supposed to call the embassy in Ottawa and negotiate
for our passports? And exactly how were we supposed to get
out of our apartment building, which I repeatedly described
to Yossi as a death trap."

In the end, Pollard concluded that his Israeli handlers
had merely been inept. "Perhaps the disaster was not the
result of any sophisticated miscalculation but rather something more primal: the one human trait I've never been
able to factor into my thinking is someone's capacity for
stupidity and this was a classic case of just such a phenome-

non if there ever were one. The quality of tradecraft exhibited by Rafi in this affair was less than poor—it was criminally irresponsible."

Pollard also feared that the Justice Department would quietly place Israel on the Criteria List. "The results would have been disastrous," he said. "The American Zionist movement could have been classified as a subversive ideological threat, equivalent to communism and Islamic extremism; the tax deductibility of donations to Zionist organizations would in all likelihood have been called into question; leading personalities of the movement might have been subjected to intrusive surveillance; and severe export controls could theoretically have been applied to sophisticated arms sales to Israel."

One reason why Pollard feared that that kind of dire scenario could develop was because of the nature of some of his interrogation. Justice Department officials were becoming increasingly convinced that there were other Israeli spies operating in Washington—that Pollard was not necessarily an isolated incident. With good reason, they operate on what they call the cockroach theory: for every cockroach you actually see in a kitchen, you better believe that there are many more hidden in the plumbing.

Pollard claimed that the Justice Department wanted him to implicate other spies. They wanted to know whether any American Jewish leaders were part of an Israeli spy network. While attached to a polygraph machine, for example, Pollard was asked to read lists of Jewish names and to point out alleged Israeli spies. He refused to do so. The former U.S. Attorney for the District of Columbia, Joseph diGenova, has denied this.

"This emasculation of Israel's support base in the U.S. was Weinberger's ulterior objective in this case, which went far beyond the mere prosecution of one individual who was neither indicted for having assisted a belligerent nor accused of having intended to harm the United States," Pollard later said. "Certainly, by blackening the moral character of an agent, one simultaneously discredits his cause as well—and that was the whole objective of this carefully orchestrated judicial farce. Anyone doubting this need only review the violence of Weinberger's denunciation of me which I'm sure was designed, in part, to curry favor with the Arabs and thereby help to rebuild the administration's tarnished credibility with them following its disastrous arms-for-hostages deal with Khomeini.

"Although the Arabists in Washington ultimately failed in their attempt to use my case as a means of realizing their hidden sentencing agenda, it was not for want of trying. What is inexplicable is that in light of Weinberger's well-publicized animosity towards Israel, due no doubt to his suffering from a 'Kreisky' or 'Amalek' complex, my handler should have done everything in his power to prevent him from getting his hands on me. From my perspective, this was the major mistake in Rafi's operational handling of the affair."

Sofaer and other members of the U.S. delegation left Israel impressed by the degree of cooperation they had received. Indeed, on December 20, the State Department issued a formal statement which made this clear. "The United States team has concluded in full cooperation with the government of Israel its mission related to certain activities by which officials of the government of Israel received classified documents of the United States government in an unauthorized manner," the statement said.

> The government of Israel has confirmed that it has returned to the United States all such documents in its possession or under its control. Through the cooperation of the government of Israel, the United States team has had full access to the persons with knowledge of the facts relevant to the mission. The government of Israel has informed the United States government that it has taken necessary action to disband the unit involved. The government of Israel reiterated to the United States team its statement that the persons concerned acted without authority

and against its policy, and in taking appropriate steps in this regard the government of Israel has acted to prevent any repetition of such activities. The United States government regards these measures as constituting the cooperation contemplated by the two governments. Within the context of their cooperation and after their discussions, the United States and Israeli teams have agreed to consider what concrete measures may be necessary, if any, in the future.

The statement went on to note that the Justice Department was still in the midst of prosecuting cases related to the matter, "and therefore comment would be inappropriate. No further statement on this subject will be made until an appropriate occasion is presented. Based on the solid foundation of deep friendship, close affinity and mutual trust, both governments reaffirm their determination to continue their close cooperation in all fields."

Anne, after her arrest, spent nearly one hundred days in the District of Columbia jail before she was released on bail. "I was locked in a tiny, windowless, roach- and rat-infested cell for 23 and one-half to 24 hours a day," she later wrote in a letter to Leon H. Charney, the New York lawyer who briefly represented her in the case. "I was deliberately denied essential medical treatment and prescriptions for my numerous health problems, and almost died as a result of this. My hair even turned gray."

She said she was constantly forced to listen to "the numerous death threats made to me by my fellow neo-Nazi and Moslem inmates as they discussed aloud how they would 'kill the dirty Jew bitch.'"

During her initial incarceration, Anne found herself

forbidden to speak to anyone and I was not permitted to breathe fresh air or see the sun. Initially, I was also denied the right to receive reading or writing material, and moreover, for the entire period of incarceration, I was forbidden to communicate with or see my husband, which is nothing short of torture for a couple as close as we are.

The odors I smelled were mixed with the unbearable stench of my continually unworkable toilet and sink which prison officials would not fix for days. My skin sweated constantly in the intolerable high-humidity heat. I could not drink the water because it was mixed with sewer gas. I lacked a moment's privacy because I was constantly watched by male and female guards, the male guards especially ogling me whenever I was allowed to take a shower. My closest companions were the families of roaches and other creatures which I daily awoke to and slept with. The cell was so bare it lacked even sheets and towels. Its horrors continually reminded me of scenes from Poe's "The Pit and the Pendulum." To this day, I wonder how I came out of that jail alive.

She continued: "These ghastly restrictions were deliberately designed to either mentally break me or kill me, and I later learned that these restrictions were ordered by high-level government officials, who were outraged over my vow of silence to all law enforcement officials. Additionally, these officials had hoped that by slowly destroying me, they could convince my husband to cooperate with them. It was a vicious circle that nearly cost me my life."

Anne lost nearly sixty pounds during those three months of prison. "I was ridden with untreated, severe abdominal pain which I later learned was exacerbated by my lack of medical treatment and the conditions I was kept under."

By the end of February 1986, Anne's lawyer, James Hibey, managed to secure her release from jail on bail. By then, it had become apparent to U.S. investigators that she had not been a Chinese spy. And it was also apparent—based on what they had heard directly from the Israelis—that she was not operationally involved in the Israeli espionage network.

She may have known what her husband was doing, but she never collected or transmitted documents.

What was clear was that the prosecutors were hoping to win the Pollards' full cooperation as part of a plea-bargain agreement. By releasing Anne, they expected her husband to start cooperating—which is exactly what happened.

By March, both Pollards were cooperating fully, although formal plea-bargaining agreements were not completed and signed until May 23. In exchange for their pleading guilty and for their full cooperation, the government would not seek the maximum possible sentences. What was clear was that Anne was hoping that her cooperation would help win a reduced sentence for her husband. He, of course, hoped that his cooperation would save his wife from having to return to prison.

On June 4, 1986—a sunny, beautiful day in Washington—both Pollards returned to the U.S. District Court, which again was packed with reporters. They came before Judge Aubrey Robinson III, a seemingly ice-cold black jurist appointed during the Carter administration. Despite his very stern demeanor, he had a good reputation as a fair and astute judge.

The Assistant U.S. Attorney, Charles Leeper, told him that a U.S. Grand Jury had that morning returned an indictment against Jonathan Jay Pollard, who was brought before the judge. Robinson, looking down from the bench, asked Pollard whether he wished to enter a plea of guilty. Pollard said yes.

"Have you had an opportunity to read that indictment?" the judge asked.

"I have," Pollard replied in a barely audible whisper. He wore a light gray business suit with a smart white handkerchief stuffed into the upper outside breast pocket. It was clear that he had lost a great deal of weight since his first court appearance some six months earlier.

Anne, awaiting her turn to appear before the same judge, sat at a nearby table, her eyes weepy. She came to the hearing in a fashionable black dress, her red hair cut shorter. She, too, had lost quite a bit of weight. Indeed, she looked much better than she did during her initial court appearance.

In response to questioning from the judge, both Pollards acknowledged that they were prepared to enter into a plea agreement and that they would forgo their right to a trial. Robinson advised Pollard that he could still be sentenced to life irrespective of the agreement. Pollard replied that he understood. The judge then asked Anne whether she understood that she faced a maximum five-year sentence. "Yes, I do," she replied.

He then asked Assistant United States Attorney David Geneson whether the government had any opposition to her remaining released on bail until sentencing. "We have no opposition to the status as it is, your honor," the prosecutor said.

Anne was permitted to return to her Falls Church, Virginia, apartment where she was temporarily living with her father. Her husband was sent back to the federal prison in Petersburg.

By the end of May 1986, U.S. law enforcement authorities began to leak word that Pollard had been part of a broader, more organized operation. The Americans, of course, were by then fully aware of Avi Sella's role and Israel's effort to conceal it. "The Israelis lied to us," one U.S. official bluntly told the Los Angeles *Times.* "This was no small-time rogue operation; it was much more systematic than that. This was a very expensive operation that they ran. There's no embassy slush fund big enough to cover that sort of thing."

By then, it was also apparent that Pollard and his wife were going to accept a plea-bargaining deal. Pollard, in order to win leniency for his wife, was cooperating with the authorities, revealing critical details of the operation that the Israelis had withheld, including the full extent of Sella's role and the Israeli promise to deposit $30,000 a year for a decade in a Swiss bank account.

Abraham Sofaer, the State Department's Legal Affairs Adviser, returned to Israel with some aides to confront the Israelis with this new information. Why had Israel attempted to cover up Sella's role? Israel's response was that Sella had played only a minor part in the operation.

But the Americans remained angry. FBI Director William H. Webster said that Israel had provided the United States with only "selective cooperation," despite promises of full cooperation. He described this lack of cooperation as "disappointing but, considering the nature of intelligence gathering, it's really not surprising."

U.S. officials threatened to revoke the immunity from prosecution granted to the Israeli operatives, including Eitan, Yagur, and Erb. That promise had been provided in exchange for truthful testimony. None of the Israelis had been completely honest.

It quickly became apparent that the U.S. authorities wanted to interview Sella. But the Israelis balked.

Leonard Garment, a powerful Washington lawyer who served as President Richard Nixon's White House Counsel during Watergate, received a telephone call from Ken Bialkin on June 6, 1986. Bialkin, himself an influential New York lawyer and past chairman of the Anti-Defamation League of B'nai B'rith and the Conference of Presidents of Major American Jewish Organizations, was in Tel Aviv where he had just discussed the Pollard affair with an old friend, Chaim Zadok, a former Israeli Minister of Justice. Zadok was representing Aviem Sella and had asked Bialkin to recommend a good Washington lawyer to get involved in the case on Sella's behalf. By then, Sella had been identified by the U.S. Justice Department as a "co-conspirator" in the Pollard espionage ring. The air force officer had two Tel Aviv lawyers: Zadok, and his own brother, Menachem Sella, who was a partner in Zadok's law firm. It was all a family affair since Zadok was also Menachem Sella's father-in-law.

This was not the first time that Garment had been associated with the Pollard affair. Shortly after Pollard was arrested, Garment received a telephone call from Israeli Ambassador Meir Rosenne asking if he could come over to discuss the case. To Garment's surprise, Rosenne was accompanied by Moshe Arens, who had been requested by Prime Minister Shimon Peres to help in the Israeli damage control operation. Arens was going to meet that evening with Shultz. He and the other Israelis who were involved in the discussions with the Secretary wanted Garment to assess the overall situation. Arens had come to Washington with Avraham Shalom and Ram Caspi. What was the mood in Washington? How angry was Shultz? What would Israel have to do to ease the very serious strain that had developed in the relationship?

Garment made some calls to key Reagan administration officials. He later told the Israelis that the situation was very serious indeed. He urged them to come clean—the United States would learn everything in any case. By cooperating with the Americans in the investigation, he suggested, the matter could be resolved once and for all.

But now, some six months later, Garment was being brought back into the case. The Israelis had earlier concealed Sella's involvement. They probably feared that no one in Washington would believe Israel's "rogue" operation story if a high-ranking Israeli Air Force officer were shown to have been involved.

On June 9, Garment flew to Israel. On the flight, he read the Justice Department documents and newspaper clippings on the case. He had no idea what was in store for him over the next several weeks. He had been involved in all sorts of Israeli-related matters during his twenty years in Washington. President Nixon had occasionally used him as a diplomatic back channel to convey and receive messages from Prime Minister Golda Meir; he had developed a relationship with Secretary of State Henry Kissinger during the golden age of shuttle diplomacy in the Middle East; and he was personally close to several Israeli ambassadors over the years. But he was still unprepared for what he was about to witness.

Garment would remove himself from the case within a few weeks after he concluded that Israel had no intention of fully cooperating with the United States.

CHAPTER TWELVE

The Weinberger Memo

The plea-bargain agreement in hand, both sides began to focus on the sentence. In exchange for Pollard's cooperation, the U.S. government promised to ask for a "substantial" sentence, but not life. Pollard was moved to the federal prison in Petersburg, Virginia. His wife was still out on bail. She visited him almost every weekend.

Judge Robinson, in the coming months, would be bombarded with memorandums from the government and the defense attorneys. He, and he alone, would decide how long Pollard would have to serve and whether Anne would have to return to prison. At the time, veteran court reporters had speculated that he would probably get ten to fifteen years—and become eligible for parole after about five years. They assumed that she would receive a suspended sentence and would not have to return to prison.

The prosecutors carefully prepared their papers. They realized that the damage assessment presented to Robinson by Defense Secretary Weinberger would probably be the single most important document. Exactly how much damage to U.S. national security had Pollard done? Weinberger's affidavit was designed to answer that question in a cool and authoritative manner.

Citing security concerns, the U.S. government refused to release Weinberger's forty-six-page statement to the public.

It was submitted to Judge Robinson in secret, although Pollard and his lawyer were permitted to read it and draft their response.

The classified Weinberger memorandum, subsequently obtained under the Freedom of Information Act albeit with certain sections blacked out, described what it said was "the significant harm caused to national security by the defendant."

"The defendant has substantially harmed the United States, and, in my view, his crimes demand severe punishment," Weinberger wrote. "Because it may not be clear to the court that the defendant's activities have caused damage of the magnitude realized, I felt it necessary to provide an informed analysis to the Court so that an appropriate sentence could be fashioned."

Weinberger, in his paper, did not say what that sentence should be.

"It is my purpose," Weinberger stated,

> to explain the nature and significance of the defendant's actions as I perceive them to have affected the security of the United States. I have detailed a considerable quantity of highly sensitive information, and therefore request that the Court review this document and deliver it under Court seal back into the hands of its bearer immediately upon completion of review. I also request that no one else be permitted to review this document unless it is necessary as a matter of law to do so, and then only if proper clearance and access is ascertained. Should the document again be required by the Court, or by any Court with jurisdiction over this case, it will immediately be made available. I have directed that this document be retained by the Director of Naval Intelligence who will be responsible for its safekeeping and further delivery to the Court as required.

A major theme in the memorandum was that the United States can indeed suffer enormous national security damage even when secrets are shared with friendly countries, like Israel. Thus, Weinberger said he wanted to "dispel any presumption that disclosures to an ally are insignificant; to the contrary, substantial and irrevocable damage has been done to this nation."

He pointed out that intelligence information disclosed to a hostile nation "can be used to produce counter measures, promote disinformation techniques, and even permit the more efficient and effective utilization of resources in manners inimical to U.S. interests." But information provided to friendly countries, he insisted, could prove just as damaging.

> Unauthorized disclosures to friendly powers may cause as great a harm to the national security as to hostile powers because, once the information is removed from secure control systems, there is no enforceable requirement nor any incentive to provide effective controls for its safekeeping. Moreover, it is more probable than not that the information will be used for unintended purposes. Finally, such disclosures will tend to expose a larger picture of U.S. capabilities and knowledge, or lack thereof, than would be in the U.S. interest to reveal to another power, even to a friendly one.

Weinberger acknowledged that the U.S. and Israel routinely share intelligence information. But he maintained that the information obtained by Pollard went way beyond the scope of the official exchanges.

> In this case, the defendant has admitted passing to his Israeli contacts an incredibly large quantity of classified information. At the outset I must state that the defendant's unlawful disclosures far exceed the limits of any official exchange of intelligence information with Israel. That being true, the damage to national security was complete the moment the information was given over.

Weinberger gave many examples of the type of information compromised. "Ideally," he said, "I would detail for the

Court all the information passed by the defendant to his Israeli contacts; unfortunately, the volume of data we know to have been passed is too great to permit that. Moreover, the defendant admits to having passed to his Israeli handlers a quantity of documents great enough to occupy a space six feet by six feet by ten feet."

The Defense Secretary said that the secret memorandum had been prepared "based on my personal review of relevant information and my discussions with personnel who are knowledgeable about the data described herein." His purpose in preparing the document, he said, was "to explain the nature and significance of the defendant's actions as I perceive them to have affected the security of the United States."

The memorandum was divided into three parts. The first dealt with the categories of information compromised. It included what Weinberger described as "brief but specific examples of the actual documents passed." The second part dealt with what the Defense Secretary said was "the harm I perceive to have occurred, again with specific examples." The third section sought to "capsulize the overall significance of the defendant's activities."

In the document released under the Freedom of Information Act, the entire first section was deleted. But chunks of parts two and three were left intact.

Weinberger, in the damage assessment section, said that "the breadth of disclosures" was "incredibly large." Accordingly, he added, "the damage to U.S. national security interests resulting from those activities is similarly broad." He detailed what he said were "the more pertinent aspects of damage to U.S. national security as I perceive them."

One major setback involved the ongoing U.S.-Israeli intelligence-sharing agreements. The United States and Israel officially share a great deal of information on a quid pro quo basis. But the Pollard operation, Weinberger said, reduced Israel's incentive in sharing information with the United States since it had a weakened incentive for obtaining American secrets. It already had those secrets.

"It should be obvious," Weinberger added,

that the United States has neither the opportunity
nor the resources to unilaterally collect all the
intelligence information we require. We compensate
with a variety of intelligence sharing agreements
with other nations of the world. In some of these
arrangements there is virtually a full partnership
which stems from recognition of common and
indelible interests [a reference to the existing U.S.
agreements with the Anglo-Saxon countries—Britain,
Canada, and Australia].

But other agreements, Weinberger continued, were
"fashioned on a quid pro quo basis." As an example, he cited
the United States's willingness to share with an ally "certain
types of intelligence information in exchange for desired
information or other valuable assistance." These exchanges,
he said, are very carefully considered.

Once such agreements are entered into,

decisions to disclose particular classified documents
or items of intelligence information are made by
high level officials after a careful evaluation of the
costs of disclosure to our national security versus the
benefits expected to be obtained if disclosure is
approved. In some instances, especially sensitive
intelligence information that is sought by an ally is
traded because the ally agrees to furnish equally
sensitive information vital to U.S. security interests.

The preparation of information to be shared is complex
because "all criteria must be balanced against one another."
Weinberger said, for example, that "the requirement to protect sources and methods of information acquisition, as well
as the requirement to protect the substantive information
received, must conform with the recipients 'need' for that
information and the expectation of benefit for the United
States."

Thus, the end product of some intelligence-gathering operation may be exchanged with a foreign country, but the
exact sources and methods used to obtain that information

must be protected by all means. All intelligence services are extremely sensitive to the need to make certain that these sources and methods—whether agents or electronic intercepts involving broken codes or photographic surveillance—are not accidentally compromised.

"This usually means that substantive information is redacted from the original documents containing the information prior to disclosure," Weinberger said.

Pollard, however, delivered to the Israelis original documents that had not been edited by intelligence specialists to make certain that information which could indicate the exact sources and methods was removed.

"The defendant has specifically identified more than 800 U.S. classified publications and more than 1,000 U.S. classified messages and cables which he sold to Israel," Weinberger wrote. "To the best of my knowledge, not one of the publications he provided them was authorized for official release to Israel in unredacted form."

Thus, the "actions of the defendant have jeopardized the substantive intelligence information he provided to the Israelis, as well as the sources of that information, by placing it outside of a U.S. controlled security environment." Weinberger said the United States now faced "difficulties in reacquiring damaged sources of intelligence acquisition which have been compromised." The United States "must expect some amount of risk to accrue directly to U.S. persons from the defendant's activities." He added that the risk with which he, as Secretary of Defense, was particularly concerned "is that U.S. combat forces, wherever they are deployed in the world, could be unacceptably endangered through successful exploitation of this data."

The Defense Secretary also said that Pollard had abused the various honor systems in the U.S. intelligence community, which are supposed to limit officials from obtaining only that information for which they have a "need to know." Pollard, in addition, violated his responsibilities as a secured "courier" who could carry classified documents from one government building to another.

"The United States, and virtually all of those who cooperate with us by sharing intelligence, have developed a system of protecting classified information which depends on the reliability of individuals for its effectiveness," Weinberger said. "It is also a system which varies its requirements for protection with the sensitivity of the information at stake."
All classified material

> is required to be placed in proper storage,
> appropriate to its classification level, and all
> personnel who have custody are accountable for
> ensuring that proper procedures for protecting it are
> followed. The system necessarily depends on the
> integrity and reliability of the individual. So long as
> an individual is accountable for classified material in
> his custody, we can generally assume that personal
> interest will guarantee its safekeeping. It is when an
> individual obtains custody of classified material for
> which he is not responsible that safekeeping is
> jeopardized. In such an instance, there is no real
> incentive to adequately protect such information.
> One example of an occasion when this happens in
> the normal course of business is the necessary use of
> couriers to carry highly sensitive information from
> one location to another. The defendant frequently
> acted as such a courier, and it was his abuse of this
> system, a system necessarily dependent on the
> integrity of the individual, which permitted his
> espionage activities to occur. Moreover, in a situation
> such as this one, there is every incentive to use the
> acquired information in a person's self-interest.

In addition to the collection of intelligence, Weinberger maintained that Pollard's activities also "have harmed U.S. foreign policy." He cited the Israeli air strike against the PLO headquarters in Tunisia, noting that that country was a friend of the United States.
Weinberger offered the following advice to the judge as far as "an appropriate sentence" for Pollard was concerned:

Punishment, of course, must be appropriate to the crime, and in my opinion, no crime is more deserving of severe punishment than conducting espionage activities against one's own country. This is especially true when the individual spy has voluntarily assumed the responsibility of protecting the nation's secrets. The defendant, of course, had full knowledge and understanding of the sensitivities of the information unlawfully disclosed. To demonstrate that knowledge, I have attached copies of non-disclosure agreements which he voluntarily executed. Should the Court require further information or explanation of anything contained herein, you may provide the bearer of this document with your requirements and I will respond to them.

Pollard and his lawyers, Richard A. Hibey and Gordon A. Coffee, were permitted to read Weinberger's secret memorandum to the judge in order to prepare their rebuttal, which they submitted to the court on February 27, 1987. In it, they sought to reject the notion that Pollard's activities had caused great harm to the United States. Hibey later backed up this point by noting that very little of their rebuttal was classified secret by the U.S. intelligence community.

"In this case, notwithstanding its sensational features, where an enormous volume of information was transmitted improperly, it was done without the intent to, and without the result of, damaging the national security," the lawyers wrote.

This case is lacking the essential ingredient that would make this a heinous crime: the beneficiary was not, and is not, the enemy, but one of our closest friends. By this, we do not argue that what Mr. Pollard did was right, or that it does not merit punishment. However, the punishment must be appropriate to the actual severity of his criminal conduct. Applying that measure, no harm has come to this country. Accordingly, Mr. Pollard's sentence ought to reflect this indisputable fact.

In challenging the Weinberger memorandum, Pollard's lawyers said that it contained "a blizzard of contentions notable for the emphasis on the phrases 'may have,' 'could have,' and 'possibly has.' "

They also charged that the affidavit was not actually written by the Secretary of Defense. "In the true spirit of overkill that characterizes the Government's assessment of damage in this case, the attempt to make more out of what is the real injury to the national security is demonstrated by this technique of having the Secretary sign the affidavit rather than the true author(s)," they wrote, pointing out that the Defense Secretary did not personally sign a similar damage assessment in another pending espionage case in Virginia. "The point is noted here because this Court should not be bulldozed into not considering a challenge to a document just because it was signed by a cabinet secretary."

The Pollard rebuttal claimed that the Weinberger affidavit had "engaged in unbridled speculation on the potential damage" but failed to note specific instances of actual damage:

> While this speculation would be germane if Mr. Pollard had only been apprehended yesterday, over fifteen months have elapsed since his arrest. During this time, the United States has debriefed him extensively, conducted exhaustive reviews of the documents delivered by him to the Israelis, and had the opportunity to observe any material alteration of the relationships between it and the Government of Israel, allied nations and friendly Arab nations. The United States should have developed a concrete assessment of the damage by now, thereby obviating the need for any speculation. The United States' reliance on speculation therefore underscores the tenuousness of its claims.

The major point repeatedly made by the Pollard defense was that no U.S. secrets actually went to a hostile power, like the Soviet Union. The only reference to the Soviet Union in the Weinberger document involved the danger of a Soviet mole in Israeli intelligence. But the government simply raised this possibility "without any proof," according to the Pollard rebuttal.

"The Government has argued that the sheer volume of the information provided has made this one of the worst espionage cases in U.S. history," the rebuttal continued. "Again, this pandering simply fails to recognize the most salient of all facts in the case: the enemy was not the recipient of the information. Volume per se is irrelevant if it is not reflective of injury."

According to the Pollard rebuttal, Weinberger

> nowhere alleges that the United States has lost the lives or utility of any agents, that it has been obligated to replace or relocate intelligence equipment, that it had to alter communication signals, or that it has lost other sources of information, or that technology has been compromised. Indeed, the memorandum only discusses the *possibility* that sources may be compromised in the future, thus requiring countermeasures. The absence of any countermeasures taken in the aftermath of Mr. Pollard's conduct therefore is perhaps the truest barometer of the actual damage, or absence thereof, to the national security.
>
> Consequently, the methodology of this damage assessment is seriously flawed for lack of a "clincher." Its focus on damage is not in the compromise of the substantive information but rather on the intangible, unproven speculation that we shall be unable to negotiate effectively with the Government of Israel over intelligence sharing for some time. One may assume that if there were evidence of this, it would be presented in these papers. Certainly, after the passage of eighteen months since the Israelis began receiving information from Mr. Pollard, such a development would have surfaced by now—if it in fact has happened; it has not.

Weinberger, in his secret pre-sentencing affidavit to the judge, made a major point of Pollard's role in the Israeli air strike against the PLO's headquarters in Tunisia. He argued that U.S. relations with a friendly Arab country had been damaged. In the process, U.S. foreign policy interests would be undermined. The Tunis raid was evidence of Israel's use of Pollard-obtained information to cause damage to the United States.

Pollard had indeed provided the Israelis with information on the exact location of the headquarters, including aerial reconnaissance and a complete description of all the buildings there. This and other related data obtained by Pollard enabled the Israeli Air Force to evade detection and to bomb those headquarters on October 1, 1985—just some seven weeks before Pollard's arrest.

Weinberger, in his memorandum, went on at great length about the potential damage that this raid could have inflicted on U.S. interests, especially if Arafat had been killed. This was an example of Israeli aggressiveness prompted by a clear military advantage over its enemies, according to the Defense Secretary.

In particular, Weinberger said, U.S. relations with Tunisia had been injured because of the raid. But Pollard's defense rejected this argument. "Secretary Weinberger misses one key distinction," they said. "The raid on Tunis was not directed against Tunisia, but was a surgical strike aimed at a terrorist organization. While relations with Tunisia may have been ruffled over the attack [though there was no rupture of ties], it is interesting that President Reagan, architect of U.S. foreign policy, stated immediately after the raid that other nations have the right to strike at terrorists 'if they can pick out the people responsible.'"

In addition, the lawyers argued, the Israeli raid was not a product of newfound intelligence data provided by Pollard but rather "an application of Israel's consistent policy of retaliating for terrorist actions against its nationals." The Israelis undertook the raid only after three Israeli civilians were murdered by a PLO terror group in Larnaca, Cyprus.

Pollard's lawyers conceded that the information provided

by him "undoubtedly furthered the [Tunis] attack, but it did not induce it. Indeed, the information most likely minimized the loss of Israeli and Tunisian lives, which would be in the best interests of U.S. policy, by permitting a more accurate attack against the PLO headquarters."

Weinberger, according to Pollard's lawyers, did not indicate in his affidavit whether the alleged damage to U.S.-Tunisian relations was the result of the actual attack or the United States's failure to condemn it immediately. "Again," they said, "assuming that the raid would have taken place regardless of Mr. Pollard's passing of information to the Israelis, Mr. Pollard may have minimized the damage to U.S.-Tunisia relations by reducing the number of Tunisian fatalities."

Indeed, Reagan himself tended to endorse the Israeli operation. When questioned by reporters on how the Israelis could be certain they were striking at PLO members, the President replied: "I have always had great faith in their intelligence."

Pollard's lawyers included other arguments in their defense to rebut Weinberger's charge that the Tunis raid had undermined U.S. foreign policy interests. "Is the Israeli raid different from the U.S. raid on Tripoli?" they asked.

> Is it not fair or accurate to distinguish the two on the basis of our friendship with Tunisia versus our enmity with Libya? Each was a violation of sovereign territory. Each was carried out for the same purpose: to retaliate against terrorists in their known locations. Each was praised by our President as responsible reactions to terrorism. After 15 months, since Mr. Pollard's arrest, our relations with each of those countries has not changed. Therefore, the Secretary's policy analysis is less an analysis and more a convenient theory of injury which bears no relation to reality.

In Pollard's personal statement to the judge, he went one step further in defending his decision to provide the Israelis with information about the PLO operation in Tunis. "Perhaps the most direct role I played in helping to eradicate this terrorist threat to humanity occurred in the fall of 1985 when the Israelis decided to raid Yasser Arafat's headquarters outside Tunis," Pollard wrote.

> As I understand it, the retaliation was targeted specifically against the PLO's Force 17 group, which had been responsible for the murder of three defenseless Israeli civilians at a marina located in the Cypriot port of Larnaca. I spent two hectic weeks collecting information pertaining to Libya's air defense system and the PLO's disposition of anti-aircraft weapons, which evidently contributed significantly to the mission's success.

Pollard pointed out that that same Force 17 group had also killed three U.S. ambassadors "over the past decade with total impunity and was in the process of organizing additional terrorist acts against American diplomatic interests abroad when the Israeli air strike destroyed its command organization."

Pollard justified his contribution. "As far as I was concerned," he said, "this constituted a perfect example of where I thought my actions were of service to both Israel and the United States which, at the time, seemed unable or unwilling to protect its citizens abroad."

He was praised by the Israelis for his contribution. Both Yagur and Sella, he said, "stressed the fact that the mission could not have been undertaken without the information I made available."

Was there any damage in American relations with other Arab states as a result of the information passed to Israel by Pollard? Weinberger argued yes, but he did not include specifics in his affidavit. Pollard's lawyers noted that Israel had not attacked any Arab country since the Tunis raid with one exception. "Israel has had a longstanding policy, which predates Mr. Pollard's involvement with them, of targetting terrorist bases located in Lebanon," they said. "Those air strikes are the only exception to this proposition. If the information given by Mr. Pollard had altered the military balance, as Secretary Weinberger contends, Israel surely would have begun hostilities against Syria, in light of that country's provocative behavior in Lebanon."

Weinberger, in his affidavit, raised the possibility that Israel might share some of the information obtained by Pollard with third countries. The purpose would be for Israel to win some corresponding benefits from those countries. Trading intelligence on the international marketplace, after all, is by no means unusual.

Pollard's lawyers, in their brief, argued that there was no evidence produced by Weinberger that Israel had actually engaged in such activity. They said that "fears about what Israel might do with this information by sharing it with third countries, are completely unfounded, unless, of course, the Secretary is willing to state that information Israel has lawfully received is also subject to improper sharing. If that is the case, the danger here is not peculiar to the compromised information; it extends to all of it—compromised and uncompromised alike."

They went on to point out that the "heinousness of any espionage must take into account the intent of the recipient of the classified information to harm the United States. There is no evidence in the damage assessment of Israel's intent to injure the United States by reason of its having illegally received the classified information from Mr. Pollard. Israel is simply not the enemy—it is not the Soviet Union—it is not a Warsaw Pact nation—it is not China—it is not even India."

Israel, by contrast, enjoys a "special relationship" with the United States. "It is our staunch, steadfast ally. The worst that has been said about our loss in this case is that our negotiating posture in near term intelligence exchanges [with Israel] might be jeopardized," the lawyers said, adding that after fifteen months of investigation, "no evidence of this appears."

They then outlined benefits which the United States obtained by closely aligning itself with Israel. "Israel," they said, "also has undertaken operations from which the United

States derived substantial benefit. In past year, Israel has frustrated numerous terrorist activities against U.S. targets and provided information to be used in U.S. intelligence activities or actions against terrorism." In the publicly released text of the defense memorandum, the next several lines containing specifics of Israel's contributions were deleted by intelligence censors.

Weinberger, in his memo, also raised the possibility that Pollard could have been the victim of a "false flag" espionage operation. That involves a situation where the offender is duped into believing that he is giving information to a perfectly benevolent recipient when in fact the ultimate recipient is the enemy.

But Pollard's lawyers showed that he had been careful to determine that he was not involved in any "false flag" operation:

> Again, we reiterate that the Court should assess the actual damage, not what it could have done. All the indicia of the "flag" pointed squarely to Israel and nothing in Mr. Pollard's experience belied that. Thus, Mr. Pollard knew then-Colonel Sella . . . to be an Israeli military hero who led the bombing raid on the Iraqi nuclear reactor site in 1981. While residing in New York, Sella's wife was nationally active in the Anti-Defamation League [of B'nai B'rith].* In addition, Sella provided Mr. Pollard the entree to Yossi Yagur and Irit Erb, who became his long-term handlers. Most significantly, he met at length with Rafael Eitan, the ultimate controller of the operation. Throughout the course of his operation, Mr. Pollard questioned all of these individuals at length to satisfy his curiosity, and to establish their bona fides. Even the best trained agents could not have known the

---

*Mrs. Sella was not active in the ADL. Her only connection with the organization involved her employment in the New York law firm of Kenneth Bialkin, a former national chairman of the ADL.

details or events on which these individuals were quizzed. The specter of a "false flag" was, in reality, therefore, non-existent.

In arguing that the information Pollard gave Israel had damaged U.S. interests in the Middle East, Weinberger suggested that a stronger Israel upsets the balance of power in the region and therefore makes armed conflict more likely. But Pollard's lawyers contended that that assertion was absurd.

"If the United States truly believed that, it would not provide Israel with the most sophisticated military equipment and generous foreign aid. Instead, one of the bulwarks of U.S. policy in the Middle East is to ensure that Israel maintains a clear military superiority in the region."

They quoted from a classified U.S. report entitled *The Arab-Israeli Military Balance,* prepared by the U.S. intelligence community, which said that "the United States sells some of its best and most advanced equipment to Israel on a timely basis, occasionally even before some U.S. forces receive it."

Pollard's lawyers further rejected Weinberger's contention by suggesting the contrary—"with the knowledge of military superiority, Israel would not experience the insecurity which fuels wars in the Middle East."

When *The Washington Times* first reported on this section of the defense memorandum, Israeli Ambassador to the United States Meir Rosenne personally telephoned Weinberger to ask whether in fact this was true—that the Defense Secretary had suggested that a stronger Israel would upset the balance of power in the region to the detriment of the United States. Weinberger refused to comment on the substance of the classified document. But he did tell Rosenne twice during their conversation: "Pollard should have been shot."

Weinberger, in a separate, unclassified memorandum to the judge, said that the information Pollard gave the Israelis was

intentionally reserved by the United States for its
own use, because to disclose it, to anyone or any
nation, would cause the greatest harm to our national
security. Our decisions to withhold and preserve
certain intelligence information, and the sources and
methods of its acquisition, either in total or in part,
are taken with great care, as part of a plan for
national defense and foreign policy which has been
consistently applied throughout many
administrations. The defendant took it upon himself
unilaterally to reverse those policies. In so doing, he
both damaged and destroyed policies and national
assets which have taken many years, great effort and
enormous national resources to secure.

Weinberger urged the judge to be firm in his sentencing.
"I respectfully submit that any U.S. citizen, and in particular
a trusted government official, who sells U.S. secrets to any
foreign nation should not be punished merely as a common
criminal," he wrote.

Rather, the punishment imposed should reflect the
perfidy of the individual's actions, the magnitude of
the treason committed, and the needs of national
security. Here, although the defendant had executed
an oath to protect and safeguard classified
information, he betrayed the public trust and the
security of the United States in exchange for money.
I believe these facts should be weighed heavily in
fashioning the sentence to be imposed in order to
protect the public confidence in our law, and restore
the public's confidence in our ability and
commitment to protect U.S. security.

By early January 1987, it was apparent that the United
States and Israel were not going to reach an early agreement
on Avi Sella. Justice Department officials refused to offer
Sella immunity from prosecution in advance of question-

ing—something they had extended to Rafi Eitan and the other Israelis involved. The Americans felt that they had been burned by their earlier agreement.

The Israelis, for their part, were becoming increasingly convinced that they already had provided enough "full cooperation" with Washington. Indeed, they insisted that there had been unprecedented cooperation in such an espionage case. They were angry about the U.S. smears being leaked against them. Enough was enough. Why couldn't the United States simply drop the matter?

The Americans bitterly rejected these Israeli complaints. The United States, after all, had been the victim of Israeli espionage—not vice versa. Yes, Israel had cooperated, but not fully. And while Israel had disbanded LAKAM, Rafi Eitan had received a nice, cushy job as director of Israel Chemicals, the largest government-owned company in the country. That, of course, was not seen as punishment. As far as Washington was concerned, it was promotion for a job well done.

Thus, the loose ends of the Pollard case were going to fester.

But Sella's air force career could not be put on permanent hold. He was, after all, extremely popular. As commander of the Ramon Air Base, he had performed very well—as usual. Air Force Commander Amos Lapidot, Chief of Staff Moshe Levi, and Defense Minister Yitzhak Rabin agreed, after careful consideration, that Sella should not be punished for having followed instructions in establishing the initial contact with Pollard. They were also under strong pressure from inside the IDF not to sacrifice Sella for the sake of American-Israeli relations. In recent weeks, a group of senior Israeli Air Force officers had met twice with Rabin to insist that Sella go unpunished because he had acted in good faith.

Sella, as a result, was promoted to command the large Tel Nof Air Base near Tel Aviv—traditionally seen as a stepping stone to becoming Commander of the Air Force. After a few months, he would receive the rank that goes along with the command: Brigadier General.

Word of Sella's promotion deeply rankled Washington. It was seen as a direct slap in America's face. Israel had promised to "call to account" those officials involved in the "rogue" operation. Yet they were now actually receiving promotions.

On March 3, 1987, the United States responded by formally indicting Sella on three espionage charges. He was accused of conspiracy "to deliver to Israel information related to the national defense of the United States"; of causing documents "to be delivered to Israel knowing that they contained United States national defense information that would be used to the advantage of Israel"; and of unlawfully receiving "classified information from an employee of the United States." If convicted, the charge sheet said, he could be sentenced to a maximum of life in prison and fined $500,-000.

Rabin reacted bitterly. "We believe that we have carried out our own commitments in regard to this case and it is painful to us that the issue is continued and dragged [on] and we hope that there will be ways to remove this source of problems in the relations between our two countries," he said, insisting that it was "total nonsense" to claim that the Pollard operation had official sanction.

Sella's promotion—as far as the Pollards were concerned—could not have come at a worse time.

CHAPTER THIRTEEN

The Sentence

It was March 4, 1987, another sunny day in Washington, the date on which Jonathan Jay Pollard and his wife, Anne Henderson Pollard, were to be sentenced. They had been arrested fifteen months earlier. The room was packed. Reporters arrived at the U.S. District Court on Constitution Avenue just a few blocks from Capitol Hill very early—around twelve-thirty. The sentencing hearing was scheduled to begin at 2:00 P.M., but even ninety minutes ahead of time a long line had already formed outside the wood-paneled room. There were dozens of pushy journalists and courtroom artists waiting in a winding line along the marble wall of the corridor. There also were about twenty of Pollard's former colleagues at Naval Intelligence, including Commander Jerry Agee, his boss. All of them wore business suits—not their uniforms. Both Pollard's father and his father-in-law were waiting outside. Carol Pollard, the prisoner's sister, was also there.

Everyone stood in line quietly until the guards began to allow the observers inside—one at a time. They frisked everyone with portable metal detectors, even though each had earlier been screened when entering the building downstairs. Despite the presence of numerous guards, there was an immediate rush; angry words were exchanged as people rudely pressed forward. Eventually, after tense moments during which some reporters feared that there would not be enough room inside, everyone was cleared to enter.

After a few moments, the Pollards were brought into the courtroom, accompanied by their grim-faced lawyers. She was represented by James Hibey and Elizabeth Liebschutz, he by Richard A. Hibey and Gordon A. Coffee. They sat at a long table on the left side of the courtroom. Jay and his lawyers were on one side of the table, facing Anne and hers. On the other side of the room was the prosecution, led by the dapper U.S. Attorney for the District of Columbia, Joseph E. diGenova, who sat at the head of the table facing the judge. DiGenova was accompanied by two assistant U.S. attorneys: Charles S. Leeper and David F. Geneson. Everyone stood while Judge Aubrey Robinson, an imposing figure, entered the room and took his seat. He looked down at everyone from his elevated bench in the front of the courtroom, then casually nodded toward the court clerk. He clearly had been through this exercise before.

At exactly 2:10 P.M., the clerk began the proceedings. There was total silence as he declared: "Criminal Case Numbers 86-207 and 86-208, Jonathan Jay Pollard and Anne Henderson Pollard." He read out the names of the government and defense attorneys.

"Could we have the defendants and their counsel come forward," Robinson said, looking around the courtroom. The Pollards and their lawyers approached the bench.

"The defendant Jonathan Jay Pollard is before the court for sentencing, having entered a plea of guilty to conspiracy to commit espionage, in violation of Title XVIII, United States Code, Section 794 (c)," Robinson said, reading from a typewritten piece of paper. "Is that correct, Mr. Hibey?"

"That is correct, your honor."

"And the defendant Anne L. Henderson is before the court having entered a plea of guilty to one count of conspiracy to receive embezzled government property, in violation of Title XVIII, United States Code, Section 371, and accessory after the fact, to possession of national defense documents, in violation of Section 793 (e) and 3 of Title XVIII. Is that correct, Mr. James Hibey?"

"That's correct, your honor."

"Now, have counsel and the defendants had an opportunity to review the presentence report in this case?" Judge Robinson asked.

"We have, your honor," Richard Hibey replied first.

"Yes, we have, your honor," his brother added.

"Very well," Judge Robinson said. "Then I think that the defendants can have a seat at counsel table."

Judge Robinson called on Richard Hibey, a big man with a strong voice, to offer Jonathan Pollard's appeal for leniency. Over the months, Pollard had become critical of Hibey, but did not dismiss Hibey. "I don't know," Pollard had said, "I think it's too late to change."

Hibey, wearing a dark pin-striped business suit with a white shirt and red tie and reading from notes, recalled that Pollard had pleaded guilty and had cooperated with the United States government in its investigation. In exchange, the government had specifically agreed not to ask for life.

In arguing for a reduced sentence, Hibey acknowledged that Pollard was "undeniably guilty," but maintained that there was no evidence "of any intent to injure the United States." He recalled that Pollard had been specifically charged with espionage "on behalf of Israel," not against the United States. The lawyer looked at Pollard, who was sitting very upright in his chair.

"In the beginning," Hibey said, "he did it for nothing. Later, he received money for his efforts. The money corrupted him. His motivation to help Israel was irreparably soiled by the addictive effect of taking money for his work. His conduct violated his trust as a keeper of the nation's secrets, and when he was found out, he lied long enough to allow his handlers to flee the jurisdiction of the United States.

"Your honor," Hibey continued, "there is no excuse for this conduct, and we offer none to absolve him of his crimes."

But the defense attorney then sought to put the case into perspective. He argued that the actual damage to the

United States was minimal. Israel, an ally of the United States, was the recipient. "In short," he said, "Israel is not and has never been an enemy of the United States. Thus, your honor, any claim of damage, we submit, must be understood in terms of its severity. Here, thank God, the damage is simply not severe."

Hibey went on to describe Pollard's family. "You have, I believe, received a letter from his father, who is the head of the family," he said to the judge. "Dr. Morris Pollard and his wife are griefstricken over what has happened to their son and their daughter-in-law. But I bring this up, your honor, because I think it is important to understand the background of the defendant before the bar of this court. And that background includes an appreciation of his parents and his family, and that, because, your honor, I believe the evidence would show, if the court accepts what has been written to the court about this family, that they have been close and caring and loving and cognizant of their ethnic heritage and at the same time dutiful and law-abiding citizens.

"This is not a plea to return Mr. Pollard to his family and to his wife immediately," Hibey continued. "That is fantasy. But the man is thirty-two years old. His parents are seventy years old, at least. They have been confined to the strictures of penal institutions which govern the visitation of prisoners. Those restrictions have been especially arduous here, for the family lives in Indiana and the defendant has not been housed there. The number of hours that they have to visit one another are sharply limited and then in highly secured circumstances, unlike other prisoners who have visitation rights. I bring these points up to you, your honor, obviously to point out the depth of the tragedy that has befallen the family as a whole and to ask you to keep that in mind when you decide the sentence that Mr. Pollard must serve."

Hibey noted that Pollard had been targeted by extremist groups in prison. "In short," he said, "his life is in danger."

The prison system itself had already recognized the dangers facing Pollard. Over the past fifteen months, he said, Pollard had been "essentially isolated, and presumably, that isolation will continue. . . . The problem is simply this: There is hard time and there is hard time. I suggest to the court, your honor, that what we are going to be faced with here is the hardest of time, as indeed his previous fifteen months in prison have attested to that in many, many meaningful respects."

Given the nature of the charge, Hibey added, the prospect for parole would be slight. "I believe that one can expect that there will be no parole, that he will do all of the time that the statutes require, less good time, before he will be released."

He appealed to the judge for mercy. "There is room, therefore, your honor, for leniency while at the same time justice will be served. Thank you."

Hibey then turned away from the judge and walked over to Pollard's table.

Judge Robinson motioned for James Hibey, already standing, to begin his pleading on behalf of Anne. Although he clearly resembles his brother, James Hibey is not as heavy, has a higher voice, and gives the impression of being more intense, less self-confident.

He stressed the differences between the two cases: "As eager as the government is to paint Mrs. Pollard with the same broad brush that they paint Mr. Pollard, the facts in her case, stripped of all of the government's inflammatory rhetoric, demonstrate that they are two vastly different cases."

He argued that Anne was not a spy for Israel or China. "She did not participate in the operational aspects of this affair. She never participated in obtaining, copying or delivering any classified documents or information to anyone."

She was not "a mercenary, driven by need and greed" but simply "a wife, albeit a knowing wife, who was motivated by love for her husband. She acted out of genuine concern and love for him, not out of any desire for money."

Anne had not asked her husband to bring home classified documents about China. "Mrs. Pollard took no notes on the intelligence information contained in the PRC documents," Hibey said. "She essentially ignored the intelligence information contained in those documents and did not relate any of that information to her colleagues at CommCore or to anyone at PRC Embassy."

Her removal of the documents from the apartment and her signal to Sella about the troubles were attempts merely to help her husband, the lawyer argued. "And, indeed, even now it is her love for him which gives her the support and strength to get through these difficult times. She sees her husband vilified by the government and in the press and she feels a need to set the record straight."

Hibey paused to look at Anne. It was obvious that she was in pain; her arms were around her stomach. He recalled her devotion to her husband during his hour of need.

"In almost any other context," he continued, "that kind of conduct would be virtuous. In this case, it was criminal. She understands that, and while, in a pure sense, she does not regret helping her husband, she is terribly sorry that any of this ever happened."

Hibey then recalled Anne's suffering as a result of the affair. He recalled her horrible experience in the District of Columbia jail. "Effectively, she was locked down for twenty-four hours a day in a windowless cell, without exercise, without sometimes any communication from any of the other inmates. The only thing she would hear would be threats, threats to her, for being a spy."

Hibey also noted that Anne has suffered from a stomach disorder that required constant care and medication. "While at the jail, there were occasions on which she did not receive that medication and once, or finally, through the efforts of counsel, when she did receive it, it was frequently not given to her in a timely fashion. Because of her condition, she was unable to eat the jail food."

He took a deep breath, then continued: "The truth of the matter is, your honor, that she is daily in pain, sometimes so debilitating that it totally consumes her. I have witnessed it. In fact, her doctors presently are of the opinion that she should be hospitalized."

He also spoke of Anne's love for Pollard and how much she missed him while she was in jail. "Perhaps most significantly, during that time, she was unable to see her husband but once. Other inmates would be given the opportunity, through the jail chaplain, to do so, but for some reason they could not get together to talk. For her, and I suspect for him, that is as serious a punishment as she suffered while in jail.

"The continued separation from her husband has been devastating to her," Hibey went on. "Indicative of the type of relationship that they have, she has attempted to visit Mr. Pollard virtually every weekend while he has been incarcerated at Petersburg. She has driven 256 miles round trip each time to see him, sometimes three times a week; on a Friday and then again on a Saturday and then again on a Sunday.

"Finally," he concluded, "because of her medical and her legal bills, she is now penniless and deeply in debt. All of this has resulted in sixteen months of living hell. The stress and pressure she has been under, and the anxiety she has endured has been unbearable. She simply is not the same person who was arrested some sixteen months ago. In spite of all of this, she has cooperated, even before her plea, with the government. She has taken the requested polygraph examinations. She has been interviewed several times by FBI and NIS investigators, and she has testified for the Grand Jury." He said that her testimony helped the government indict Sella.

Hibey, referring to the Richard Feen incident, denied that Anne had tried to recruit him. "That simply is not true. . . . The bottom line is that she didn't attempt to recruit this friend, and this friend is not the victim that the government has attempted to portray him as.

"Now," he continued, "with regard to Mrs. Pollard's knowledge of espionage by her husband, she has never denied that she knew of his activities. What should be clear, however, though, is that when Mr. Pollard first told her of his desire to help Israel, she did not know what precisely he contemplated. Indeed, at that point, neither did he. His ideas had not crystallized. It was not until November of 1984 that she became aware of his transfer of documents, and that was after she saw and discovered documents in the apartment. She never knew of the contents of those documents that he was providing to the Israelis. She never obtained, analyzed or delivered them to the Israelis for her husband."

Hibey, turning toward Anne who was sitting facing the

judge, described her as "a loyal American who never spied or did anything to hurt this country." He pleaded that she not be returned to prison.

Then he paused, looked for a final time at his notes and into the eyes of the judge. "Thank you," he said.

His brother then stood. "Your honor," he asked, pointing toward Anne, "may we have a brief recess?" Her face clearly showed that she was in pain.

"How brief?" the judge asked.

"Long enough for her to be attended to. That is all."

"I want to finish tonight," Robinson said sternly.

"I understand that," Hibey said. "We all do. Five minutes perhaps?"

"Let's take a ten-minute recess," the judge said, pounding his gavel.

In the back of the courtroom, the spectators stood and stretched. They could see Anne leaving the room accompanied by two female guards. Pollard and the lawyers also joined her. There was no doubt that she was in pain—both physical and emotional.

Bernard Henderson and Morris Pollard, sitting in the back row, were understandably nervous and upset. The Hibey brothers had made a strong case for their clients; their arguments had been well reasoned; they both were articulate and to the point. At that moment, it appeared that Anne would receive some sort of suspended sentence. Among the reporters sitting in the courtroom, the consensus during the break was that the judge would not send a sick woman back to jail. Pollard, on the other hand, would probably receive twenty-five years although he would be eligible for parole after about ten years.

"Mr. Pollard," Judge Robinson said in resuming the hearing, "do you wish to allocute on your own behalf?"

Pollard, wearing a handsome dark suit, walked to the front of the room, just below the bench. The months in prison—during which he lost over fifty pounds—may have been difficult but he certainly looked a lot better than when he first appeared in that building at the end of 1985.

He began to address the judge, without any notes. He had been rehearsing his remarks in recent months. At one point in his life, he had been enrolled at the Notre Dame Law School; now was his chance to demonstrate what kind of lawyer he could have been. Pollard was articulate and that quickly became evident. With the exception of some very brief remarks made during his earlier court appearances, this was going to be the first time he would be heard by the press. He knew that this would be his day in court—his last chance to explain why he acted as he did.

"I thank the court for this opportunity to address it today," he began, looking up at the judge. "I will keep my comments as brief and to the point as possible."

"I have as much time as is necessary," the judge said, perhaps concerned about his earlier admonition that he wanted to complete the hearing by the end of the day. He probably did not want to leave any impression that he was being unfair.

Pollard then began his appeal. "Over the past fifteen months which I have been held in isolation," he said in a soft-spoken but clearly audible voice, "I have had more than enough time to reflect both upon my motives and upon the impact of my actions on behalf of the government of Israel.

"I have come to the inescapable conclusion that while my motives may have been well meaning, they cannot, under any stretch of the imagination, excuse or justify the violation of the law, particularly one that involves the trust of government, and there is no higher trust than [for] those in the intelligence community. The only one that I could imagine would be higher would be the court system.

"Having said that, it is cold comfort for me to realize that I was not intending to hurt the United States but to further an ally. That is cold comfort. It doesn't matter that what I did may benefit this country over the long run. That can't excuse or justify the breaking of the law."

Pollard, his eyes fixed on the judge, took a breath and continued. "I could go through a list of things that I wish I could use to justify an act such as mine, but unfortunately the inescapable conclusion is that I must admit wholly and unequivocally my criminal culpability before the court.

"In retrospect, I wish that I had thought about alternative courses of action. They were available. If I saw something that was wrong, I should have exhausted the legal processes that were at my disposal. They are called the chain of command. I should have gone to the Inspector General of the Navy. I should have gone to the Director of Naval Intelligence, the Chief of Naval Operations, the Secretaries of Navy and Defense and, even if I had to, the President of the United States, to make my case. But instead, I broke faith and took the law into my own hands.

"Unfortunately, what I failed to remember was that whenever a civil servant can no longer abide by the political constraints of the administration in which he serves or for whom he serves, he really only has one obligation, both to himself and the nation, and that is to resign in order to maintain his personal and his civic responsibility.

"What I have done, in short, your honor, was an act of intellectual laziness. I broke trust. I ruined and brought disgrace upon my family. I have inadvertently strained relations between two otherwise amicable nations. And in spite of the fact that I neither intended nor wanted to take monetary compensation for my actions on behalf of the Israelis, I did. And there is no way around the fact that I crossed a line.

"Perhaps the act itself that I did of providing information to the Israelis might have been perhaps a little bit more understandable for some people, if there hadn't been a monetary issue. But unfortunately, your honor, that is not the case. There was the element of money and I cannot avoid it and I will not avoid it."

Again, Pollard paused to collect his thoughts. So far, he sounded very apologetic about his activities. But this was understandable. He had to show his deep remorse.

"The other aspect of what I have done," he continued, "which is coming crashing down around me right now, is the fact that I violated another trust, and that was the trust of my wife."

His voice cracked. He spoke in a hushed tone.

"Usually," he said, "when a man and woman decide to get

married, it is with the assumption that each will safeguard the interests of the other and put their priorities in that order. Unfortunately, I sacrificed her, inadvertently, but the end result is here, on the altar, I think it is safe to say, of political ideology. There is nothing virtuous in that. I don't care what end you serve. And for fifteen months, I have tried to rationalize it but it is inescapable. You can't. I wish I could, because no man would like to be in the position that I am in right now, not for himself but for his wife.

"So what I did, your honor, was that I violated, in essence, two trusts; one, to the nation—and I say it again, it doesn't matter, ally or otherwise, a law was broken—and I violated another trust, which in some respects, your honor, is a little bit more ancient and perhaps a little bit more sacred, and that is the trust that a wife implicitly has in her husband.

"What I did was put my wife, your honor, in a situation where I called out to her and without any sense of self-preservation, she responded. I had no right to do that at all. And I would hazard to say that you may have seen some very criminal individuals before your court right now. . . ."

The judge, who had been looking at a piece of paper, looked up and interrupted Pollard: "May have?"

"Or," Pollard quickly corrected, "you *have,* but I don't think, your honor, and I don't want to be presumptuous, but I don't think you have had anybody before you who has felt more rotten at what he has done to the trust of his wife.

"What I should have done long ago was recognize the infectious nature of an ideology and resigned. That is what I should have done. And instead, your honor, what I did was take the law into my own hands. I appointed myself, as I have read somewhere, Secretary of State. . . ."

"Defense," Robinson said.

"Defense and, ultimately, the President."

Robinson again began to interrupt. But Pollard quickly added: "Everything."

"Security Council, DIA," Robinson said.

"NSA, DIA, Alphabet City," Pollard added, shaking his head with a faint attempt to be cute.

"You name it," Robinson said.

"And while I am alone, as I said before, I can rationalize in my moments of desperation the possible good that might come of it, it is cold comfort, because we are, I guess, at the bottom, your honor, a nation of laws."

"You guess?" the judge asked sternly.

"We *are* a nation of laws, and not. . . ."

"You are not convinced of that, are you?"

"I am very convinced of that," Pollard replied. "We *are* a nation of laws, not a collection of individuals that go off in twenty different directions, defining what they consider to be the national interest.

"If everybody followed my course of action, I can tell you what the net result of that would be. It would be nothing short of Lebanon. And that is an eventuality that I would never, under any stretch of the imagination, like to see here."

Pollard's reference to the "infectious nature of an ideology"—i.e., Zionism—was a surprise. Yes, he was bitter because of the Israeli government's decision to abandon him. But his comments today went considerably beyond his earlier remarks. He appeared to be condemning the entire Zionist movement. Maybe this was because he was trying to save his skin, and his wife's.

Pollard's voice then became a bit stronger as he continued: "I took sectarianism to an illogical extreme." No rationalization, no justification, no explanation, no mitigation for the breakage of a law.

"In conclusion, your honor," Pollard said, his voice even softer than it was at the start of his appeal, "I hope that other people in my position will watch very carefully the result of this kind of arrogance and draw the right conclusions. The penalties will be swift. They will be applied, and they will be felt deeply.

"The only thing, your honor, I can beg the court for at this time, as humbly and as sincerely as I can, is that it take that second violation of trust that I committed into account, and if it has any mercy in its heart, any mercy at all, that it be extended on behalf of my wife, who was, your honor, in my opinion, and in the opinion of others who have witnessed this situation at close hand, as much a victim of my culture-arrogance as anyone else.

"I took advantage, and she now must pay the penalty, which I think is a real and unmitigated tragedy, which I am the responsible party. I can't express any deeper remorse than the fact that I recognize I broke the law. I should not have done it. There were alternative means at my disposal, that I was lazy and did not use, and that I hurt badly a woman who was relying upon my good judgment to maintain the integrity of one of the oldest institutions that thinking man ever had, and that is marriage. And that is something I will have to live with long after this case is but a distant memory. Thank you."

He walked back to his table and sat down. On the whole, Pollard appeared to have strengthened his hand. He certainly hoped to have helped Anne.

The proceedings continued without a break. Anne stood and walked very slowly toward the judge. Her arms were clutched around her stomach. She was wearing a gray suit over a black silk blouse with a high collar.

"Your honor," she began in a barely audible voice, "I am speaking from my heart and not from any text that I have written. What I want to tell you is of the deep love and respect and admiration that I have for my husband, that my husband is by far the most important thing that has ever come into my life and will forever be that; that I would never, and I must be candid with you, I would never do anything to hurt him and I would only do to help him [sic] in any way I thought was correct.

"I pray to God every single day that I will be reunited with my husband. That is all I live for. It is just, I want more than anything to raise a family with him, grow old with him and live the rest of my life with him. I can't think of a man who would be a more wonderful father or more caring or more concerned than Jonathan Pollard. He is the most wonderful man I have ever laid eyes on or met in my entire life."

Everyone in the courtroom strained to hear her remarks.

Reporters sat at the edge of the benches, trying to listen and take notes. It was not easy.

"I know that he undertook his actions because he believed that at the time he was doing good for both the United States and Israel and he believed at the time that by strengthening Israel, a vital strategic ally, he was indirectly strengthening the United States, considering the special relationship which both nations share.

"My husband and I are vehemently anti-Communist and we would never do anything to harm this country or hurt this country in any shape or form. We are dedicated and patriotic Americans and we are also loyal to Israel. We look to Israel as a, shall I say, as the end of the Holocaust, as a nation or state that represents the end of the systematic extermination of Jews or of mankind in general. And we would never, as I said, never, never do anything to harm this country.

"I cannot lie and say I was not aware that my husband was assisting Israel at the time, but I can say that my husband fully assured me that he was doing nothing in his power to hurt Israel—or rather," she added, correcting herself, "to hurt the United States, that he was not compromising information against the United States or doing anything to harm this great nation, which is our homeland, which is where our families live, which is our birth place and is, to us, extremely special.

"I love Jay very, very much and when he called me in his eleventh hour, I responded because I felt that was what a wife should do. I felt that I was, while assisting my husband, not causing any harm to the United States at all. I did not compromise information. I did not disclose anything to any foreign national. I have never committed espionage in my life, nor would I ever. I would never do anything to damage this country.

"I just pray every day that I will be reunited with Jonathan Pollard. He is everything in the world to me. He is so special. I need him so much right now. He is my soul, my best friend ever, my intellectual conversationalist, my best friend. I mean, he is my greatest love. He is everything in the world to me wrapped up in one."

By now, she was crying. She tried to compose herself, but could be seen visibly shaking in front of Judge Robinson.

"I never thought," she continued in a very low voice, "that God would bless me with somebody as good and wonderful as my husband, and it has just disheartened me to see the consistent negative reports on him, because anyone who knows him knows what a good and wonderful person he is and that he would, if someone called him at three o'clock in the morning and needed something or an emotional problem or whatever, my husband would be the first one to get out of bed to help them because that is the kind of person he is."

Again, the tears flowed. "I'm sorry," she cried. "I am so sorry for what happened. I can't change history but I can say, I am very sorry to have seen two nations come to this point who share such a close relationship in such a political case. I am very, very sorry to have seen this happen.

"I greatly respect Israel and I greatly respect this country and I want nothing but the two to be good friends. The two come through for one another time and time again. In terrorist incidents, where my husband and I are absolutely outraged over the barbaric and the heinous acts that occur, I am happy to see that the two nations work together sometimes, or singly, to avert those type of incidents. I am happy to see that, I believe, both countries are working to avert an Arab-Israeli war, and I believed at the time that my husband was doing everything in his power to preserve human life."

Her voice suddenly grew a bit louder as she was winding up. "Again," she said, "I am sorry for what happened. At the time, I believed it to be correct. My husband pleaded with me. He had just, as you know, the previous day, asked me to remove certain items from the house should he ever use this word [i.e., "cactus"], and it came through his call and I did it. And I can't say that I would never not help him again. However, I would look for different routes or different ways of doing that.

"I am just so sorry this incident has gotten so blown out of proportion. I am very, very sorry for it to have happened. I am sorry for it to have hurt relationships between two countries. I pray that one day Jonathan and I will have children together and that that will be something that will occur in the near future, and I pray, I pray to you for leniency and for mercy, especially for my husband, who is everything in the world to me. Thank you very much."

She walked back to her chair. As she sat down, she wiped her eyes with tissues. Her hand reached out to touch her husband's.

The judge called on Assistant U.S. Attorney Charles Leeper. He approached the bench with his notes. Leeper is a tough, no-nonsense prosecutor; physically, he resembles the gruff lieutenant on the popular television program "Miami Vice," although Leeper is much more articulate.

"Your honor," he began in a booming voice, "I intend to keep my remarks mercifully brief, and I will be addressing only the case of United States against Jonathan Pollard." He said that David Geneson would later address the matter of Anne's sentencing.

Leeper glanced quickly at his notes. "In reading the version of the offense that this defendant has written—the defendant's version of the offense—I was struck by the frequency with which he would make a point or attempt to make a point by literal references or biblical references. And there was one in particular at page 14, that struck me. At that time or at that place in his pleading, the defendant said, 'Despair is the unforgivable sin.' As I was growing up, I was taught that there are, in fact, two sins that are unforgivable, and they are arrogance and deception. And in fact, it is in the Book of Proverbs, at Chapter Sixteen, where we are told, where we learn, that there are many sins that the Lord has, but the two that his soul detests are haughty eyes and lying tongue.

"And in fact, arrogance and deception is what that reference means. And it is arrogance and deception which drove this defendant to commit the acts, the criminal acts in this case, and they are also those two character traits, arrogance and deception, typical of the way he has sought to defend and excuse the things that he has done."

Leeper restated the government's arguments about the grave harm committed to U.S. national security. "It seems that this defendant believes that if he keeps repeating the words to this court, 'This case does not involve the Soviet Union,' that your honor then will swallow the position that he is taking that he caused no harm to the national security when he sold those thousands of pages of TOP SECRET and code word documents. . . . Now, in taking that position, this defendant is saying, 'Jonathan Jay Pollard is right,' he says, 'but the Secretary of Defense, in his sworn declaration to this court, is wrong when he states that as a result of Jonathan Pollard's activities enormous damage has been wrought to the national security.'

" 'Jonathan Jay Pollard is right,' he says, 'but the President of the United States, when he issued Executive Order 12356, was wrong when he said that the disclosure, the unauthorized disclosure, of TOP SECRET information to any nation, would cause or could be expected to cause exceptionally grave damage to the national security.'

" 'Jonathan Jay Pollard is right,' he says, 'and every administration since 1948, since the creation of the Israeli state, Republican and Democrat alike, have been wrong when they determined that the disclosure policies should not permit the disclosure to Israel of the kinds of secrets that this defendant sold.'

"This defendant," Leeper declared, "has admitted that he sold to Israel a volume of classified information ten feet by six feet by six feet. So if it was stacked up right here in front of where he is sitting, it would be as long as this table, a little bit wider and well above his head.

"Are we to believe that he studied each one of those documents, those TOP SECRET code word documents, before he delivered them to his handlers? Are we to believe that he conducted a page-by-page review of each document weighing the impact of its disclosure on our foreign relations, determining the need that Israel had for that particular information, assessing whether or not Israel was capable of affording the same measure of protection to that document as we could?"

Leeper, who had come to understand the facts of the case about as thoroughly as anyone, continued to paint a picture of Pollard as a dangerous, greedy, and treacherous spy who sold out his country for money. "He has told us that every day for over a year, he would grab handfuls of daily messages, throw them into a suitcase, messages which included information, TOP SECRET information, about the location of U.S. ships, the location of U.S. training exercises, the location of various U.S. training stations, and we are to believe that before he stuffed those messages in his suitcase he conducted this careful analysis.

"Is there no limit to how gullible Jonathan Jay Pollard thinks we all are? It would be impossible for him to have conducted that kind of analysis for more than one percent of these documents, and it is doubtful that he did that. And the reason that that is so is because he just didn't care. He made a judgment up front—Israel, right or wrong. And once he made that judgment, he was on automatic pilot. He never looked back. He no more understands today how much damage he has done to the national security than he understood back then when he was stuffing that stuff in the suitcase. He didn't care then. He doesn't care now."

Leeper looked again at his notes. He spoke of Pollard's family. "I have met Mr. Pollard's mother and father, and this defendant has as fine a group of parents as any man could want. And that this man would commit this crime, without considering the impact on his parents, makes it all the more reprehensible. A thirty-two-year-old man should not be heard to come in here, after having committed this thoughtless crime, which deeply hurt his parents, and ask your honor to consider their grief and their pain in granting him some leniency."

Again, Leeper paused, clearly confident in his arguments. He was scoring points with the judge and the spectators, and doing so succinctly. The momentum was clearly with him. The judge kept nodding in agreement.

Leeper charged that Pollard, in his written pleadings, had

displayed "blind contempt" for the U.S. military and intelligence community, even alleging anti-Semitism in the Navy. "Well, what Jonathan Pollard doesn't say in this pleading is that when the United States government learned on the night of October 10th, 1985, that the *Achille Lauro* terrorists, the murderers of Leon Klinghoffer, a United States citizen, were fleeing Egypt by plane, it was United States Navy fighters that took off from an aircraft carrier, in the middle of the night, intercepted that plane and forced it to land in Italy. Now, this action was taken at great personal risk to those military personnel. It was taken, despite the fact that it would have obviously unsettling effects on our friends in Egypt and in Italy, but certainly, it was taken without reference to the religious beliefs of the victim in question, Leon Klinghoffer."

Leeper said that Pollard's perspective "has become so skewed and his view so warped that at the very first opportunity he has, he is going to be about the business of telling everything he knows to the Israelis."

He looked at his papers. "Well," he continued, "what can we do to protect against that? What can be done to protect our national security from the damaging conduct of people like Jonathan Pollard?"

Leeper cited Pollard's utter disregard for signed agreements, including his refusal to obey the plea agreement which restricted his access to the press. "On January 3rd, 1985, right in the midst of this conspiracy, Jonathan Pollard signed a security agreement. Your honor has seen it. It was attached to Secretary Weinberger's declaration. It is not classified. And he stated therein, 'I will not discuss or reveal any classified information except in the performance of my official duties. I take this obligation freely, without any mental reservation or purpose or evasion.'

"That was in the middle of the conspiracy. He gets caught. He is arrested. He decides to plead guilty and he comes in here, on June 4th, 1986, and again he looks your honor in the eye and says, 'There is a plea agreement, your honor, that I have signed. I acknowledge its contents and I agree to live up to the terms and conditions of the plea agreement,' one of which includes a requirement, almost a housekeeping requirement, that would cause little trouble to this defendant to follow, the man who claims to have learned his lessons after fifteen months, a requirement that if he wishes to speak to the press, all he has to do is to submit the information he wishes to disclose to the Director of Naval Intelligence, the very same man he says now he should have gone to fifteen months ago.

"He looked your honor in the eye on June 4th, told you he would abide by those conditions, and he wasn't telling your honor the truth, because on any number of occasions, as recently as a couple of weeks ago, for example, on January 29th, he sat down with a reporter and imparted information which we maintain and have demonstrated to the court is, in some instances, classified, and never bothered to follow that procedure."

Pollard, Leeper said in summing up his statement to the judge, simply cannot be trusted to keep his word. "And I close by saying, your honor, that what these three documents demonstrate, in my view, is that when it comes to protecting against further disclosures of U.S. secrets, Jonathan Jay Pollard is not a man of his word. And in combination with the breadth of this man's knowledge, the depth of his memory and the complete lack of honor that he has demonstrated in these proceedings, I suggest to you, your honor, he is a very dangerous man. Thank you."

Leeper had done well, but many courtroom spectators still remained convinced that Pollard would receive a twenty-five-year sentence.

The judge motioned for the other Assistant U.S. Attorney to come forward. David Geneson approached the bench. He looked less hostile and intimidating than Leeper, although that image was merely superficial. Geneson was tough and unrelenting. Jewish himself, he was especially bitter about what the Pollards had done.

"Your honor," he said, "I also will be brief."

"Are you getting tired?" the judge asked.

"I expect everyone here may be a little tired."

"No, no, judges and lawyers don't do anything in court so we have plenty of time," Robinson said sarcastically.

Geneson reviewed the government's charges against Anne. "Counsel has said the government has been strident," he said, "without fear of appearing unsympathetic to this defendant's age, physical maladies, personal relationship with her husband, the government believes that this conduct is without serious mitigation or explanation. There is no rationale, be it political, ideological, practical or personal, for the fact that she assisted Jonathan Jay Pollard in undermining this country's national security.

"Being knowledgeable about his conduct, from its inception, in detail, understanding its implications, accepting the fruits, the benefits, the monetary compensation, the two luxurious trips taken within an eight-month period, she also sought and obtained from her husband classified, secret PRC documents, used those documents, examined them, took notes on them, left her fingerprints on them, and then kept them, along with many other classified documents that her husband was storing in their apartment, thereby leaving them additionally exposed to compromise to people who should not, above and beyond her, be accessing them."

Geneson held a yellow legal pad in front of him. He looked down at it, then continued his statement. He cited Anne's effort to dispose of the documents in the apartment once Pollard had been stopped for questioning. He also referred to her meeting with Sella.

"Your honor," Geneson continued, "something has happened recently which sheds a great deal of light on what is going on in court here today. And the court already knows what I am referring to, but I think it bears mentioning. I had the opportunity to watch '60 Minutes' this last Sunday night, to watch an interview of defendant Anne Henderson Pollard. Unfortunately for this defendant, so did millions of other Americans. She was interviewed. When she was asked whether she understood what she was getting into, her response was, 'Very much so.' She went on from there to discuss some of the factual details of the espionage operation."

He noted that Anne, during the interview, had failed to express any remorse. And indeed, when asked by Mike Wallace whether she would do it over again, she replied: "I feel my husband and I did what we were expected to do, what our moral obligation was as Jews, what our moral obligation was as human beings, and I have no regrets about that."

Geneson then repeated the phrase, "I have no regrets." He looked up from the pad and toward the judge. "That is my emphasis, your honor," he said.

"This defendant," he continued, "comes to this court with a mask of contrition and remorse. She is terribly sorry, according to her counsel, according to herself, as to what has happened. Your honor, the government suggests she is terribly sorry that she is caught."

Geneson began to speak with a louder voice. "She shows, your honor, and showed in the forum of Sunday night on '60 Minutes,' that she does not believe that what she and her husband did is wrong; that her problems are actually everyone else's problems. But moreover, the government believes that, based upon how she appeared, what she said, how she acted, in a much less emotional environment this past Sunday night, if given the opportunity, she would do the same thing as what she did before.

"We believe, your honor, that this defendant does not merit the consideration that this court reserves, that this court would bestow, upon a defendant who recognized the criminality of their acts, who was willing to take responsibility for them. She characterizes her conduct in terms of a political crime. This is not a political crime, your honor. It is a criminal act. The government would suggest, your honor, and the government requests, that this court impose a sentence of incarceration reflective of her lack of remorse and contrition and commensurate with the severity of the acts in which she was engaged. Thank you."

Geneson returned to his table. His boss, diGenova, wearing a very smart, gray double-breasted suit with a matching handkerchief in the outer pocket and sitting majestically at the head of the table, appeared pleased by the work of his two assistants. He was the coach; they were his quarterbacks.

The judge called James Hibey to offer a rebuttal. "Your honor," Hibey began, "I will try to be very brief."

"I have plenty of time," the judge said.

Hibey, glancing at his handwritten notes, charged that Geneson's points "really are hollow." Projecting both anger and frustration, he urged the judge to consider all the facts and circumstances. He repeated that Anne had been motivated by her "love for her husband. It is overreaching, we would submit, to suggest that Mrs. Pollard assisted in undermining the national security of this country. The facts simply do not bear it out."

Hibey addressed the "60 Minutes" interview. The judge interrupted him. "Did you know about it?" he asked.

"No, your honor, not until it was done."

"I didn't think so," the judge said scornfully.

"And as misguided as it would have been and was," Hibey continued, "you have to understand, as I am sure virtually everyone in this courtroom does, that the format of that program is such that things are taken in and out of context. And what Mr. Geneson quotes from probably are his own notes, perhaps not. The transcript, and I watched carefully and I watched it several times, the transcript indicates that when she said, 'And I have no regrets about it,' she wanted to continue. She says, 'My acts,' and then Wallace cuts her off and doesn't give her an opportunity to say anything more.

"I spoke to her the next day, after I watched it, and what she didn't regret, as I have told you today, is that she helped her husband. She regrets that there was any criminal activity involved. There was no appreciation for that as it was happening, but that show makes her look like someone who is without remorse, or regret, and it just does not accurately portray her.

"She would not, as Mr. Geneson suggests, do the same thing all over again. She indicated to you today that she would help her husband, but she would find other ways. She recognizes that this was a criminal activity. She would not engage in criminal activity again."

James Hibey took a second to catch his breath. He was speaking loudly and emotionally. The judge did not appear all that interested. "What I am suggesting to the court is she *has* been punished enough," Hibey said. "She will continue to be punished, simply by the very virtue of her separation from her husband. We ask the court to consider it all and show some mercy and place her on probation." Hibey sat down.

Richard Hibey then approached the bench to defend Jonathan Pollard. He acknowledged Pollard's guilt—"We are not saying there was no injury. But it is not the injury that calls for the imposition of a substantial or maximum sentence."

Hibey again insisted that the damage to American national security had not been serious.

Judge Robinson interrupted. "That depends entirely upon what credence I give to what I have read, doesn't it?" he asked.

"That is correct," Hibey replied, "and that, in the final analysis, your honor, is what I have to rely on. Obviously, all of us, and understandably so, are restricted by the laws involving the discussion in open court of classified information, and that is why this court has had a substantial amount of classified information before it."

Robinson raised his arm to stop Hibey. "Well," the judge said, "then I would ask you to just think and not articulate."

"Yes, sir."

"But I would ask you to think about the Secretary of Defense's affidavit, as it related to only one thing, and I won't even pinpoint it, as it related to only one area with reference to one particular category of publication, and I fail to see how you can make that argument."

"Your honor," Hibey said, "I must say, in all candor, that I—my recollection of the Secretary's affidavit is not so precise that I can be responsive to you, even in a generalized sense."

"Would you like to come to the bench and I will refresh your recollection to what I am referring to?"

"Yes."

"I want you to understand very clearly where I am coming from."

"Yes, your honor."

"Do you want to come up, Mr. Leeper?"

At that point, Hibey, Leeper, and diGenova walked toward the judge for their secret conversation. They spent about two minutes with Robinson before everyone returned to their places. There was no indication what specific piece of intelligence mentioned in the Weinberger affidavit was being cited by Robinson.

But later it would become clear that the discussion involved Pollard's handing over to the Israelis the extremely sensitive U.S. handbook on communications intelligence cited in Weinberger's secret memorandum. Clearly, Judge Robinson was convinced—like Weinberger—that the transfer of this book alone was extremely damaging to U.S. national security.

When Hibey resumed his statement in open court, the subject of the damage done by Pollard in the release of the communications handbook was simply dropped.

"I do not believe that the case has been made here that Mr. Pollard has violated the classified information rules that have governed us during the period of our preparation for this sentence. I don't stand here and tell you that I agree or otherwise advised or knew or approved of any discussions he had with the media, particularly just one person," Hibey said.

The reference was to Pollard's newspaper interviews.

"You don't take the position, do you, that they are in compliance with my order?" the judge asked Hibey.

"I don't believe they are—I don't believe," the lawyer corrected himself, "that he is in violation of your order because—and that, because, your honor, of what we argued yesterday in our pleading, that the information that was discussed is, in fact, unclassified information."

"But before any information was to be discussed, what was ordered to be done, Mr. Hibey?" the judge asked. "That is all."

"Oh, I understand that, your honor. I understand that."

"What was ordered to be done, across the board?"

"That on the occasion of discussing classified information, there should be notice to the government," Hibey said.

"No, no, no," the judge quickly shot back angrily. "That is not the way it read at all. Do you want to get it out? Give him the file and look at it again. Refresh your recollection."

"Very well," Hibey said. A clerk brought the May 23, 1986, plea-bargaining agreement to the lawyer. "Paragraph Nine?" Hibey asked the judge. The judge looked at his copy and nodded. Hibey started to read that paragraph to himself. It says:

> Mr. Pollard understands and acknowledges his legal obligation to refrain from the unauthorized disclosure, either orally or in any writing, of classified information derived during his employment by the United States Navy and/or in the course of the activities which resulted in his arrest in the above-mentioned case. Should Mr. Pollard at any time author any book or other writing, or otherwise provide information for purposes of publication or dissemination, he hereby agrees to first submit said book, writing or information to the Director of Naval Intelligence for pre-publication review and deletion of information which, in the sole discretion of the Director of Naval Intelligence, is or should be classified. Furthermore, at the time of his acceptance of the instant plea offer, Mr. Pollard agrees to execute an Assignment to the United States of any profits or proceeds which may be obtained by, or become payable to, Mr. Pollard in connection with any publication or dissemination describing his employment by the United States Navy, his espionage activities on behalf of the government of Israel, or the facts and circumstances leading to his arrest in this criminal case. The Assignment is attached hereto as Exhibit A, and is incorporated herein by reference.

Hibey looked up at the judge. He acknowledged that Pollard had made a mistake. "The whole action was ill-advised, unauthorized, there is no question about that in my mind.

What I am still trying to point to is the fact that the information itself was unclassified."

But Judge Robinson again pointed out that that decision was not Pollard's to make. Pollard was no longer in any position to decide what should or should not be classified. Hibey conceded that Pollard had granted the interviews without the required pre-clearance procedures. He did not ask why the government had decided to let a journalist into the prison in the first place.

Instead, he looked again at his notes and began his final summation. He stressed how Pollard had cooperated with the government's investigation. He said that Sella's indictment was largely the result of Pollard's testimony before the Grand Jury. "If that man goes to trial," Hibey said, "the evidence against him must largely rest upon the testimony of Mr. Pollard. And there we will hear the argument that Mr. Pollard has told the truth.

"And so, in the end, we are asking for a judgment tempered with mercy," he concluded.

Hibey walked back to his chair. He looked at Pollard, who was staring at his wife. Anne was still clearly suffering.

The judge noticed that Anne was in visible pain. "You don't need another recess, do you?" he asked.

"No," Richard Hibey said. "We are prepared to go forward."

Robinson again looked at Anne, who was now weeping. "Is she all right?" he asked.

"Yes, sir," Hibey replied quickly.

"No," Pollard shouted, shaking his head as he saw his wife clutching her arms around her stomach. His anger at Hibey was evident.

Hibey quickly rose and said: "May we have a break, your honor?"

"How long do you need?"

"Five minutes."

"All right. Five minutes then, please."

The recess lasted for more than five minutes; it was closer to fifteen. Anne was almost hysterical in the adjacent room where she, Pollard, their lawyers, and the guards had gone. Inside, Pollard tried to comfort her. He threw his arms around his wife, told her not to worry. He tried to be brave, although he was convinced a life sentence awaited him. His only hope was that Anne would be spared a return to prison.

"Is there anything further from counsel?" the judge asked as the session resumed. The lawyers shook their heads.

Judge Robinson then began his formal sentencing. Inside the courtroom there was total silence. In the back row, Dr. Morris Pollard and Bernard Henderson were understandably tense. They looked bitter and confused.

"Would the counsel come forward and the defendants come forward," Robinson said. The lawyers and the Pollards moved to the front of the courtroom. They stood below the judge. The climax of the hearing had come.

"I think I should state for the record that during my entire tenure in this court, I have never had more voluminous submissions in connection with the sentencing of a defendant than I have had in this case. And in addition to those voluminous submissions by each side, I have also received numerous communications directed to the court with respect to this procedure.

"I have read all of the material once, twice, thrice, if you will, and I have given careful consideration, not only to the submissions, but to argument of counsel, and I pronounce sentence as follows:

"With respect to the defendant Jonathan Jay Pollard, who is being sentenced for violation of Title XVIII United States Code, Section 794 (c), I commit the defendant to the custody of the Attorney General or his authorized representative for his life."

Upon hearing the word "life," Anne began to scream hysterically. "No, no, no," she cried, collapsing on the floor. The two female guards picked her up. The lawyers asked her to calm down. The spectators gasped. It was a stunning sentence, harsher than almost everyone had expected. The judge, after a very brief delay, continued.

"I am required, by law, to impose a $50 assessment," he said. "There will be no fine."

Helped to her feet and only slightly composed, Anne was still crying when the judge looked at her. He wanted to announce her sentence quickly.

"With respect to the defendant, Anne Henderson Pollard, I commit the defendant Anne Henderson Pollard to the custody of the Attorney General or his authorized representative on the first count of the information to a period of five years."

Again, there was an uproar in the courtroom. Anne again gave out a shriek. She earlier did not believe she would be going back to jail. Only the day before, in a telephone conversation with a reporter, she spoke of her plans to organize support groups around the country on behalf of her husband. At least, she would be free on the outside, able to visit him. She would be able to talk to the press. But her hopes were quickly dashed.

Robinson pounded his gavel. There was still bedlam in the courtroom but he continued. "With respect to the second count of the information, I commit the defendant to a period of five years to run concurrent by the counts. And as required by the Comprehensive Crime Control Act, I impose a $50 assessment on each count. There will be a special designation with respect to the place of incarceration."

Anne's lawyer, James Hibey, quickly spoke out. "Your honor," he shouted, "could I request that she be allowed to remain on bond pending that commitment and designation and allow her to submit herself directly to the institution?"

"That request is denied," Judge Robinson said firmly. "Recess the court," he told the clerk.

It was exactly 5:05 in the afternoon, some three hours after the sentencing hearing began. Reporters scurried to find telephones. The guards dragged Anne out of the courtroom. By now, she was screaming, completely overcome with hysteria. There was nothing Pollard could do to help her. Indeed, federal marshals forcibly separated them.

In the back row of the courtroom, the two fathers shook their heads in disbelief.

Outside the courthouse, diGenova met with reporters. "It is likely he will never see the light of day again," he boasted. Technically, he acknowledged, Pollard could become eligible for parole after ten years. But because of the harm done to America's national security, diGenova said, Pollard probably never will be freed.

CHAPTER FOURTEEN

When Fantasies Become Nightmares

Immediately after his sentencing, Pollard was moved from Petersburg to a federal prison hospital in Springfield, Missouri. Anne was sent to the federal prison in Lexington, Kentucky. In the months that followed, they would not be allowed to see each other. They were permitted to talk on the telephone only a few times. And their mail was heavily censored.

In a May 19, 1987, letter to me from prison, Pollard expressed surprise that correspondence was reaching him. "I, too, was pleasantly surprised or, should I say, relieved to hear from you again," he wrote.

> In light of what has been going on with my mail, I suppose I should be thankful that any of it manages to reach me. Whatever antediluvian creature is responsible for screening my letters to Anne has been single handedly responsible for destroying the government's strategic stockpile of magic markers. My letters to her have been effectively reduced to little more than free standing adverbs, adjectives and conjunctions. I haven't been able to make any sense

273

out of what they've chosen to censor and can only conclude that their principal objective is to harass us as much as possible.

In that regard, I thought it was rather humorous that a section of one letter pertaining to an interview of Caspar Weinberger which I'd heard on National Public Radio had been blacked out ostensibly for "security" reasons. Having been involved with this type of prison-related censoring a few years ago, I'm well aware of the fact that the first priority of such efforts is to "sit" on the mail for as long as possible in order to frustrate correspondents and thereby reduce their incentive to write. It's sadistic but makes perfectly good sense, especially if the navy has nothing better to do with its largely useless officer corps.

In Springfield, Pollard underwent a series of psychological tests. For his own protection, he was again put in an isolated cell, away from other prisoners, many of whom were mentally ill. At night, he could hear their constant wailing and ranting. He grew a beard because he feared that the razor blades he was given had been previously used by other inmates; they could have AIDS. But on the whole, the physical situation in Springfield was an improvement over Petersburg.

"I must admit that the officials at Springfield have been trying their best to make things as civilized as possible for me, which I deeply appreciate given the fact that I'm being held in solitary confinement and will probably be kept in this status for the indefinite future," he wrote. "Needless to say, every day is a struggle against the twin constants of prison life: namely, despair and ennui."

He said that "the near total isolation and lack of control over my life can be absolutely overwhelming at times." But he was determined to survive. "I try to follow a very strict personal regimen since it would be incredibly easy to simply give up and become a mental vegetable. I don't know whether you can imagine what it's like to be locked down twenty-three hours a day, but it's somewhat comparable to emotional strangulation." Pollard's cell was air-conditioned and he was allowed one hour of exercise a day "in a rather small grass-covered courtyard equipped with a few park benches.

"Luckily," he continued, "I've been permitted to purchase a radio which has put me back in contact with the outside world." He said that there was a National Public Radio station broadcasting out of nearby Southwestern Missouri State University. "I can listen to the BBC's World News Service as well as Garrison Keillor's 'Prairie Home Companion'—which I realize betrays my carefully obscured Midwestern roots!"

He also said he had accepted Anne's advice "to put this monastic life to some good by catching up on all the reading which my previous frenetic professional schedule had precluded." Pollard said he had just finished George Lee Walker's *The Chronicles of Doodah* and a Primo Levi anthology ("I was heartbroken to hear of his recent death—yet another [Holocaust] witness gone"). He said he was about to "lay siege" to Vasily Grossman's *Life and Fate.* "I hope I'm out of prison before I finish this monster."

But for Pollard, Springfield was worse than Petersburg in one crucial area. In Virginia, he used to see Anne on weekends while she was out on bail awaiting sentencing. Despite her ill health, she would make the three-hour drive from Washington to Petersburg every Friday, returning Sunday evenings after visiting hours. Even then, when he would regularly see her, he missed her terribly. And her medical problems merely compounded his anguish. He and Anne, he said, had a "perfect relationship. I can't imagine my life without her." He felt incredibly guilty that he had brought her into this mess.

But in Springfield, there were no visits from Anne on weekends. There was only news that she was suffering from her medical problems in Lexington. In another letter, he said that in early June 1987 she had been "severely beaten by a deranged inmate." He also said that she was not receiving the proper medical treatment. Her weight was under ninety pounds.

Dr. Morris Pollard, following a visit to Lexington, said that

Anne was constantly "bent over" in pain. Jonathan Pollard was furious. "The fact that she hasn't been scheduled for an endoscopy in over three months is absolutely outrageous given the precarious nature of her gastrointestinal system," he wrote. "The prison authorities basically have told her that if she wanted access to such 'extraordinary' health care that she should have turned me in when she 'discovered' my so-called treasonous activity rather than protect me. Pathetic, isn't it?"

He said she spends "most of her time curled up in pain begging for the occasional Tylenol capsule. You know, Anne's brutal treatment is all the more remarkable given the fact that she was never charged with espionage and her 'heinous' loyalty to me stands in marked contrast to the case of Mrs. [Edward] Howard who, even though she facilitated her husband's defection to the Soviet Union, has not even been indicted for obstruction of justice let alone conspiracy. Is there a double standard being applied here or am I missing something?"*

On March 29, 1987, Israel announced that Avi Sella would not, after all, become commander of Tel Nof. America's anger was too much for the Israeli leadership. They belatedly recognized the blunder they had made; they were anxious, even at this late date, to try to limit the damage. Sella, despite being a war hero and a brilliant pilot, would have to be sacrificed.

For a final time, he assembled his men, many of whom had tears in their eyes. "I'd like to talk to you about the publication of my name in the news media," he said in a soft voice. "I'd like you to know that what occurred was in the national security interest of the State of Israel. What was at stake was the saving of many Jews' lives."

---

*Edward L. Howard was a former CIA employee who offered his services to the Soviet Union and then defected to the Soviet Union just as he was about to be arrested by the FBI.

In a formal letter of resignation to Air Force Commander Amos Lapidot, Sella explained why he had to step down. "I have long desired the post I was assigned only a few weeks ago, a post which is the dream of any commander in the Air Force," he wrote. "Ending my role before I had realized as much as a tiny part of my thoughts and plans is a source of profound sorrow for me, yet I have reached the conclusion that I owe it for the causes for which I have fought and for which I shall continue to fight together with my colleagues in the Air Force.

"The deterioration in United States–Israel relations and my concern for the future of those relations and the ties with United States Jewry," Sella continued, "have brought me to ask you to relieve me of my post as commander of Tel Nof Base." He said he did not want to be "a burden to either the country or the Israel Defense Forces. . . . The circumstances of my case are known to you now, as they were before, and this is not the place to repeat them."

Sella, after stepping down from the command of Tel Nof, was named to head the Israel Defense Forces staff college. Eitan, earlier, had been named to head Israel Chemicals.

Yagur, Pollard's second handler, has not managed to cope well since his flight to Israel. Alone among the major Israelis involved in the affair, he has accepted personal responsibility for the tragedy, especially for Pollard's incarceration. He does not work, although he continues to receive a government salary. He has bitterly feuded with Eitan and Sella and the other Israelis involved. He feels terribly guilty about having testified before the Sofaer delegation. He never wanted to cooperate, but was flatly ordered by the government to do so.

Pollard, to this very day, remains confident that "what I did will be significant to the defense of the [Israeli] State and to the defense of American interests." He also feels that his actions have resulted in the saving of Jewish lives. "If nothing else," he said, "an Israeli boy or girl is going to be saved. However, here I am, rotting."

Still, Pollard's dream about strengthening Israel had turned into a horrible nightmare, especially for himself, his wife, and the American Jewish community. Paranoid about anti-Semites in America, he had managed to provide them with some fresh ammunition. And, while he wanted to shore up American–Israeli relations, he wound up damaging them.

With hindsight, Israel's decision to cooperate only partially with the United States in the prosecution of Pollard was a blunder. Israel should have either cooperated fully or not at all, citing national security considerations. In the process of providing only selective information to U.S. investigators, Israel got the worst of all possible worlds. U.S.-Israeli relations were seriously strained and one of Israel's own agents was sentenced to life in prison, largely because of the initial evidence against him made available by Israel. Israel must accept the responsibility for this entire tragedy; it mishandled the matter from the start.

Israel should never have run Pollard in Washington—no matter how important the information he obtained. The risks were not worth the benefits, even if they were significant. Later, the information about Pollard's espionage activities that Israel initially provided to the United States actually set the stage for his decision to plea-bargain with the U.S. government and to cooperate in the investigation. Pollard confessed and began to tell all only after discovering that Israeli officials, whom he had trusted and with whom he had worked, had already presented the United States with a considerable body of evidence against him. Feeling betrayed and abandoned, he began to inform the prosecutors of even more incredible details involving the scope of the espionage ring—details left out by the Israeli officials. For example, Israel returned only 163 of the more than 1,000 documents taken by Pollard, according to court papers.

Once Israel itself confessed to the crime—albeit insisting that a "rogue" intelligence unit had run amok—Pollard decided that he had little choice but to follow suit. He was confronted with the very damaging testimony of Eitan, Yagur, and Irit Erb, the secretary at the Israeli Embassy in Washington who routinely photocopied documents obtained by Pollard. And what made matters worse was the fact that they had described him as a mercenary, simply out to get rich selling American secrets to Israel. He, of course, insisted that he was motivated by his love of Israel and his concern for its security.

Israeli officials maintained that they deliberately stressed the money aspect of the operation, convinced that this would limit the damage to the American Jewish community. If Pollard were simply spying for money, the "dual loyalty" accusation could be muted. But if Pollard had acted out of idealism, other American Jews would also become suspect. This explanation makes sense. There was a deliberate desire among Israeli officials to limit the fallout on American Jewry.

U.S. law enforcement officials have acknowledged that Israeli cooperation, even if incomplete and misleading, had been instrumental in convincing Pollard to confess. Without the leads and evidence provided by Israel, Pollard could have remained silent—his right under the U.S. Constitution—and the government would have had a very hard time convicting him. Certainly, the enormous scope of his espionage activities over the eighteen-month period would almost assuredly never have been uncovered if both he and the Israeli government had made a decision to stonewall. The handful of documents discovered in his apartment the first night he was picked up for questioning were not enough in themselves to earn him a lengthy prison sentence.

Israeli officials have privately conceded that they panicked when Pollard was arrested outside the embassy. Prime Minister Peres and his national unity government were clearly concerned about the ramifications of the scandal on U.S.-Israeli relations. They thought they were embarking on a damage control operation. They apologized and cooperated—but not completely. The decision to cover up Sella's role in the affair deeply angered the Americans. After Pollard was arrested, Israel should have done one of two things: it should have either hung tough and remained totally silent—an action that would have been grudgingly understood by hard-nosed U.S. intelligence officials—or it should have cooperated fully and accurately with the Americans.

By taking a middle position—partial and even misleading cooperation—Israel managed to bring the worst upon itself. U.S. officials thought that Israel was playing them for fools. The promotions of Eitan and Sella understandably made things even worse. Dr. Edward Luttwak, the U.S. defense expert, said that Israel's refusal to punish those officials involved was merely "an act of self-indulgence," a reckless disregard of its broader interests in maintaining close ties with the United States.

One inescapable conclusion of the Pollard affair is that Israel's famous chutzpah can be a source of weakness as well as strength. It has enabled Israel to survive in a very dangerous part of the world. Yet it also has engendered a widely held attitude among Israeli officials that Israel can get away with the most outrageous things. There is a notion among many Israelis that their American counterparts are not too bright—that they can be "handled," thanks partially to the pro-Israeli lobby's clout in Congress. The political leadership in Israel occasionally shows disdain even for the American Jewish community, despite the enormous moral, financial, and political support it has received over the years. Israeli officials have often convinced themselves that, in the end, the politically active Jewish leadership in the United States will not set itself against Israeli policy. But Israel is not totally to blame for having arrived at this attitude. Both the U.S. government and the American Jewish leadership have often reinforced its haughty viewpoint.

Eitan must have been certain that if the Pollard operation were exposed, he could handle the fallout. The incident would be covered up. Israel was dealing with an extremely friendly White House. Casey, at the CIA, was the most pro-Israeli official there since the legendary James Jesus Angleton. Pollard has repeatedly asserted that Eitan assured him that he would be protected.

On the whole, the United States has benefited from its close relationship with Israel, which has become a strategic asset in the eastern Mediterranean. In the area of intelligence sharing, the United States has probably received more than it has provided. Israel, for example, has made available to the United States a great deal of captured Soviet military equipment. It has shared with Washington the lessons it has learned in combating Soviet-made weaponry. And there has been extensive cooperation in the area of counterterrorism. Indeed, former U.S. Air Force intelligence chief Maj. Gen. George F. Keegan has said that "Today, the ability of the U.S. Air Force in particular, and the Army in general, to defend whatever position it has in NATO owes more to the Israeli intelligence input than it does to any other single source of intelligence, be it satellite reconnaissance, be it technology intercept, or what have you."

Still, in the Pollard affair, Israel demonstrated a reckless disregard for the American government. Israel, after all, is still the junior partner in the U.S.-Israeli relationship. Ze'ev Schiff, Israel's leading defense editor, would later tell *The Washington Post* that the Pollard affair was "the worst blunder I remember since I started my work here."

Why did Eitan run Pollard in Washington? Some U.S. officials argue that the operation was not necessary since Israel gets a great deal of information through official channels. But Israeli officials apparently are not convinced of this logic. They feared that the United States was not supplying Israel with everything. And what the United States was not supplying, Pollard would later show them, could be essential, especially in the area of sophisticated reconnaissance photography and electronic intercepts where Israel's own capabilities are limited.

There have been some very real repercussions from the Pollard affair. In the relationship between Israel and the American Jewish community, it has been a truly watershed event. Together with other decisions and actions taken by Israel in recent years, the affair has ensured that American Jews are now far more ready to criticize Israel. They still overwhelmingly support that country, but not nearly as blindly as they once did. This was underlined in interviews I conducted with Jewish leaders.

"There has been a very real erosion," says Phil Baum, associate executive director of the American Jewish Congress. "This is very clear in my mind. It has been very damaging." He notes that increasing numbers of American Jews are even rejecting the very notion of Israel's centrality to world Jewry. Instead, there is a trend toward "the preservation of the Diaspora." Baum suggests that the American Jewish leadership—before Pollard—would have been unlikely to oppose the Israeli government as vocally as it has on such sensitive issues as arms sales to South Africa and the emigration of Soviet Jewry. Thus, in March 1987, American Jews weighed in very heavily in urging the Israeli government to curtail its military-to-military relationship with the Pretoria regime. And Israel did indeed respond by announcing that it would not enter into any new arms sales with South Africa. On the matter of Soviet Jewry, American Jewish leaders told the Israelis that Soviet Jews should have the right to emigrate to Israel, the United States, or any place else they may want. Israel has insisted that the Soviet Jews should immigrate only to Israel. There has been an open rift between significant chunks of American Jewry and Israel on this question, and Baum believes that the Pollard affair was largely responsible for this changed relationship. Because of that Israeli blunder, he maintains, American Jews have become emboldened to challenge Israeli decisions openly and forcefully.

Morris Abram, a former chairman of the Conference of Presidents of Major American Jewish Organizations, reflected this trend when he said that Israelis had to accept the viability of the Diaspora. "The Diaspora has always been important," he says. "The Diaspora is not to be dismissed. That is not to deny the centrality of the [Israeli] State. . . . The whole thrust of the people is centered in that small state. But the responsibilities of the people are much greater than what happens in Jerusalem."

There is today a consensus in the American Jewish community that Israel was reckless in originally running a spy in the U.S. intelligence community—irrespective of the potential gains. "I'm concerned that the Israelis have not come to terms with its meaning here," says Tom Dine, executive director of the American Israel Public Affairs Committee, the pro-Israeli lobbying organization in Washington. "Who needed it? Why were they so stupid? If they wanted these things, why didn't they ask? Isn't the U.S.-Israeli relationship close enough? You could have gotten it." Dine, like many other American Jewish leaders, was also personally angered by the Pollard affair. "A criminal act was committed—treason against my own government," he says. "And in this case it's a Jew." But he expressed confidence that the damage will prove short-lived. "I think it has caused a pause. I think it has caused apprehension. But I do not see it shaking the American-Israeli relationship."

Democratic Senator Frank Lautenberg of New Jersey, a Jew, agrees that Israel acted "very stupidly, very badly." Since the Pollard affair erupted, he has spotted a change on the part of American Jews—"They have bent over backwards to show that they are Americans first."

But the damage to the overall U.S.-Israeli relationship has been contained. And this, according to Hyman Bookbinder, formerly of the American Jewish Committee, is testimony to the built-in strength of the special relationship between Washington and Jerusalem. He notes that the Pollard affair has generally been seen as an "aberration." Americans have placed the affair into proper perspective. "You've got to remember the bigger picture," he says. "Israel is still a good ally." As someone who has been involved professionally in trying to strengthen American-Israeli ties, Bookbinder maintains he felt a special satisfaction in seeing the potential damage from the Pollard affair contained. "I don't mind telling you that I get personal as well as professional satisfaction in saying that we've probably done our job pretty well. If the basic bond has been so strong as to permit this thing— at least up to now—to be relatively without cost to Israel or to U.S.-Israeli relations, I think that gives us grounds for satisfaction."

Still, the Jewish community for the most part believes that Israel was incredibly inept and insensitive when it refused to punish those Israeli officials directly implicated. There was deep and understandable U.S. resentment at Israel's behavior. "I think it was handled very poorly by Israel," says former U.S. Supreme Court Justice Arthur Goldberg. "First they described it as a 'rogue' operation and then they promoted those characters. That wasn't very sensible. It shows a lack of sensitivity."

Former Secretary of Commerce during the Carter administration Philip Klutznick agrees: "It was such a pitiful thing the way it was handled." He offers some advice to Israel. "I think they have developed a sense of superiority about these kinds of things—some of them. I don't want to generalize. And I don't think there's any question but this will put a shadow on several things. There are enough people in our government who are not Jewish who will use this. And they will be more difficult to deal with. On the other hand, there are enough people in our government who are Jewish who will be very reluctant to do certain things that are perfectly legitimate for fear that they will be misunderstood." Thus, there will be a lasting impact.

"You don't ever sweep things like this under the carpet," Klutznick continues. "Let's start with that premise. I don't think it will be as devastating as some of the extremists say. But there will be an effect. Governments don't deal with governments. People deal with people. And there will be people in our government who may use this. Place yourself in the position of a person in responsibility."

Democratic Representative Henry Waxman of California, a Jew and one of Israel's best friends on Capitol Hill, believes that the Pollard affair has also hurt Israel's image in Congress: "I've heard more criticism of Israel after Pollard than before. Many more questions are being asked about Israel's economic independence—their constant need for U.S. aid. When is Israel going to be self-sufficient?"

And Stuart Eizenstat, a former White House official in the Carter administration, comments that "the Pollard affair was not a cataclysmic event in the sense that it has produced a sea change of difference. But it was one of a series of things that have happened to sort of shatter images of Israel. We are much less willing to accept on face value the things that are happening there. In that respect, it's not necessarily all bad because I think that when you have a false stereotype of a country, even one in which we have such a close relationship, then it's not healthy. You're much better off seeing the country with all its warts."

In the aftermath of the Pollard affair, American Jewish leaders have been willing to criticize Israel openly—something they historically had been reluctant to do, fearing that it would tend to undermine Israel's bargaining positions. "Many people in the Jewish community were suddenly, in my terms, liberated from the chains which they had up to this point," says Hyman Bookbinder, "the chains being never to criticize Israel publicly." But even the top Jewish leaders discovered that they could criticize Israel "and that doesn't mean the end of the world. It doesn't really break our love for one another and our hopes for one another. It is a better relationship today."

Both the U.S. and Israeli governments have clearly tried to limit the long-term damage to their overall relationship, but it is still going to take a long time to heal the wounds completely. It makes no sense to belittle the enormity of the disaster. There has been a genuine sense of dismay in official Washington. Yet despite the problems, the official day-to-day relationship has bounced back in a rather impressive and remarkable way. Both countries recognize that they share too many military, economic, strategic, and political interests to allow the Pollard affair—no matter how distasteful—to overly upset their de facto alliance.

But the long-term impact may be even more serious and permanent. "The most lingering damage of the Pollard affair is going to be between American Jews and Israel," says Harry Wall, the Jerusalem-based representative of the Anti-Defamation League.

This sense has been backed up by recent public opinion surveys. An April 1987 poll released by CBS News and *The New York Times* showed that most Americans did not expect the Pollard affair to inflict any lasting damage on U.S.-Israeli relations; indeed, for many Americans, the Pollard scandal was a nonissue. Only 18 percent of non-Jews were even aware that Pollard spied for Israel. In contrast, 62 percent of Jews could name the country Pollard spied for.

Both Jews and non-Jews thought that the U.S. government should take no action against the Israeli government because of Pollard. Do most American Jews place the interests of Israel above those of the United States? By two to one, the public said no. Among Jews, the margin was seven to one.

Here are some of the other questions and findings of the survey:

A U.S. citizen named Jonathan Pollard was recently convicted of spying for a foreign government. Do you know which country he was spying for?	Total	Jews	Non-Jews
Israel	19%	62%	18%
USSR	13	5	13
No opinion	68	33	69

Pollard was convicted of spying for Israel. Do you feel angry, do you feel embarrassed, or do you feel sympathetic towards him?			
Angry	48	34	48
Embarrassed	12	27	11
Sympathetic	7	13	7
Other	7	9	7
No opinion	26	17	27

Pollard was sentenced to life in prison. Do you think that sentence was too harsh, too lenient, or was the sentence the right one?			
Too harsh	16	40	15
Too lenient	9	2	9
Right one	57	43	58
No opinion	18	15	18

Do you think the Pollard spy case will cause serious damage to relations between the United States and Israel, or will it blow over fairly soon?			
Serious	19	8	19
Blow over soon	65	76	65
No opinion	16	16	16

Certainly, the most severe ramifications have involved Jews serving throughout the U.S. government in sensitive foreign policy and defense jobs. For them, the old accusations of dual loyalty have been revived. A hunt for other "Pollards" was started. There was genuine nervousness among Jewish circles in Washington. It was not so much that their non-Jewish colleagues said anything sinister or nasty; it was more of an uneasy feeling that the Jews themselves had inside. Many of them sensed that their associates were looking at them differently. Jews began to feel somewhat more awkward and conspicuous.

Dr. Edward Luttwak believes that the Pollard affair has already had "a disastrous effect" on Israel's friends in the American defense establishment. In the past, he said, U.S. security officers used to worry about granting TOP SECRET security clearance to individuals with questionable contacts involving Communist and other unfriendly countries. Now, they are investigating very closely all ties with Israel. Does someone visit Israel often? Does someone make financial contributions to Israeli causes? Does someone have relatives in Israel? "These questions are now becoming part of America's standard operating procedure," Luttwak says, adding that Israel has shown that it was indeed prepared to penetrate the inner sanctums of the U.S. intelligence community.

A Jewish official in the Justice Department, who did not want to be named, said it was still "too early to tell" whether the Pollard case would have all that much of a long-term damaging impact on the status of Jews in the U.S. government. He predicted, however, that Jews applying for sensitive government positions involving security clearances will "be subjected to stricter" background checks by the FBI.

Indeed, on January 9, 1989, a civilian employee of the U.S. Defense Department lost his TOP SECRET security clearances because three of his sons live in Israel. The official, who asked that his name not be revealed, was told by his supervisors that he was losing his clearances because of tighter security procedures imposed since the arrest of Pollard. "They don't want to take any chances now," said the official, who has worked for the Defense Department at a sensitive Air Force base in the midwest for twenty-five years.

Pentagon sources confirmed that there has been a dramatic tightening of security clearance procedures since the
arrest of Pollard and several other highly publicized spies in
recent years, but denied that Israel was the only foreign
country targetted. They said that, for example, almost no
one with close relatives living abroad or married to foreign
nationals could work on highly classified black intelligence
programs or on the stealth bomber and a limited number of
other very high-technology weapons systems. ("Black" is a
budgetary term used to refer to those intelligence operations that are not specifically named in the annual U.S. federal budget, but for which funding is provided from that
budget.) Pollard, during part of his six years in the navy,
worked on various black programs.

Pentagon sources also strongly denied that American Jews
were automatically losing—or being denied—clearances.
They pointed out that there were numerous high-level Jewish officials working in very sensitive national security positions. Still, the sources acknowledged that top American
security personnel were today indeed taking a much closer
look at all employees' associations with Israel. Thus, counterintelligence experts were asking employees' more specific questions about Israel than they had in the past.

Thus, in a separate case that has come to my attention,
another U.S. official married to an Israeli woman has been
waiting for over a year to receive what were supposed to be
routine security clearances. "It should have been done a
long time ago," the official said, suspecting that his wife's
nationality was the major obstacle standing in the way.

In an interview, the Defense Department employee from
the midwest said that he had filled out routine security clearance update forms over a year ago. In those forms, he noted
that three of his sons—who range in age from twenty-six to
thirty—currently live in Israel. The sons are observant Orthodox Jews; the father is not. Two of the sons are married
to American women while the third is married to an Israeli.
The oldest son has served as a paratrooper in the Israeli
army. The father and the sons were all born in the United
States.

On January 9, the employee said, "just one hour before quitting time, I was called into the office of my department head."

"Your clearances have been lifted," he quoted his boss as having said. "It was not done by us, but by Washington."

The employee was told that he had not done anything wrong and that his work over the years was excellent. He was immediately escorted back to his desk where they asked him to "clean up" the classified documents. "They wanted my badge right away," he said.

He was reassigned to another department involving unclassified information. Because he has continued to work there, he asked that his name, unit, and the exact nature of his work not be publicly disclosed.

The employee said that he was subsequently told by other officials that he lost his clearances as a result of Pollard's arrest. "They told me that the Pollard affair changed all the rules," he said. "They said I fall under the new rules."

But he said that he had also learned that two other colleagues had recently lost security clearances; in one case, it was because a wife was from France, and in the other case, it was because the official had close relatives living in Canada.

The employee said he likes his new unclassified job and wants to continue working there. "I have no desire to leave," he said, noting that he has accepted the Defense Department's decision. "I'm not bitter. It's like the old saying, 'God moves in mysterious ways.' Security also moves in mysterious ways. Ours is not to wonder why. . . ."

Another Jewish official at the Defense Department said: "It has had a terrible effect on the morale of the Jews. It has come up in a number of conversations with senior people. . . . Many of my Jewish friends in the government have told me that they have felt very, very peculiar. They have found themselves on the defensive." This official, who also did not want to be identified, was very angry at Israel. "There is a sense of betrayal," he explained. "The Israelis may not have considered this aspect. What I have gathered from the various Jews I have spoken to is that the Israelis didn't take into account the impact on the U.S. Jewish community, and what a difficult position this places us in. A lot of people are saying, 'The Israelis are arrogant. They don't care about the American Jewish community. They only want to take our money. And they just don't give a hoot.' "

The Pentagon official sensed that non-Jews now look at Jews "in a funny way. There is a terrible sense that people seem to have been put on the spot. I haven't felt it very personally. But among the Jews in the government, it is the subject of discussion . . . and the reaction is that it's almost like betrayal. How could they do this to us, as American Jews?"

The Pollard affair also has resulted in less willingness on the part of Jews in the government to deal with Israel. Some have even stopped showing up at the Israeli Embassy in Washington for diplomatic receptions. They are not certain that they want to be seen with Israelis. Even non-Jews who may be sympathetic to Israel have curtailed their cooperation.

A Jewish State Department official was very concerned about the impact of the affair—"Needless to say, this is a subject very close to my heart. It was with considerable trepidation that I first read of it." He said he had heard "rumors" that the "FBI was reviewing all of our files. I have no indication of that. I really don't." But he added: "Quite frankly, if I were in the FBI, I might be thinking along those lines—not out of any anti-Semitic motivations or any bigotry whatsoever. But just look at this guy's [Pollard's] profile, and say, 'Maybe, just as a precaution, we had better look at people with similar profiles—Jews who have dealt with Israel in some sort of sensitive capacity.' There are probably one hundred or so people who might fit that description—people who have worked in the embassy in Tel Aviv, people who have worked in Middle Eastern affairs. But as far as I can tell, I have not heard a comment, either directed at me or anybody else, which would cast the slightest shadow of doubt or question on Jews per se about their loyalty or anything else. I can tell you though that it has made me uneasy, nonetheless."

Over the years, the Justice Department has occasionally probed the activities of some Jewish groups, such as the American Israel Public Affairs Committee (AIPAC) and the Anti-Defamation League of B'nai B'rith. But they have come up with no hard evidence of espionage on behalf of Israel. AIPAC and ADL leaders, while aware that their activities have occasionally been investigated, firmly denied that they ever have been involved in any espionage on behalf of Israel.

In a carefully drafted statement to the court, chief prosecutor Joseph diGenova wrote that he had been informed by senior officials of the Internal Security Section that

> they are aware of no instances in which prosecution was declined wherein reliable and admissible evidence had been obtained by law enforcement officers of the systematic, clandestine provision of U.S. classified information by an American citizen to Israel. Even more significantly, these officials are unaware of any prior instance of espionage committed by a U.S. citizen on behalf of Israel in exchange for money.

On March 18, 1987, Prime Minister Yitzhak Shamir addressed a delegation of American Jewish leaders in Jerusalem. He stated that the Pollard affair was "a very unfortunate event" as well as "a human tragedy," but urged his audience to keep the matter in its proper perspective. "We are intent on maintaining and developing our close and friendly ties with the United States, and the Government of the United States has informed us that they share this feeling completely."

But many American officials remain skeptical about Israel's denials. The results of the two formal inquiry commissions in Israel (the Cabinet-appointed Rotenstreich-Tzur Committee and the separate Knesset subcommittee chaired by Abba Eban) were not taken as the final word. The Americans argue that the Defense Ministry unit that "ran" Pollard

(LAKAM) was created years ago to collect scientific intelligence. They also assert that Israeli intelligence experts had to know that only an inside American agent could supply the massive quantity and quality of satellite photography and other electronic intelligence they were getting. Israel lacks that capability, and Israeli experts knew the United States was not supplying the information to Israel officially. On August 19, 1987, Eitan told an Israel Radio interviewer that he had received authorization for all of his actions. He refused to cite names.

In fact, Pollard, in a sixty-one-page document submitted to the court, had made exactly the same point. He rejected Israel's assertion that he was part of a "rogue" operation. "Perhaps sometime in the future a more politically secure Israeli government will be able to set the record straight with the U.S. Department of Justice, but until that day arrives, it will be more expedient for Israel's fractured leadership to stonewall and deny any official involvement with my activities," he stated. On three separate occasions, "I was told that the highest levels of the Israeli government had purportedly extended their collective thanks for assistance I had provided the state." He insisted that "a Cabinet-level decision had to have been made with the concurrence of the General Staff, that the gains associated with my activities far outweighed any potential risks that might result if I were compromised." The Israeli government, Pollard said, acted predictably "by attempting to limit the damage to itself by retreating behind a plausible denial screen in which the scandal was purportedly precipitated by a group of renegade intelligence officers acting without authorization." But in rejecting this denial, Pollard pointed out that "the number and type of Israelis who were associated with this affair suggest a high degree of government awareness if not intimate supervision of their behavior." He said it was "beyond reason" to believe that this operation was unauthorized.

"Furthermore," Pollard continued, "if one takes into account both the quality and highly specialized performance expertise of the personnel who were involved in this affair, it seems unlikely that their collaboration could have been the product of random selection: a near famous ex-Mossad assistant chief of operations, then assigned as a special adviser to the Prime Minister; a highly decorated member of the air force; two science attachés; and a leading international arms broker* do not coalesce out of thin air."

In describing the kind of information he made available to Israel, Pollard wrote that

> the type of guidance I received suggested a highly coordinated effort between the Navy, Army and Air Force intelligence services. At the end of each month, I was given an extremely detailed list of material which was needed by the various organizations that included an explanation of why the information officially transferred did not satisfy their requirements. Although the acquisition lists appeared to have been submitted by each service separately, since dissimilar paper and formats were used by the three organizations, there was always one prioritized list which had evidently been agreed upon [by] the respective military chiefs of intelligence and bore their combined seal. While it is possible that the Mossad considered this affair to have been "unauthorized" because they were evidently never a party to it, the same cannot be said of the General Staff, which was intimately involved with identifying which type of scientific and technical intelligence was to be the object of my activity.

Pollard went on to note that he was "routinely provided with finished technical assessments of the material which had been passed to the Israelis. The turnaround time for these assessments was very quick and when I inquired how this was accomplished, I was told that a special team of analysts had been established back in Israel just [to evaluate]

*This last person cited by Pollard was a reference to the Israeli identified in court papers only as "Uzi." His full name has not been disclosed.

the operational applicability of all the next information collected." He said that most of the information came from satellite photography and signal intelligence studies. Israeli experts were aware that this information was not coming from "official" channels. Pollard was never told how large the group of experts analyzing the information was, but insisted that "it had to have been rather well staffed with extremely competent scientists in light of the volume and diversity of the material I collected."

Shimon Peres and Yitzhak Shamir—the two prime ministers who were in office during Pollard's espionage—as well as the two defense ministers who served during the operation—Moshe Arens and Yitzhak Rabin—have steadfastly denied ever knowing about him. According to Knesset investigators, Eitan showed some of the original documents obtained by Pollard to Rabin. But the Defense Minister, during questioning before the Israeli investigatory panels, insisted that Eitan never told him about Pollard. He assumed that Eitan had other sources for such documents. Where else could Eitan get them? Rabin speculated that LAKAM could have had sources in Britain or some other NATO ally that would be in a position to receive this kind of U.S. document.

Since the trial and sentencing the overall mood in Israel toward Pollard has shifted, especially because of the life sentence, which was considered much too severe. Officially, Pollard was still an orphan. But unofficially, he was developing into an Israeli hero. Senior government officials—political, military, and intelligence—became committed to trying to help him get out of jail and to bring him to Israel.

Pollard had been a loyal agent. He had been brought into the espionage ring by Rafi Eitan, one of Israel's best spies. At the time, Eitan was employed by both the Defense Ministry and the Prime Minister's Office. Even if he had exceeded his authority, Israel still had a responsibility to get Pollard out.

But the Israeli government faced a continuing dilemma.

Israeli leaders had to stick to their story that the operation was unauthorized. They feared that U.S.-Israeli relations could suffer if they publicly announced any shifting attitude toward Pollard. It would be awkward politically.

In the meantime, Pollard's $2,500 per month salary has been doubled. The tradition in the Israeli intelligence community has always been that captured agents serving in prison continue to receive their salary, only doubled. Pollard would have a nice little nest egg when he finally settled in Israel.*

Ironically, Pollard would almost certainly not receive security clearances in Israel. The Israeli intelligence community—like others—is extremely reluctant to trust someone who has been proven to be so unreliable. The Israelis, moreover, can be as hard-nosed about protecting their national security interests as the United States or any other country.**

By the summer of 1987, top officials in Israel began more forcefully to underline their firm commitment to Pollard. They confirmed that the Israeli government was responsible for raising the approximately $200,000 in legal fees for the Pollards' lawyers. Yes, some private and highly publicized Citizens for Pollard groups had collected funds on city street corners. But that was largely for show. Only a modest sum was raised, a tiny fraction of the money sent to the lawyers. What was most important was that the organizations could be used as a cover to protect the Israeli government's very active, behind-the-scenes involvement.

---

*The Israeli government will probably deny this, but authoritative sources in Israel have told me it is so.

**This was underscored during Israel's handling of Mordechai Vanunu, the former nuclear technician at the Dimona nuclear reactor who provided the London *Sunday Times* with details about Israel's very secret nuclear development program. Vanunu, an Israeli, claimed that he was motivated by his conscience. A self-described peace activist, he said he wanted to stop a nuclear war from erupting in the Middle East. Using a blonde agent named "Cindy," the Israeli intelligence services lured Vanunu from Britain to Italy and then brought him back to Israel, where he stood trial behind closed doors. In the spring of 1988, he was convicted and sentenced to eighteen years in prison.

Israeli intelligence officials knew that Pollard was originally motivated by his love of Israel. The money was largely
an Israeli idea designed to corrupt Pollard and to make sure
he did not quit the operation. The Israelis also knew that
they bungled his rescue operation. There should have been
a workable plan to save the Pollards before their arrest.

The Israelis, moreover, felt very guilty that they were
effectively forced to hang Pollard by cooperating in the U.S.
investigation. They did something that was truly unprecedented in the annals of covert intelligence operations—they
made available evidence to convict their own agent. How
would this impact on other Israeli spies?

Thus, although Pollard may not have been part of a Mossad operation, the Mossad still had a clear interest in seeing
him freed. Other Israeli agents, sitting in dangerous spots
around the world, were waiting and watching to see
whether Israel would save Pollard. They were naturally
wondering what Israel might do to help them if they were
ever exposed.

But there was still another unresolved problem. U.S. Justice Department investigators remained convinced that
Pollard was not an isolated incident. They seriously suspected that at least one other American citizen working
inside the U.S. government was spying for Israel.

Their fears were based on more than just a hunch. During
their many hours of interrogating Pollard, they discovered
to their absolute horror that the Israelis had been rather
specific in "tasking" him to obtain certain TOP SECRET documents. Indeed, Pollard was often asked to obtain classified
documents by their code numbers and titles. U.S. counterintelligence agents quickly concluded that Israel must have
had at least one other agent on the inside providing the
names of the documents. Perhaps that agent did not have a
"courier card," like Pollard.

DiGenova, the chief prosecutor in the case, publicly
raised this possibility in an interview with journalist Lally
Weymouth in *The Washington Post* on March 15, 1987.
"Direct and circumstantial evidence indicates that we
should be concerned as a government about how Jonathan

Pollard was originally tasked before he ever gave over information," he said. "What did they show him when they
tasked him?"

Pollard was constantly questioned about other Americans
involved in the espionage ring. Indeed, he charged that the
government interrogators had threatened to "smear" him
beyond recognition for "my refusal to implicate other Jews
in what was held to be a conspiracy reaching up to the
highest echelons of the American Zionist establishment."
He added: "I had so many 'confessions' thrown at me by the
NIS regarding this it got to be a joke after a while."

Defense Minister Rabin confirmed that the United States
was pressing Israel to name others involved in the operation.
"Let me make it clear," Rabin told a gathering of American
Jews in Jerusalem on March 16, 1987, "there are no Americans or non-Americans that serve as spies for Israel against
the United States." He charged that American prosecutors
had tried to tempt Sella into avoiding indictment by naming
other Americans spying for Israel. Rabin maintained that "a
key figure in the prosecution of Pollard" had approached
Sella's American lawyer and said: "From my point of view,
Sella can be Chief of the Israeli Air Force if you give me
another name or names."

Pollard was clearly pleased by the changing attitude toward him in Israel and the American Jewish community.
When he was first arrested, he was very sad and bitter about
the fact that he had received virtually no sympathy for his
actions. He was an outcast. But since then, things had altered. "I think that people are slowly waking up to the fact
that certain elements within the administration did indeed
have a private sentencing agenda, which had nothing to do
with my supposed crimes. I was nothing more than a conve-
nient means to an end."

In the American Jewish community, it was indeed becoming okay to express some sympathy for Pollard and his wife.
Their families worked around the clock to establish "Justice
for the Pollards" committees, and they were meeting with
increasing success. Their immediate objective was to win
Anne's release, citing humanitarian concerns about her

deteriorating health, but they also wanted to get Pollard out of prison.

Many American Jews did not feel a need to run away from Pollard in order to prove their own loyalty to the United States. Pollard said he was especially pleased by an article that appeared in *Tikkun,* a Jewish magazine published in San Francisco. The article was entitled "J'Accuse: American Jews and L'Affaire Pollard." And he was thrilled by the second reaction to him in Israel following his life sentence. "Judging by the volume of mail I've received from Israel," he said, "I can't see how any government could let me languish in prison for the rest of my life."

Pollard also felt that after reading a transcript of an interview with Robert Dasa on Israel television, "perhaps I shouldn't complain about my abandonment." Dasa, an Egyptian Jew, had spent several years in an Egyptian jail for his role in the ill-fated Lavon affair bombings in Cairo in 1954. He was eventually allowed by the Egyptians to go to Israel. "If the word 'empathy' has any meaning, it certainly describes the feelings I have for that man," Pollard said.

Alfred Frauenknecht, the Swiss engineer who had spied for Israel in the 1960s, told an Israeli newspaper that he could personally identify with Pollard because he, too, had offered to pass on information to Israel solely out of concern for Israel's security. "I understand that there was a need to punish him in order to deter other spies," Frauenknecht said. But he called on Israel not to "throw Pollard to the dogs."

Shortly after the life sentence was imposed, Harvard law professor Alan Dershowitz wrote an article in the April 28 issue of *The Washington Times* charging that the punishment had been grossly excessive. "In a democracy," he declared,

> it is dirty pool for the government to make charges
> and then to hide behind the curtain of national
> security when asked to substantiate them. If charges
> cannot be substantiated publicly, then they should

not be made publicly. The Defense Department cannot expect the American people to accept its gross exaggerations at face value, especially when they fly in the face of common sense.

Pollard's parents immediately contacted Dershowitz. "What took you so long?" was his first comment to Dr. Pollard.

Jonathan Pollard, around that same time, became publicly critical of Hibey. Pollard charged that his interrogators were constantly trying to get him to implicate others in his espionage network. "I repeatedly apprised my 'lawyer' about this but he felt it was insignificant."

Pollard welcomed Dershowitz's involvement in the case. But in the meantime, the Hibeys temporarily remained in charge of the Pollards' unsuccessful appeals for sentence reductions. "I trust Dershowitz implicitly," Pollard said. "I know I should have gone to him nineteen months ago. Although I've only talked to him a few times, I can sense that he is an honorable man who understands the essentially political nature of this case."

In August 1987, Pollard, once called the "Hoosier Poet," wrote the following poem, which he entitled *Gilboa Revisited:*

> I knew the battle was lost
> even as the enemy gathered in the plains below—
> my sentence as certain as the hatred behind it.
> Yet still I stayed and fought out of loyalty to a mad
>   father
> who led me to that desolate mountain
> and left me as a victim of his arrogance
> and misjudgment.
>
> So, there I stood at day's end—
> defiant before my enemies, imploring the fallen
>   King:
> Will you not fight?

Will you not arise
and prove the justness of our cause?
Will you not shield this son
whose loyalty you took for granted?

But you said not a word
my old and rotting father.
You just lay there rigid
denying any responsibility as the sentence was
    passed.
And I fell at your feet
unrecognized by your cold, indifferent eyes.

But it was not your body this time
that hung above the city gate
for ridicule and scorn—
it was mine.

So, tell me, father
how long am I to serve as a symbol of Philistine
    strength
before David is allowed to end this demeaning
    spectacle
of Hebrew impotence?

In the summer of 1988, Pollard was moved from Springfield
to the federal prison in Marion, Illinois, a maximum security
facility reserved for the worst and most dangerous criminals
in the country. He remained in isolation. At one point, he
went on a hunger strike to protest delays in receiving his
mail. At another point he protested his wife's alleged medical mistreatment in prison. Throughout, he has remained
hopeful that he eventually will be allowed to settle in Israel.
As he wrote to me, "I don't know how long it will take, but
I hope that one day in the not too distant future, we can sit
down in Israel and try to reconstruct this nightmare."

EPILOGUE

Operation Blowback

In the introduction to this book, I asked a series of key questions about Pollard and this mysterious case, and I pointed out that I had been very confused following my first interview with him in the Petersburg, Virginia, federal prison in 1986. So many questions were left unanswered.

In *Territory of Lies,* I sought to tell the story of what exactly happened—how this young man from South Bend wound up spying for Israel and how he was betrayed. I have tried to report the details as fairly and as completely as possible, without the interference of too many of my own opinions—the reader is entitled to a straightforward account, one that places this extraordinary case of espionage in its proper perspective.

Still, as I read and re-read the manuscript, I concluded that some holes remained to be filled, that some answers to key questions may have gotten lost in the course of this book's extensive reportage—indeed, some questions may never be completely answered. Moreover, there has been a great deal of misinformation about the case from the very start. This continues today, and in some respects the case has not yet been closed. So let me try to answer the remaining questions in this epilogue.

Question: Why did the Israelis do it? Weren't they getting enough information from the United States officially?
Why risk the overall U.S.-Israeli relationship?

Answer: In the real world, as I pointed out earlier, all
countries spy—not only on their adversaries but on their
friends as well. This is called "friendly espionage." Friends,
after all, can take actions that may have very serious and
damaging consequences. Therefore, although the United
States and Israel are allies, their interests do not always over-
lap—no two countries, no matter how close, always see eye
to eye. The United States occasionally has disagreements
with Britain, Canada, Japan, Mexico, Israel, and other countries. Thus, the United States understandably and legiti-
mately wants to know what's going on in Israel—and vice
versa.

Israeli operatives, led by Rafi Eitan, wanted to know what
information the United States was not officially sharing with
Israel. Even if Israel could collect information withheld
from them by the United States from other sources, a reliable confirmation—a second source—would be very important. Countries are often reluctant to act on intelligence
from only one source.

The United States and Israel both suspect that the other
occasionally provides disinformation in order to advance
some particular foreign policy objective; they believe that
intelligence reports are doctored. "Friendly espionage,"
therefore, can be used to obtain confirmation of the veracity
of intelligence information that has been officially provided.
It's all part of the game.

For both countries' intelligence communities, secrets are
their jewels—they must be protected at all costs. And, while
the United States and Israel may be friends, they do not
share all their secrets. Indeed, each believes the other tries
to obtain the other's secrets clandestinely. These suspicions
have certainly increased as a result of the Pollard affair.

In the course of the Pollard operation, the Israelis discovered that the United States had a wealth of largely technical information with which it was not willing to provide Israel. Some of the information involved the military capabilities of friendly Arab countries, such as Egypt, Jordan, and Saudi Arabia. The United States does not normally share information about these countries with Israel. Israel, likewise, certainly does not share all the intelligence it gathers with the United States because of the danger of the Arabs' learning about some of it from their American contacts.

The Israelis also wanted to know the extent of U.S. espionage in Israel. Rafi Eitan, as I reported, was in fact obsessed by this question. Pollard was reluctant to provide Israel with this kind of information, but he did hand over photographs of Israeli military installations taken by U.S. reconnaissance satellites—demonstrating to the Israelis exactly what reconnaissance capabilities the Americans (and, presumably, the Soviets) had. This information placed Israel in a better position to devise appropriate countermeasures, including better camouflaging techniques, which, in turn, would make it more difficult for the United States to spy on Israel.

Both the United States and Israel are very concerned about the Soviet Union's, or any other country's, hostile penetration of each other's intelligence communities—and with good reason. Both have been compromised over the years. A whole host of Soviet spies have operated in the United States—the sensational Walker family spy ring being the most recent. Soviet spies have been captured in Israel as well, and at least two—Shabtai Kalmanovich and Marcus Klingberg—are currently serving prison terms there.

As I have stressed throughout *Territory of Lies,* all countries' intelligence services are primarily concerned with protecting their sources and methods in the collection of vital information. Sometimes it takes years to plant an agent; other times it can take years to crack a code. Developing appropriate technical means of gathering intelligence can cost huge sums of money. Very often, friendly countries do not exchange certain information because they fear it would compromise these very sensitive sources and methods: The other country might innocently initiate some action which might tip off a hostile force that it has been penetrated.

For example, during World War II Prime Minister Winston Churchill decided that British towns and villages about to be bombed by the Nazis could not be warned in advance because that might signal to the Germans that their secret codes had been broken. If warned of an impending attack, British citizens would of course take defensive action; they would scramble for shelters. German spies would certainly pick this up, and their codes would immediately be changed, thereby setting back Britain's overall war effort. Churchill and other British leaders simply had to swallow hard and accept the fate of the bombing raids because the alternative would be even more disastrous.

It was this same rationale that prevented the United States from telling Israel about planned Palestinian terrorist attacks and some other threats facing Israel. And Israel, of course, would similarly be afraid to inform the United States about any terrorist operations against American targets if some highly placed Israeli source could be endangered in the process. All intelligence officials grudgingly accept this logic without question.

Almost all of the highly classified documents Pollard provided to Israel—and they involved literally thousands of pieces of paper—were stamped NOFORN, meaning that the information was "not releasable to foreign nationals." Some of those documents could be provided to certain friendly foreign countries, but *only* after U.S. government specialists went through each page, blacking out any information a trained foreign intelligence expert could use to determine how the United States originally collected that information.

What seriously undermined Pollard's case with Judge Robinson was the fact that he did not black out or "redact" information on any of those pages. Even if he had, however, it would hardly matter because Pollard would not have been qualified to make the appropriate determinations: He was not in a position to appreciate what was authorized for release to Israel and what was not. When Israel provides the United States with similar intelligence documents, it, too, edits out certain information which could compromise its own means of collection and always removes its own code-words.

Question: Was Pollard justified in spying for Israel? Was the United States holding back vital information, necessary for Israel's very survival?

Answer: The information that Pollard provided—as documented in this book—was very important. Israeli intelligence officials are firm in pointing out that Israel certainly would have survived another war with the Arabs if Pollard had never crossed the line. But they add that Israel's efforts have been made easier as a result of Pollard's espionage. If there is another full-scale war with Syria in the near future, some Israeli soldiers who might otherwise have died will live because of what Pollard did, and the extent of losses to very expensive Israeli military equipment, especially fighter aircraft, will be reduced. Thus, I can certainly understand why some Israelis concluded that the operation was worth the risk. Israel's survival in the Middle East depends on good intelligence.

Even so, with hindsight, the benefits to Israel did not outweigh the costs—even if the full impact of those costs occasionally remain blurred to the public. As the Rotenstreich-Tzur commission concluded: "There was no room for the recruitment and running of Pollard."

Pollard and his supporters have argued that the information that he provided to Israel had actually been authorized for release as part of a secret annex to the 1983 U.S.-Israeli agreement enhancing the two countries' strategic cooperation. They have accused Weinberger of breaking that agreement. "The hard reason why I did what I did was because I had become aware of Mr. Weinberger's agenda in Washington in regard to Israel," Pollard said in a November 20, 1988, interview with Mike Wallace on "60 Minutes." That agenda "was, fundamentally, to place Israel in a position where she would be forced to make an unenviable choice between a ruinous war or shameful peace."

Weinberger was not Israel's best friend in the Reagan administration by any means: He had been deeply angered by Israel's invasion of Lebanon in 1982; he often clashed with his Israeli counterparts, Defense Minister Ariel Sharon and, later, Moshe Arens. Within the highest echelons of the Reagan administration, Weinberger was usually the most critical of Israel, but it was also true that under his watch at the Pentagon the overall U.S.-Israeli military relationship reached new heights. Things began happening in that relationship that would have been considered unheard of only a few years earlier. Military cooperation between the two countries was dramatically expanded, and it was Weinberger who signed agreements with Arens, and later with Rabin, institutionalizing much of this cooperation.

But Pollard has become deeply embittered toward Weinberger largely because of, in my opinion, the classified damage-assessment memorandum which the then-Defense Secretary sent to Judge Robinson. As I reported in Chapter 13, this document convinced the judge that Pollard had caused very severe damage to U.S. national security interests.

During my first interview with Pollard, in November 1986, he barely mentioned Weinberger's name. Pollard was certainly angry, but not specifically at Weinberger. In fact, he spent most of the time during that first interview railing against his Israeli handlers for abandoning him and against the Israeli government for disowning him. During my next interview with him, at the end of January 1987, his deep hatred toward Weinberger was repeatedly expressed. The difference, in my opinion, was that Weinberger's memo to the judge had been submitted earlier in January, and Pollard had been permitted to read it. He was outraged. He sensed that the judge, upon reading it, would sentence him to life even though the plea agreement said the government would seek only a "substantial" sentence. His intuition was right. He blamed Weinberger personally for what he saw as a betrayal of that plea agreement.

In all cases involving espionage, the Pentagon—often in the name of the defense secretary—must routinely submit lengthy documents to the court. Because they involve national security secrets, they are usually submitted *in camera.* The Weinberger memo in the Pollard case, therefore, was by no means all that unusual.

Using very strong language, Weinberger detailed the extent of the damage caused by Pollard's activities. He suggested that it was absolutely terrible—among the most damaging spy cases in American history. In the process, Weinberger spelled out the possible worst-case scenarios as far as damage to U.S. national security was concerned: What would happen, hypothetically, if the information Pollard provided to Israel wound up in the hands of the Soviet Union? That was certainly possible given the fact that Soviet spies have been found inside the Israeli intelligence and defense establishment. There may, perhaps, be others who have not yet been discovered.

Weinberger also raised the possibility that Israel, for whatever reason, might trade some of this sensitive information with other parties, including some hostile to the United States. Once the information was out of America's control, after all, there would be no way to determine what was done with it.

Other high-ranking U.S. intelligence officials, in private conversations with me, have expressed concern that Israel theoretically could have made some of the information available to South Africa in exchange for something that Israel needs. They acknowledged, however, that there is no evidence that this has happened. Intelligence officials also wonder if, in order to win freer emigration for Soviet Jews or to improve Israel's overall relationship with the Soviet Union, Israel would be prepared to hand over information gained from Pollard to the Soviets? They have, they concede, no evidence that any such deal occurred.

But the American fear of—and the potential for—a worst-case scenario continues to exist. There is, after all, a global marketplace for intelligence where information is sold and resold. It's a strange trading ground where even warring nations occasionally barter information. Representatives of the CIA, MI5, KGB, Mossad, and all other European, Asian, South American, Arab, African, and Communist intelligence agencies come to this "market" to buy, sell, and trade information that is classified "secret." And they are especially interested in learning about the sources and methods used to collect this kind of intelligence—they want to know if they have been penetrated by a "mole."

Thus, U.S. counterintelligence experts have pondered this question: If Pollard has unleashed U.S. secrets into this marketplace through Israel, what will be the impact on U.S. interests and security?

Since Pollard's arrest, officials have undertaken an exhaustive "blowback" operation to determine whether any American agents or other technical intelligence gathering sources and methods were compromised by information provided to Israel by Pollard. This investigation continues.

Those worst-case possibilities may be very far fetched and, perhaps, unrealistic, but U.S. counterintelligence experts clearly worry about them, and that concern was vividly conveyed in the Weinberger memo to the judge. In the memo, there was no flat assertion that any of these worst-case possibilities had in fact occurred. The possibilities were merely raised, and the judge, no doubt, was understandably alarmed. Judge Robinson's decision to sentence Pollard to life was also designed to serve as a warning to other American officials not to spy for friends or foes.

Question: Was the U.S. holding back infromation from Israel that should have been made available under their intelligence-exchange agreements?

Answer: None of the information that Pollard provided— not one page—was authorized for Israel in its unredacted form. Many of those pages certainly could (and probably should) have been released with certain sections censored— as is done when classified documents are made available to the public under the Freedom of Information Act. United States officials privately acknowledge this, but, as part of the ongoing bargaining process with their Israeli counterparts, they insist that withholding information is necessary in order to try to put pressure on Israel to provide parallel information. The give-and-take process of all international intelligence exchanges is part of the politics of the market- place. Israel, like any other country, doesn't give unless it receives.

Thus, exactly when information should be made available to Israel is a decision that the president, the secretary of state, the secretary of defense, the director of the CIA, and other top policymakers must make. They must decide how much information should be made available—and in what form. Pollard, as he admitted in court at his sentencing hear- ing, had no right to make those decisions on his own.

Some of the information that Pollard provided Israel— especially in the area of highly-sensitive communications intelligence—was so sensitive that it would not be author- ized for release to Israel or to any other country under any circumstance whatsoever. This, too, was spelled out in the Weinberger memo. That Pollard, a relatively low-level ana- lyst, could access this kind of information is incredible and underscores the shabby state of the U.S. intelligence com- munity.

Question: Did Pollard act alone inside the U.S. intelli- gence community or was there a mysterious "Mr. X," a second Israeli spy who still remains at large?

Answer: Almost from the day of Pollard's arrest, U.S. in- vestigators have been looking for a "Mr. X." As I have re- ported in this book, investigators were alarmed by the de- tailed tasking of Pollard, who was asked to collect specific documents, which his Israeli handlers' often cited by code names. Only a highly placed inside source, the Americans suspected, could have provided Israel with that kind of in- formation.

"Mr. Pollard was given very, very specific tasking instruc- tions by his handlers," said diGenova. "He would be told not just areas of information which were required of him. In many instances, he would be given the names of specific documents and their numbers to retrieve." According to diGenova, many in the U.S. intelligence community "be-

lieve that someone else in the American intelligence community or military establishment was giving [the Israelis]
that information to give to [Pollard]."

Pollard, during hundreds of hours of polygraphed interrogation, recalled those specific documents. He dazzled the
interrogators with his incredible memory. But he has maintained throughout that he was unaware of any other Americans involved in the spy ring. The Americans believe him
but they have not dropped the matter because even if there
were other Americans, Pollard probably would not have
been told their identities. After all, he had no need to know.

Scores of counterintelligence experts from the Navy, the
FBI, the CIA, the DIA, the Justice Department, the National
Security Agency and other branches of the U.S. government
have been looking for Mr. X. Finding him has been a very
high priority. Government experts have had at their disposal the most sophisticated electronic surveillance and
communications intercept capabilities; they have gone over
the files of scores of suspects. So far, they have met with no
success.

It should come as no great surprise, therefore, that I, too,
have been unable, with my very limited resources, to learn
the identity of Mr. X—if, in fact, there is such a person or
persons.

Israeli officials have steadfastly denied the existence of a
Mr. X. They claim that there were other ways for Israel to
learn the code names; perhaps they had sources in other
NATO countries where these kind of documents could have
been circulated officially or in unfriendly countries which
might have obtained the documents clandestinely. Perhaps
they learned of the code names from some of the original
documents provided by Pollard or even those provided officially by the U.S. government, which might have contained cross-references to other documents.

But if a Mr. X does in fact exist, my own sense is that he
is long gone, that he almost certainly has been removed
from the U.S. government. Discovery of a second Pollard,
Israeli officials recognize, would represent a major disaster
for U.S.-Israeli relations. The American Jewish community

would be justifiably outraged. Thus, since Pollard's arrest, the highest officials in Israel have assured me that the Israeli intelligence community has cleaned up its act in the United States. The risks of running another spy in Washington, the Israelis have now belatedly concluded, outweigh any conceivable benefits. Most—but not all—U.S. officials believe the Israelis have stopped spying against the United States.

In the course of the search for Mr. X, Pollard has claimed that he was shown what he has called "a master list of American Jews" also suspected of being Israeli spies—a charge denied by diGenova. "He is totally fabricating the notion that anyone ever showed him, or anybody else, the list of the names of American Jews, prominent or otherwise. It is an outrageous falsehood, and it is an example of the level and the depths to which he has stooped in order to try and extricate himself from a situation that he and he alone is responsible for."

Pollard's charges that anti-Semitism played a role in his conviction and sentencing have outraged U.S. officials. DiGenova has noted that five of the key players in the government's team involved in the case—Mark Richard, Deputy Assistant Attorney General; Judge Abraham Sofaer, the State Department's Legal Affairs Adviser; and Assistant U.S. Attorneys Stephen R. Spivack, David Geneson, and Charles Roistacher—are Jewish. To which Pollard has replied: "And there were kapos also during the concentration camps."

Beyond the ongoing mystery of Mr. X, there are other reasons why the Pollard affair will continue to remain in the headlines. The U.S. and Israeli governments continue to search for some sort of diplomatic formula to tie up the loose ends that have strained American-Israeli relations. The Justice Department is still formally threatening to prosecute Eitan and Yagur despite the fact that they had earlier been granted immunity in exchange for their "full cooperation." There is, of course, no chance that Israel would hand the two over for prosecution—they have refused to hand over Sella, who has been formally indicted. But any formal indictments against Eitan and Yagur would put additional political pressure on Israel.

Talks continue between high-level U.S. and Israeli officials on the matter of Eitan and Yagur, as well as the future of Sella, who is completing his Ph.D. at Tel Aviv University. There has been extensive discussion on both sides about a deal that would have Israel liberalize its existing extradition treaty with the United States. The Americans want to gain custody of American-Jewish criminals who flee to Israel where they can obtain automatic citizenship under Israel's Law of Return. So far Israel has balked at changing the treaty.

As a gesture of good faith, the Justice Department has agreed that retired Air Force Major General Amos Lapidot and retired IDF Chief of Staff Moshe Levi can now enter the United States without fear of arrest.

There have been persistent reports in the news media that some sort of international spy swap involving Pollard may be in the works. The Soviet spies in Israeli prisons—Kalmanovich and Klingberg—would supposedly also be involved. Writing on December 2, 1988, in *The Washington Post,* syndicated columnists Jack Anderson and Dale Van Atta suggested that the complicated trade would work like this: "The United States would send Pollard and his wife, Anne Henderson Pollard, to Israel. Israel would release a captured Soviet spy to the Soviet Union. As the last link in the chain, the Soviet Union would lean on Syria and Iran to negotiate the release of one or more American hostages being held by terrorists."

While I have no doubt that Israeli officials would welcome such a deal, there is considerable opposition inside the U.S. government, especially in the Justice Department. Top U.S. officials do not want Pollard released. Although sentenced to life, he will become eligible for parole after serving 10 years, and they want him to serve at least that much.

Question: Was Pollard part of a rogue operation or did he have high-level authorization? And how high did that authorization go? Was there an official Israeli cover-up?

Answer: The two official Israeli investigatory commissions concluded that Rafi Eitan decided to run Pollard on his own. "In spite of the fact that he sometimes initiated meetings with the political level, he did not consult with the relevant ministers on the recruitment and running of Pollard," the Rotenstreich-Tzur report said. The Eban panel added: "Rafi Eitan bears full and direct responsibility for the decision to recruit and run Pollard. He did not report this to his superiors, and thus received no approval therefor."

Some of the members of the two commissions told me privately that they felt very uncomfortable in placing all of the blame on Eitan. In fact, one panelist said: "We agreed to this language out of a certain sense of patriotism." He suggested that higher-ranking officials, including some ministers, probably suspected that Eitan had a spy or spies in Washington but were willing to shut their eyes to it. They did not ask questions; they did not want to know the full extent of the story. And Eitan, anxious to make certain that his operation continued, saw no need to tell them. In the world of covert operations, certain things are best left unsaid.

One of the Knesset investigators compared Eitan's decision to deliberately keep the top leadership in the dark to former U.S. National Security Adviser John Poindexter's decision not to inform President Ronald Reagan about the diversion of profits from U.S. arms sales to Iran to the contra rebels in Nicaragua.

In any case, I could come up with no hard evidence that Peres, Shamir, Rabin, or Arens knew about the Pollard operation although I, too, suspect that at least one or two of them probably knew that Eitan was running a spy in Washington. They are simply too experienced in these kinds of matters not to have known or suspected. But even if they suspected that a spy was in place in Washington, they almost certainly did not know his name was Pollard, that he was being paid, or any other specific details of the operation. In order to maintain plausible deniability, they would not want to know these kind of details.

Eitan, for his part, has said publicly that he was authorized to recruit and run Pollard. He has refused to say who provided him with that authorization, although, as I have reported in this book, a lifetime of experience in spying (in-

cluding in the United States) must have convinced him that
that authorization was simply built into his LAKAM man-
date. He was a trained spy, and he was doing exactly what
he was supposed to do. Given the importance of the information provided by Pollard, I can understand Eitan's thinking.

Let's look at a hypothetical case where the tables are
turned: What would an American intelligence official operating out of the U.S. Embassy in Tel Aviv have done if a
well-placed Israeli military intelligence analyst had approached him and offered to provide vital documents af-
fecting the most important national security interests of the
United States, including the fate of American citizens? Let's
say, for whatever reason, the Israeli government was unwilling to provide the United States with this information officially—perhaps the information could compromise Israel's
own intelligence sources and methods. How would the
Americans react?

They, no doubt, would be nervous—as were the Israelis
when Pollard walked in. They would be concerned about
being set up or compromised politically. But I have no doubt
that after careful consideration and with the utmost precautions the Americans, too, would be prepared to see exactly
what kind of information the Israeli could provide.

And if, in fact, the Israeli citizen then began to transfer
tremendous quantities of highly classified Israeli documents
to his American handlers—in exchange for money over an
eighteen month period—and if he were eventually exposed
and arrested, I doubt very much whether the Israeli judicial
system would treat the spy very leniently. He would almost
certainly wind up spending many years in jail even though
the information went to Israel's ally.

There would be one major difference between the way
Israel and the United States would handle this kind of
"friendly espionage." The Israelis, almost certainly, would
maintain a very low public profile. There would be a secret
trial and very little publicity. Israeli law would permit this.
After all, Israel's basic interests in maintaining its strong
relationship with the United States would prevail over any
other considerations.

If there had not been such a rash of spy cases in the United States earlier in 1985, Pollard's arrest almost certainly would have been handled differently by the United States. For one thing, it probably would not have generated the enormous media publicity that it did. The Americans would have tried to play down the affair—anxious not to unnecessarily endanger or undermine U.S.-Israeli relations. The Americans are aware of the fact that, in the hardball world of international espionage, all countries spy.

"I don't think Mr. Pollard could have picked a more inauspicious time to have committed espionage against the United States," said diGenova. "His draw that evening at the table was pretty bad."

Turning off the Pollard spigot—despite all of the warning signs—proved to be too difficult and painful for Eitan and his colleagues. They apparently assumed, arrogantly and recklessly, that they would not get caught. And they must have been convinced that, even if they did get caught, they could contain the damage. There was no independent political overseeing of the operation—and the Israeli government is to blame for that. It is always unrealistic to assume that spies can exercise the necessary political constraint in any operation.

The high-level decision to cover-up Sella's role was understandable but stupid. The Israelis genuinely wanted to salvage Sella's brilliant career, which would crumble if his involvement were known. They also feared that the Americans would never accept the notion that the operation was unauthorized if a senior Air Force pilot was involved. But Israeli counterintelligence professionals should have known that the Americans eventually would learn of Sella's involvement. From the start, the Israelis should have assumed that Pollard—who was, after all, an amateur with no professional training as a spy—would cooperate with the Americans, especially after Israel betrayed him. The Israelis should never have assumed that Pollard would honor a code of silence, particularly since the Americans could, and did, use Anne as leverage. The Israeli cover-up undermined Israel's credibility with the Americans and resulted in the worst of all possible worlds for Israel.

Pollard should not have been so shocked by the Israeli betrayal: He became temporarily expendable because the overall American-Israeli relationship was at stake. Thus, the Israeli government's claim that Pollard was part of a rogue operation should have been anticipated. If Pollard's loyalty to Israel were as strong as he has maintained, his bitterness and anger—while certainly understandable—should have been contained even in the face of Israel's handing over evidence to the Americans to nail him.

Israeli officials maintain that Pollard—even under those very trying circumstances—should have assumed that Israel knew what it was doing and that it would eventually take steps to free him. "He should have kept his mouth shut," one hard-nosed Israeli spy said. On the old "Mission Impossible" television series, he recalled, Jim Phelps (played by Peter Graves) was always routinely advised that "the Secretary will disavow any knowledge of your activities if you are captured or killed."

The problem with Pollard, however, was that he was never professionally trained by Israel to spy. As a walk-in, he never took a basic course in espionage. After learning that Eitan, Yagur, and other Israeli officials were cooperating with the U.S. investigation, he simply assumed that Israel wanted him to follow suit. He also made many grievous errors early on. His decision, for example, to collect classified documents on China for Anne was utterly reckless. Theoretically, he had risked compromising the entire operation in order to help Anne get a job. He also foolishly collected way too many documents; not all of them were essential for Israel's security. If Pollard and his handlers had been less greedy, the operation might have continued undetected for years. Pollard's handlers, of course, should have spotted and corrected these errors. But the entire operation was basically flawed. Eitan's behavior, too, was less than professional.

Question: Was Pollard's life sentence just or was it too severe?

Answer: On the "60 Minutes" program, Pollard, clearly embittered after three years of solitary confinement in prison, referred to the Naval Intelligence officials who accompanied Mike Wallace as "the rats" who have "come out of the woodwork." Pollard maintained that his sentence "did not reflect proportional justice, it reflected political vengeance, plain and simple." He again blamed Weinberger—a charge repeated on the program by Alan Dershowitz, Pollard's lawyer.

Dershowitz acknowledged that Pollard had been "justly convicted and justly sentenced to a term of imprisonment. That's what he deserved. But the idea that he should be treated as if he were a spy who has sold nuclear secrets to the Soviet Union—what did he do? He pleaded guilty. He fully cooperated. He helped the government in its damage assessment. He spied for a country which was an ally of the United States. He tried his darnedest to give Israel only information which he believed was necessary for Israel's survival and would not jeopardize the interests of the United States. Those are not defenses, but those certainly argue against the maximum possible punishment, which is what he got."

DiGenova conceded that the government, as part of the plea bargain agreement, did not request a life sentence. "However," diGenova said, "the judge was given access to the damage assessment prepared by the Secretary of Defense. . . . And I believe that if we were able to reveal to the American people the kind of damage that was done, there would be no question about the sentence."

"That is nonsense," Dershowitz replied. "I think that it is un-American for a Secretary of Defense to get up there and use hyperbole to the American people, and then when people say prove it, he hides behind a shield of confidentiality, turns it into a sword, and says to the American people, 'Trust me, believe me, what I told the judge is true.' I don't believe him, and I think a lot of Americans don't believe him."

The "60 Minutes" report quoted unnamed government officials as saying that Pollard lied when he said that "none of the information that [he] provided Israel . . . dealt with

U.S. codes, agents, their identity, location, military hardware, war plans, intelligence collection devices, or forced depositions." The officials charged that he did in fact compromise sensitive human and technical sources of intelligence gathering. But "60 Minutes" did not provide any specific details.

Based on what I know and what I have reported in this book, Pollard did indeed damage U.S. national security interests by spying for Israel. DiGenova is right when he says that even Pollard's supporters would recognize this damage if the complete memo were released. However, much of the damage has been contained because of the exposure of the operation. Since Pollard's arrest, U.S. and Israeli intelligence officials have cooperated—albeit not completely—to repair the damage, although the Americans have remained understandably bitter about the entire affair. Pollard may not have shown much remorse in his comments to me and to others since his arrest and sentencing, but he did cooperate with the investigation, and he did plead guilty. In my opinion, therefore, he should not have received a life sentence. Judge Robinson should have gone along with the government's recommendation that Pollard receive a substantial sentence instead.

In any case, my own sense is that the U.S. and Israel will eventually reach some sort of political deal enabling Pollard to be deported to Israel. But that will take time.

I have always felt that Anne's five-year sentence was much too harsh. In fact, I don't believe she should have been forced to return to prison. For one thing, she is very sick. For another, she did plead guilty and cooperate with the investigation. Finally, while she tried to help her husband (and, inadvertently, Avi Sella) escape and, while she knew of Jay's activities, she was never operationally involved in the espionage ring. Her involvement was marginal; she was motivated by a blind love for her husband. Anne's three months in the District of Columbia jail did nearly kill her. Consequently, she should have received a suspended sentence with for a limited period of probation, which is what I assumed she would get. She already has suffered enough for her crime. That she was sent back to jail, in my opinion, was largely the result of her disastrous pre-sentencing interview on "60 Minutes," during which she showed little remorse. Her stance deeply angered Judge Robinson, who saw the program.

Question: Why did the government permit me to enter the prison to interview Pollard? Was I used so that Pollard would receive a harsher sentence?

Answer: As I wrote in the introduction, I had no idea what the government's motivation was in permitting me access to Pollard. I was happy to receive his first interviews. I continue to believe that I acted professionally and responsibly even though I am prepared to concede that the government—in seeking a stiff sentence for Pollard—used me.

After careful examination, I have concluded that the government was anxious to see what Pollard would tell a journalist. The warden at Petersburg did not allow me to enter the prison on his own; he received authorization from Washington. I easily could have been denied permission, but the government knew that any interview Pollard granted—without the authorization of Naval intelligence—would represent a violation of his plea-bargain agreement. United States prosecutors and other law enforcement officials were more than happy to let Pollard dig his own grave.

Still, words and ideas can be very powerful, and in our system, the government cannot fully control what impact they have. Pollard, in getting his side of the story out for the first time, began to change public opinion in Israel and in the American Jewish community. Before the interviews, there was very little—if any—sympathy for him. That has now changed.

Question: And finally, what about Pollard himself? Was he a destructive, dangerous spy—a mercenary—or an over-bright young man who led a rich fantasy life that centered on his becoming a superhero for the country he idolized?

Was he genuinely concerned about Israel's well-being or was he merely anxious to make some extra money?

Answer: Having interviewed Pollard, his family, friends, and scores of others involved in the case, I have no doubt that Pollard's original motivation was to help Israel. His primary loyalty was to that country. He saw information he felt Israel needed, and he decided to make it available—that was a horrible and tragic mistake. As I wrote earlier in this book, Pollard should have quit his job and moved to Israel the moment he was tempted to become a spy. But he almost certainly was also intrigued by the excitement of becoming a spy—something he had indeed fantasized about for many years. He deeply admired Avi Sella, a real-life Israeli hero; he wanted to be like Sella. And, as he has himself admitted, the money provided by the Israelis eventually did corrupt him—as they no doubt knew it would. He liked the higher standard of living. The Israelis knew he would get hooked and continue to work for them as a result. Still, the sums were not all that significant and his financial profitting was only a by-product of his original motivation.

As a result of his crime, Pollard continues to languish in prison. He broke the law; he violated the trust that the U.S. government placed in him. He entered the territory of lies without a passport for return.

INDEX